THE MITIGATION
DOCTRINE

A PROPOSAL FOR ITS REGULATION IN BRAZIL

MARCELO LAPOLLA, PHD

iUniverse

THE MITIGATION DOCTRINE
A PROPOSAL FOR ITS REGULATION IN BRAZIL

iUniverse books may be ordered through booksellers or by contacting:

iUniverse
1663 Liberty Drive
Bloomington, IN 47403
www.iuniverse.com
844-349-9409

ISBN: 978-1-6632-6137-3 (sc)
ISBN: 978-1-6632-6138-0 (e)

Library of Congress Control Number: 978166326137

Print information available on the last page.

iUniverse rev. date: 03/18/2024

ACKNOWLEDGEMENTS

My most sincere thank you to Professor François du Bois (a true inspiration I will carry all my life), Dr. Nicola Jackson, Teresa Rowe, Helen Newcombe and the staff at University of Leicester, for being by my side during these years. To my partner and brother Thiago Vezzi, who calmed me down and supported me when I needed. To my great friend Erik Navrocky, who helped me take so many steps along the way. To those who, in the years before or at the very end, inspired me and helped me make this project become possible: Eduardo Salusse, Sergio Marangoni, Eduardo Parente, Wilson Jabur, Marcello Klug, Carlos Artur Andre Leite, Eduardo Miranda, Marcel Cordeiro, João Daniel Rassi, Christian de Lamboy, Carlos Fonseca Monnerat and Gonzalo Fernandez. To all of those who supported me to keep moving or challenged me to continue. And above all, to God.

Dedicated to my beloved wife, who supported me the whole way through and brought Helena and Martin to our lives. To my parents, who pointed me to this direction. To my sisters, nephews, nieces, in-laws and Nina, who understood and tolerated my absence. To my grandmothers (*in memoriam* and in my heart). To my country, wishing to contribute with a fair society. And to anyone this might bring strength and inspire resilience to go after their goals.

"only when the law seeks to find correlation with actual developments is the legislator able to pave the way for regulation that can truly come to full fruition."

(Anne Keirse, 'Why the Proposed Optional Common European Sales Law Has Not, But Should Have, Abandoned the Principle of All or Nothing: A Guide to How to Sanction the Duty to Mitigate the Loss' (2011) 19 *European Review of Private Law* 976)

CONTENTS

CHAPTER 1

1.1 Context and outline

Most, if not all, legal systems contain the so-called "duty to mitigate loss" doctrine. This duty (or principle; the most appropriate characterization will be discussed later), in broad terms, requires victims of wrongfully inflicted damage to take reasonable steps to limit their losses. Failure to do so limits their entitlement to recover damages from the wrongdoer who inflicted the damage.[1] Although traces of this doctrine and its application can be found in several court decisions in Brazil, the requirements and limits of its application, as well as its legal basis, have not yet received much attention in the Brazilian legal system and legal literature. Associated with this is the absence of an express provision regarding the duty to mitigate in Brazilian Civil Code[2] – which is meant to contain all rules applied to private relations.

The duty to mitigate loss made its first appearance in Brazil in doctrinal writings. Before that, there is no record of its application by courts, nor significant impact of the topic in the Brazilian legal landscape, in which the binding force of contracts has historically prevailed. This was so until former Minister of the Superior Court of Justice, Aguiar Júnior, introduced it as "doctrine of mitigation" in his work, originally dated of 1991. In Chapter 6 of his work, when debating the definitive breach of an obligation, the author stated:

> "Further on this topic, it is necessary to refer to the
> doctrine of mitigation, which requires of the creditor to

---

[1] Harvey McGregor, James Edelman, Jason Varuhas and Simon Colton (general eds), *McGregor on Damages* (21st Ed., London, Sweet & Maxwell, 2020) Chapter 9, par 9-001 – 9-007; Joseph Chitty and H. G. Beale, *Chitty on Contracts* (33rd Ed. Incorporating Second Supplement, London, Sweet & Maxwell, 2020) 26-087.
[2] Available at <http://www.planalto.gov.br/ccivil_03/leis/2002/l10406.htm> accessed 7 August 2022. Throughout the thesis, citations of the Brazilian Civil Code will be transcribed from the English translation produced by Leslie Rose, *O Código Civil Brasileiro em inglês / the Brazilian Civil Code in English* (Renovar 2008).

collaborate, despite of the breach of the contract, in order
to ensure that the resulting harmful outcome of the breach
is not aggravated through his or her action or omission"
(original version: Ainda nesse tema, deve ser lembrada a
doutrina da mitigação, pela qual o credor deve colaborar,
apesar da inexecução do contrato, para que não se agrave,
pela sua ação ou omissão, o resultado danoso decorrente
do incumprimento).[3]

The topic did not receive much attention from legal commentators,
nor did it reach the courts until 2004. The first Brazilian court to ground
its decision on (or at least mention) the duty to mitigate loss was from the
state of Paraná. The ruling, however, brought together several elements
with no clear distinction of one from the other: the duty of good faith,
duty of diligence, contributory negligence and causation – besides the
"doctrine of mitigation".[4] This decision did not detail the application of the
duty to mitigate loss, but it was followed by others which, again, combined
the duty to mitigate with other principles, such as *venire contra factum
proprium, supressio, surrectio, verwirkung* and *erwirkung*, with no detailed
consideration as to any aspect regarding the application of the doctrine.[5]

In subsequent years, numerous decisions by Brazilian courts
(throughout the different jurisdictions in Brazil's constitutive states) made

---

[3] Ruy Rosado de Aguiar Júnior, *Extinção dos Contratos por Incumprimento do Devedor*
(2nd Ed., 2003, Rio de Janeiro, Aide Editora) 136. Unless otherwise indicated, all
translations into English in this thesis – as this one – are my own.
[4] TJ/PR Appeal 158909-7, 6th Civil Chamber, Judge Albino Jacomel Guerios, on
08/23/2004, by unanimous decision. In this case, the Court reduced recovery for
the period the property was vacant, for the claimant was aware of defendant's breach
and could have repossessed the land before.
[5] TJ/SP Appeal 1.029.972-4, 16th Chamber of Private Law, Judge Cândido Alem,
on 09/05/2006, by majority. Here, claimant was seeking termination and reduction
of the penalty stipulated in the agreement. The Court granted both claims, basing
the reduction on the fact that defendant was aware of the breach and still took no
action, allowing the fine amount to elevate.

express reference to the duty to mitigate loss.[6] These decisions give a sense of the current application of the duty to mitigate loss in Brazil – mostly present when decisions delve deep into the *quantum* of compensation. In one appeal decided by the State Court of São Paulo, the decision limited the recovery of damages for the claimant to the loss which the party would have experienced if he had acted reasonably (the court ruled that the claimant had chosen to experience further damage).[7] In another decision by the same court, the claimant argued that the defendant should not be entitled to receive interest over the original debt, for it would allow him to profit from his own inertia in timely collecting the debt, in a manner arguably contrary to the duty to mitigate. The Court ruled against the claimant on the ground that it was the claimant's lack of payment that caused the loss and the application of interest. The decision rejected the application of the duty to mitigate loss in the specific case, but did not deny its existence in the legal framework.[8]

Most importantly, in 2010, the Superior Court of Justice issued a decision with express reference to the duty to mitigate loss – supposedly

---

[6] Web researches in Supreme, Superior and State Appeal Court of São Paulo (http://www.stf.jus.br http://www.stj.jus.br and http://www.tjsp.jus.br), with the key words "mitigation", "duty to mitigate", "dever de mitigar", "mitigar danos" and "mitigação de danos", by the year of 2021, show numerous of results with express reference to the mitigation doctrine (over 2,000 in the Appeal Court of the state of São Paulo; 26 in the Superior Court of Justice); and 4 in the Supreme Court). None of them holds the status of a leading case, since the duty to mitigate does not figure as the main ground for any decision and is always associated (properly or not) with other existing rules.
[7] TJ/SP Appeal 992.06.073838, 30th Chamber of Private Law, Judge Edgard Rosa, on 09/15/2010, by unanimous decision. In this case, claimant was seeking recovery for damages to his property, supposedly caused by the defendant's fail to build a wall which would have potentially protected the property; recovery equivalent to the expenses in hiring alternative security during such period was reduced to half under the argument that claimant could have built the wall himself and that such security was as much needed by him and the defendant, who was his neighbor.
[8] TJ/SP Incident Appeal 1.288.546-0/2, 31st Chamber of Private Law, Judge Adilson de Araújo, on 08/25/2009.

following from good faith and the duties of loyalty and to cooperate – bringing it to the Brazilian legal scene in the following context:

"Thus, objective good faith constitutes an ethical-legal standard to be observed by the parties in all phases of the contract. This means that, during all stages of the contract, the conduct of the parties must be based on probity, cooperation and loyalty (...). This gives rise to the duty to mitigate one's own losses, or, in foreign law, the 'duty to mitigate the loss': the parties to a contract must take all necessary and possible measures to ensure that the loss is not aggravated. In this sense, the party on whom the loss falls must not deliberately remain inactive, for his or her inertia can cause unnecessary aggravation of the loss and unnecessary and avoidable damage to the other party, which infringes the duties of cooperation and loyalty." (original version: Assim, a boa-fé objetiva afigura-se como standard ético-jurídico a ser observado pelos contratantes em todas as fases contratuais. Ou seja, durante as diversas etapas do contrato, a conduta das partes deve ser pautada pela probidade, cooperação e lealdade (...). Com esse entendimento, avulta-se o dever de mitigar o próprio prejuízo, ou, no direito alienígena, duty to mitigate the loss: as partes contratantes da obrigação devem tomar as medidas necessárias e possíveis para que o dano não seja agravado. Desse modo, a parte a que a perda aproveita não pode permanecer deliberadamente inerte diante do dano, pois a sua inércia imporá gravame desnecessário e evitável ao patrimônio da outra, circunstância que infringe os deveres de cooperação e lealdade).[9]

---

[9] STJ, Special Appeal 758.518/PR, decided on 07/10/2010 by Superior Court of Justice. The court acknowledged the existence of the duty to mitigate loss, in

In subsequent years, the Superior Court kept making reference to the mitigation doctrine as regularly and constantly as if it were actually part of the Brazilian legal system, whether as a "parameter" to quantify damages,[10] or in connection with the duty of good faith and to prevent abusive exercise of rights.[11] Similarly, and also with diverse justifications as to the existing principles and provisions that allow its application, state courts have repeatedly and constantly made rulings based on the mitigation doctrine.[12] And since 2016, even the Supreme Court has mentioned the duty to mitigate loss in a few decisions, differing among each other as to its interpretation.[13]

This evidences that the duty to mitigate is now firmly established

---

connection with the principle of good faith, to reduce creditor's recovery due to his inertia in demanding his rights against defaulting tenant.

[10] STJ, Special Appeal 1.819.069/SC, decided on 05/26/2020 by Superior Court of Justice.

[11] STJ, Petition on Special Appeal 1.733.695/SC, decided on 03/22/2021 by Superior Court of Justice.

[12] TJ/SP Appeal 1019063-59.2020.8.26.0562, 22nd Chamber of Private Law, Judge Edgard Rosa, decided on 07/08/2021; TJ/SP Petition 2139107-93.2021.8.26.0000, 38th Chamber of Private Law, Judge Spencer Almeida Ferreira, decided on 07/06/2021; TJ/SP 1020621-94.2020.8.26.0100, 12th Chamber of Private Law, Judge Tasso Duarte de Melo, decided on 07/01/2021.

[13] The Superior and Supreme Courts are both courts of final appeal but constitutional arguments are exclusively for the Supreme Court to decide. This means that the same Appeal Court decision may be subject to simultaneous appeals addressed to each of these two courts. The statement in the texts is evidenced by the following Supreme Curt decisions: STF, ARE 1281443, decided on 21/06/2021, stating that the late exercise of rights by claimant (university collecting its student debt), if within the correspondent statute of limitations, is not abusive and, therefore, does not on the basis of good faith trigger the mitigation doctrine; STF, ARE 985744, decided on 20/02/2017, stating that the failure of the consumer to enter a substitute transaction (subscribing to an alternative internet service) prevented his claim for losses; STF, ARE 1070079, decided on 30/08/2017, limiting recovery from claimant who failed to act in good faith by mitigating losses incurred after the public contest he had won was void; and STF, ARE 1000876, decided on 25/10/2016, referring to the mitigation doctrine when assessing the absence of losses incurred by claimant who had his taxpayer enrollment number duplicated to someone else.

in the practice of Brazilian courts. However, as the Civil Code of Brazil fails to regulate the requirements and limits of this duty, judicial decisions have continued to base the duty to mitigate on other principles, in order to justify its application. This has prevented the development of a full understanding of this doctrine, the establishment of a coherent concept, and its consistent application. As a result of this, and although the courts keep applying it, it remains uncertain what the basis of the mitigation doctrine is in the Brazilian legal system, as well as what the principles are which justify and guide its practical application. As Chong states: "the problem is that there is no provision in the legal system clearly regulating this duty (...) There is much to be studied about the duty to mitigate loss, specially to comprehend its requisites, in order to avoid its unnecessary and, mainly, incorrect application".[14]

1.2 Research question and objectives

This thesis aims to bring greater clarity to the treatment of the duty to mitigate in Brazilian law, and to propose the formulation of an express rule which would fill what appears to be a gap in the legislation and also to harmonize the application of this doctrine by the courts. In order to achieve that, the present study will explore the conceptualization and application of this duty in countries where it is more fully developed, so as to enable the understanding of its foundations and limits, in order to develop a formulation of this duty that would be suitable to the Brazilian culture and legal system.

---

[14] Paulo Araújo Chong, 'O duty to mitigate the loss no direito brasileiro: é justo o credor ser indenizado por prejuízos que deixou de mitigar?' (2017) 1 *Cadernos Jurídicos da Faculdade de Direito de Sorocaba* 190-209 (original version: "problema é que não há previsão legal no ordenamento jurídico que estabeleça de forma clara esse encargo. (...) Há ainda muito que se estudar sobre o duty to mitigate the loss, principalmente para compreender os seus requisitos, a fim de se evitar o uso desnecessário e, principalmente, equivocado do instituto, o que pode trazer insegurança jurídica").

In order to analyze the duty to mitigate loss, it is important to determine its meaning from the strictly legal view. In the context of this thesis, the expression refers to the conduct to be expected from an innocent party in order to limit the losses suffered as a consequence of the other party's unlawful action or contractual breach. Although commonly referred to as a duty, the conduct to which it refers ("to mitigate loss") may not be required from the party to whom it refers, as this "duty" does not correspond to a right that the other party could claim.[15] The "duty to mitigate", therefore, should not be understood as someone's duty in the sense of "obligation"; instead, it refers to the conduct such party is expected to observe, so that limitations to the extension of this party's right of recovery will not be applied.[16]

In other words, the mitigation doctrine refers to the actions the party

---

[15] Michael G. Bridge, 'Mitigation of damages in contract and the meaning of avoidable loss' (1989) 105 Law Quarterly Review 398, 399: "it is quite inaccurate to speak of the plaintiff having a 'duty' to mitigate, for it is not met by any corresponding right of the defendant". Daniel Pires Novais Dias, 'O duty to mitigate loss no direito civil brasileiro e o encargo de evitar o próprio dano' (2011) 12 *Revista de Direito Privado* 89, 99: "the duty to mitigate loss corresponds to a rule which together with others determine the value of the victim's compensation for contractual or non-contractual harm" (original version: o duty to mitigate loss corresponde a uma norma que, conjuntamente com outras, determinam o valor da indenização da vítima de um dano contratual ou extracontratual). Tomas Barros Martins Comino, 'As desaventuras do duty to mitigate the loss no Brasil' (2015) Dissertation for the degree of Mestrado Profissional em Direito dos Negócios Aplicado e Direito Tributário Aplicado, Fundação Getúlio Vargas, São Paulo, 13, available at <https://bibliotecadigital.fgv.br/dspace/handle/10438/13610?show=full> accessed 31 July 2022: "The duty to mitigate the loss does not involve a duty nor an obligation, insofar as there is no related right granted to the other party" (original version: o duty to mitigate the loss não envolve um dever e tampouco uma obrigação, na medida em que não existe direito correlato titularizado pela outra parte).

[16] "There is no legal duty to mitigate loss; a claimant is free to act as it wishes in response to a breach of contract. The point is that its damages will be limited by an assumption that it has taken reasonable steps in mitigation of loss whether or not it has taken these steps": Iain Drummond, 'Is 'duty to mitigate loss' a misnomer?' (2016) <http://www.shepwedd.co.uk/knowledge/duty-mitigate-loss-misnomer> accessed 31 July 2022.

is supposed to take in order to avoid losses which will otherwise not be recoverable from the defaulting party. In sum, the mitigation doctrine stipulates that one who does not act reasonably – an abstract concept, to be further analysed in later chapters – to avoid or mitigate their own losses will be subject to limitations in the extent of his or her rights of recovery. The result is that the measure of recovery is connected to the conduct of the innocent party in dealing with the consequences of the unlawful action or breach by the other party.[17] As such, losses experienced as a result of the party's inertia – when legally expected (required) to act – may not be subject to recovery.[18]

With this conceptual aspect taken into consideration, we will – nonetheless – continue to refer to the mitigation doctrine as the duty to mitigate loss, for this is the most common language by which it is referred in the jurisdictions analysed throughout this thesis and should not, if the point just made is taken into account, lead to any misunderstanding as to its nature.

Given the absence in the Brazilian Civil Code of an express duty to mitigate, the thesis will consider: why is there no mitigation provision currently: did the legislator simply forget it, or was it thought unnecessary or sufficiently addressed by supposedly equivalent doctrines and rules that are present? The point, here, is not to argue that all countries – including Brazil, then – should enact a specific rule to regulate the application of the duty to mitigate; rather, the point is to identify how courts in Brazil have dealt with this issue in the absence of a specific provision, and to further establish whether the legislative gap presents a justifiable concern from the legal perspective which calls for a new provision.

---

[17] Gustavo Santos Kulesza, *Princípio da mitigação de danos; evolução no direito contratual* (Curitiba, Juruá, 2015) 318: "Mitigation of losses is not a duty, but a limitation to the recovery of the creditor" (original version: A mitigação de danos não é concebida como um dever, mas sim, como uma limitação à indenização do credor inadimplido).

[18] Bridge (n 15) 409: it is not the right of recovery that will be limited; it is the extent of the recoverable loss which will be affected.

To this end, the thesis will critically analyse the different doctrinal bases which have been put forward in Brazil by writers and courts to support the application of this doctrine: the principle of good faith, the doctrines of avoidable losses, *supressio* and *venire contra factum proprium*, the concepts of causation and contributory negligence and common-sense elements like reasonableness.[19] In this regard, the thesis will consider whether any of these provide an appropriate basis for applying this doctrine in Brazil, given the legal framework established by the Civil Code and the Constitution of Brazil. It will also reflect on whether these concepts and principles provide clear answer to central questions such as: When does the duty to mitigate arise: only in case of breach of contract, or also in case of an unlawful act (tort), or perhaps even more broadly? What standard of conduct does it impose and how is reasonableness measured? What is the scope of the duty: does it cover failures to reduce the loss caused or only failures to avoid aggravating the loss, how are extra costs caused by mitigation dealt with, and is the recoverable compensation reduced even by mitigating measures which were not required? On which party is the burden of proof?

This will provide a starting point which identifies uncertainties surrounding the application of the duty to mitigate by Brazilian courts, and to uncover the link between these and the absence of a specific rule regulating the principle. In this respect, the gap in legislation will be placed in the context of the Constitutional provision which establishes that "no one will be obliged to do or not to do anything if not in virtue of law", present in art. 5, II of the Constitution of Brazil. The instability as to the enforceability of the mitigation rule – evidenced through the decisions and doctrine referred to above and further analysed in later chapters – not only justifies this research, but also legitimates the intention to contribute to the Brazilian legal framework by proposing the proper regulation of the mitigation doctrine.

---

[19] See Chapter 2.

Here it is important also to explain what this thesis does not do. Because the thesis takes as its starting point the fact that the duty to mitigate is now an established part of the practice of Brazilian courts, as was shown in the previous section, and aims to make a contribution to how it is regulated, it does not engage in an in-depth inquiry into to the deeper philosophical or economic justifications of such a duty. Although reference is made, when appropriate, to such justifications in order to shed light on the nature and extent of the mitigation principle, the aims of this thesis does not require a full justification as to why a legal system should adopt the mitigation principle. In relation to Brazil, others have already done that work[20] and this thesis does not aim to repeat that.

Identifying the difficulties caused by the legislative gap will lead to considering which aspects a new provision on mitigation should address (technically, according to codification best practices, and substantively, ensuring the most appropriate content for regulating the doctrine of mitigation). In this regard, the research will then unfold to cover questions such as how far a party must go to mitigate loss and how the effects of said action will affect both parties in the course of losses, remedies and recovery. It will also be necessary to consider whose burden it will be to prove relevant matters in case of litigation. Because these matters have been faced also in other legal systems, this raises questions about the international experience, as revealed by comparative law research. What lessons can Brazil learn from the experience of other countries?

Finally, the ultimate objective is to propose and formulate a new provision to be added to the Brazilian Civil Code, which will be designed to resolve current uncertainties and tensions and to bring about a harmonious application of the duty to mitigate loss by parties and courts.

---

[20] See the Literature Review below, especially the references to the books by Lopes, Kulesza and Andrade Martins.

1.3 Structure of the thesis

The thesis will be divided into five chapters.

This first chapter provides a general outline of the topic and presents how the thesis will be developed.

The second chapter turns to Brazil, investigating in detail the local legal position. At this point, the thesis will present the rules relevant to the duty to mitigate in local legislation, and proceed to analysing its current application by the courts. This chapter will also analyse Brazilian legal writings on the duty to mitigate. This will evidence the lack of uniformity and absence of clear legal grounds for requiring mitigation. Doing this will identify the tensions surrounding the mitigation doctrine and differences of opinion regarding its existence and, ultimately, will demonstrate the need to fill a legislative gap. In doing so, this chapter will set the agenda for the comparative studies in the following chapters.

The third and fourth chapters will explore the experience of selected other jurisdictions, belonging to the Common Law and Civil Law families, respectively, as well as the texts of relevant transnational instruments. General studies of the literature will be followed by the identification of the rule concerning the duty to mitigate loss (if any) that is locally applied by courts. The objective of these chapters will be to develop an understanding of how different countries interpret and decide, through their legal systems, similar questions related to the duty to mitigate losses, as well as to identify the specific issues and difficulties that need to be dealt with. Where these exist, attention will also be paid to how any legislative or codal rules concerning the duty have been formulated.

The final chapter will build on this to develop a possible solution for the legislative gap in Brazil. It will summarize and apply the lessons that can be learnt from this comparative survey, and use these to make an original contribution in the form of a proposed new Civil Code provision to regulate the duty to mitigate loss in Brazil – benefiting from foreign experience, but yet responding to the local needs and concerns identified in Chapter 2.

The proposal will take into consideration the specific character of a Civil Code as being more than a simple collection of rules. Structured in a certain and systematic order to facilitate consultation and reference, codes "represent a homogeneous, unitary, rational system, which aspires to be a logical and complete construction, erected under the foundation of principles that are assumed to be applicable to all the reality that the law must discipline".[21] Therefore, the new rule will be designed to fit in and be compatible with the existing principles and provisions of Brazilian law.

1.4 Literature Review

Preliminary research has shown that little academic work has been directed at this matter in Brazil, and no established approach has been adopted.[22] Therefore, the local literature concerning the duty to mitigate loss is limited. There are only three book-length monographs, in Portuguese, on the topic, respectively by Lopes,[23] by Kulesza[24] and by Andrade Martins.[25] The first two investigate mitigation only in relation to contractual claims, and the scope of each is limited by the author's specific objectives. Kulesza's study analyzes the development of the mitigation principle in the light of the

---

[21] Adriane Stoll de Oliveira, 'A codificação do Direito' (2002) <http://www.egov.ufsc.br/portal/sites/default/files/anexos/11087-11087-1-PB.pdf> accessed 31 July 2022 (original version: representa um sistema homogêneo, unitário, racional, que aspira a ser uma construção lógica completa, erigida sob o alicerce de princípios que se supõem aplicáveis a toda a realidade que o direito deve disciplinar).

[22] Emerson da Silva Dourado, 'O dever de mitigar o dano (the duty to mitigate loss)' (2012) <http://www.webartigos.com/artigos/o-dever-de-mitigar-o-dano-duty-to-mitigate-the-loss/101882/> accessed 31 July 2022.

[23] Christian Sahb Batista Lopes, *Mitigação dos prejuízos no direito contratual* (São Paulo, Editora Saraiva, 2013).

[24] Kulesza (n 17).

[25] Jose Eduardo Figueiredo de Andrade Martins, *Duty To Mitigate The Loss No Direito Civil Brasileiro* (São Paulo, Verbatim, 2018).

reciprocal evolution of legal systems, focusing especially on the interaction between international trade law instruments and the domestic contract law of states, including Brazil. Lopes focuses on identifying the appropriate doctrinal basis for the mitigation principle as it has developed in Brazil in the existing provisions of the Civil Code as well as on finding an ultimate justification for the principle with the aid of the economic analysis of law. This thesis does share the concerns of these works, notably in relating the theory and practice of mitigation to the experience of other legal systems and in presenting a proposal for the insertion of a new mitigation provision into the Civil Code. However, the comparative investigation is limited and by now outdated,[26] and the proposal is presented without express consideration of alternatives or explanation of the choices made, so that there remains scope and need for further work which may challenge Lopes's conclusions and proposal. Finally, Andrade Martins analyzes the application of the mitigation principle in both torts and contractual claims, and even classifies Brazilian court precedents on the basis of whether they have "properly or improperly" applied the mitigation doctrine in the view of the writer. The author concludes that the updating of the Brazilian legal system with regards to mitigation is an urgent matter,[27] but makes no concrete proposition in this regard. Thus, although these works contain important discussions of the mitigation principle and its treatment in Brazil, and valuable insights which this thesis can draw on, none of them prioritizes the specific research questions pursued in this thesis: they do not aim to identify the difficulties to which the adoption of this principle in Brazil – in torts and contractual contexts – has given rise, in order to propose a solution to these that draws on international experience.

The remaining literature consists of a small number of journal articles,

---

[26] Only one chapter is devoted to comparison; there have been important recent developments in France (see section 4.2.2.1 below), one of the systems discussed by Lopes, and a range of relevant transnational instrument, notably the Principles of Latin American Contract Law (see section 4.4.6 below) not investigated by Lopes.
[27] Andrade Martins (n 24) 228.

conference papers, university dissertations and web articles in Portuguese, which is reviewed in the remainder of this section. There is only one treatment of the topic in English, a recent journal article by Veloso and Vieira.[28] This literature does, however, reveal a broad spectrum of views.

Professor Fradera, for instance, mentions the duties of loyalty and cooperation when proposing the limitation of victim's right of recovery.[29] Tartuce complements the analysis by relying on the abuse of rights theory, also to argue for the limitation of rights of the victim.[30] Pinheiro, on the other hand, understands causation as one of the matters that are related to the duty to mitigate in Brazil,[31] whilst Valdesoiro relates it directly and almost exclusively to causation.[32] Veloso and Vieira also base their analysis of mitigation in causation, although they do acknowledge that the Superior Court of Justice has grounded mitigation in the duty of good faith.[33]

The discussion of the nature of the duty to mitigate also shows no unanimity. Dias classified the duty to mitigate as a burden;[34] Lopes referred

---

[28] Regina Coeli Soares Oliveira Veloso and Nathalie Gurgel Vieira 'Duty to mitigate loss: a Brazilian perspective' (2018) *Revue libre de Droit* 14-26.

[29] Vera Maria Jacob de Fradera, 'Pode o credor ser instado a diminuir o próprio prejuízo?' (2004) 19 *Revista trimestral de direito civil* 109-119.

[30] Flavio Tartuce, 'A boa-fé objetiva e a mitigação do prejuízo pelo credor' (2005) <http://www.flaviotartuce.adv.br/artigos/Tartuce_duty.doc> accessed 31 July 2022.

[31] Denise Pinheiro, 'Duty to mitigate loss à brasileira: uma questão além do nexo de causalidade' (2012) <http://www.publicadireito.com.br/artigos/?cod=3e524bf740dc8cfd> accessed 16 January 2016, published during the XXI Congresso Nacional do CONPEDI/UFF, 324-353.

[32] Gabriella Michetti Mora Valdesoiro, 'O instituto do duty to mitigate the loss e seu conteúdo eficacional no direito brasileiro em case da causalidade cumulativa do artigo 945 do Código Civil' <https://repositorio.ufsc.br/bitstream/handle/123456789/114922/TCC%20-%20FINAL%20-%20REPOSIT%C3%93RIO%20-%20TERMO%20DE%20APROVA%C3%87%C3%83O%20-%20PDF%20A.pdf?sequence=1&isAllowed=y> accessed 31 July 2022 (Bachelor degree dissertation, Universidade Federal de Santa Catarina, from 2013).

[33] Veloso and Vieira (n 21) 19-20, 24.

[34] Dias (n 15) 89-145.

to it as an obligation;[35] Kulesza treated it as a principle;[36] and Fradera, mentioned above, states that it is a duty (as opposed to an obligation).

Although most authors relate the duty to mitigate loss to contractual relationships, Peixoto classifies it as a duty to act according to people's legitimate expectations, beyond any binding rules of a contract.[37] According to Veloso and Vieira, it can apply to both contractual and non-contracual (i.e. tort) liability.[38] Didier Jr. applies it to civil procedure relationships, making express references to procedural good faith and *supressio*.[39]

The fact is that there has been little work done on seeking the most adequate approach and possible harmonization of the application of the duty by Brazilian courts. Most authors have proceeded on the assumption that it derives from the duty of good faith,[40] but they have not addressed precisely which form the duty should take in the Brazilian Civil Code. Most of the literature is dedicated to exposing the origin of the duty of good faith (here, again, Kulesza), or focused on its application in specific situations (Flumignan relates it to the liability of the State;[41] Antunes

---

[35] Lopes (n 22) 196.

[36] Kulesza (n 17) 19.

[37] Alessandra Cristina Tufvesson Peixoto, 'Responsabilidade extracontratual – Algumas considerações sobre a participação da vítima na quantificação da indenização' (2008) 11:44 *Revista da Emerj* 135, 136.

[38] Veloso and Vieira (n 21) 24.

[39] Fredie Didier Jr., 'Multa Coercitiva, boa-fé processual e supressio: aplicação do duty to mitigate the loss no processo civil' (2009) *Revista de processo, São Paulo* n. 171, 48.

[40] Lopes (n 22); Renata Malta Villas-bôas, 'Duty to mitigate the loss no Direito Civil pátrio' (2013) XVI:111 *Âmbito Jurídico, Rio Grande*<http://ambito-juridico.com.br/site/?n link=revista artigos leitura&artigo id=12702> accessed 31 July 2022.

[41] Silvano J. G. Flumignan, 'A correlação entre o dano moral, o dano social e o caput do artigo 944 do Código Civil na responsabilidade civil do Estado' (2011) XXXVII *Congresso Nacional de Procuradores de Estado, Belo Horizonte*.

defends it exclusively in the context of contracts;[42] Mantovani narrows its application to contracts with the public administration[43]).

A few authors, however, have taken up the challenge of identifying a benchmark or standard for an acceptable definition and appropriate approach which could, then, become part of Brazilian law. Lopes defends the convenience of having an express rule regarding the duty and proposes the insertion of three paragraphs to the article that deals with full recovery for losses and damages caused (article 403).[44] His idea is to link the right of full recovery to diligent conduct by the claimant in avoiding the aggravation of own losses. In contrast, Comino suggests the alteration of article 945 – which deals with contributory negligence – to add the requirement of "ordinary diligence" on the part of the defendant.[45] Such proposals are, however, controversial, and authors such as Dias and Valdesoiro insist that the existing legal provisions deal adequately with mitigation.[46] This difference between authors' opinions evidences the level of uncertainty as to the connection of the mitigation doctrine to principles such as causation and contributory negligence, a point to be further developed in Chapter 2. Lopes's and Comino's proposals will also need to be considered in Chapter 5, where an alternative proposal is developed for regulating the mitigation principle in the Civil Code.

From this review it is clear that there is a growing interest in, and support for, the duty to mitigate in Brazilian legal literature. Importantly, it shows that there is also support for amending the Civil Code so as to

[42] Felipe Martins Antunes, 'O duty to mitigate the loss no direito contratual brasileiro' (2013) <http://semanaacademica.org.br/system/files/artigos/duty_to_mitigate_the_lossev.pdf> accessed 31 July 2022.
[43] Alexandre Casanova Mantovani, 'A mitigação do próprio prejuízo nos contratos administrativos' (2013) <https://www.lume.ufrgs.br/bitstream/handle/10183/90488/000914028.pdf?sequence=1> accessed 31 July 2022.
[44] Lopes (n 22) 268. The express proposition made in Lopes's doctorate thesis was excluded from its published version, but the rational remained.
[45] Comino (n 15).
[46] Dias (n 15) 50; Valdesoiro (n 31) 74.

make more direct provision for the duty to mitigate. There are however also significant uncertainties, disagreements, and gaps in the literature. As we have seen, there are diverging views on the basis and appropriate scope of the duty to mitigate as reflected in current law, and there are different opinions on how it may best be accommodated in the Civil Code. Because most of the discussion is focused on how the principle of mitigation *is* given effect through existing concepts such as the duty of good faith, the literature lacks a rigorous and systematic consideration of how the principle of mitigation *should* be dealt with in Brazilian law. As yet, there is no treatment of this topic which provides a comprehensive analysis of the doctrine of mitigation as applied by Brazilian courts and expressed in the writings of Brazilian scholars, compares this rigorously with experiences in other jurisdictions, and draws lessons from this for the further development of Brazilian law, including the possible amendment of the Civil Code.[47]

Further, as the explanation in the previous sections above of the background to the thesis and the research questions makes clear, the uneven and uncertain development of the duty to mitigate by the Brazilian courts has created an urgent need to fill a gap in Brazil's legislation, and this requires a fuller and more comprehensive treatment of the topic than is found in the existing literature. Accordingly, this thesis will seek to provide an in-depth and comprehensive analysis of the mitigation doctrine in Brazil and to determine both the needs and the best strategy for filling this gap in Brazil's legislation. In this way, the thesis will build on and extend the existing literature, making an original contribution to the literature on mitigation in Brazilian law (especially, but not only, in English) and

---

[47] This is not to suggest that Brazilian authors have paid no attention to comparing Brazilian law in this respect to other countries. To the contrary, as the frequent references to the English phrase "duty to mitigate" in the titles of the publications cited above show, the literature does link the position in Brazil to other jurisdictions. However, such comparisons are often limited and sporadic, as is exemplified by the article by Veloso and Vieira (n 27) and even the book-length treatment by Lopes (n 22) has limitations, as pointed out in the text above at footnote 25.

formulating an original proposal for the development of Brazilian law. It is hoped that this will make a meaningful contribution to legal literature in Brazil as well as to the international and comparative literature on mitigation of loss.

1.5 Research methodology and its justification

The research question set out above will be investigated mainly through the application of two related methodological approaches. In the first instance, a detailed study will be undertaken of the current state of Brazilian law and legal literature. This will take the form of a black-letter doctrinal analysis of judicial decisions and legal literature. This is designed to establish the current state of Brazilian law, and especially to uncover the uncertainties and disagreements of legal commentators that might deserve further analysis.

Secondly, the thesis will seek to develop an understanding of the foundations, limits and practical operation of the doctrine of mitigation in legal systems where it is well established or, at least, has been subject to discussion. The research will include a historical overview of the doctrine and itemize its most relevant aspects, requirements and rules for its application. Decisions and statutes from Civil Law countries, as well as from Common Law ones, and transnational instruments, will serve as examples to illustrate the doctrine's present stage of definition and enforcement. The aim of this is to provide a basis for reflection on possible reform of Brazilian law, including the formulation of an appropriate statutory text for inclusion in the Civil Code. This will therefore be an exercise in comparative law.

A comparative research methodology is particularly appropriate, even though the focus of the thesis is on Brazilian law, as it was comparison which, in the first instance, imported the mitigation doctrine to Brazil,[48]

---

[48] Veloso and Vieira (n 27) 16. Kulesza (n 17) provides an interesting analysis of the process by which this took place.

and it is comparison which might allow this development to be brought to a conclusion by providing the mitigation doctrine with an appropriate, state-of-the-art, legal basis. In this context, this methodology can be seen as "needed urgently today in a world in which law increasingly absorbs influences and ideas that have crossed national borders and have blurred traditional legal classifications".[49] Moreover, as pointed out by Kleinheisterkamp: "The degree of authority of foreign law – and the resulting problems – are certainly a striking feature of law in Latin American in general, and of Brazilian law in particular".[50]

As a comparative study, this thesis will be exploring similarities and differences between legal systems:

> "The essence of comparison is then aligning similarities and differences between data points, and using this exercise as a measure to obtain understanding of the content and range of the data points."[51]

Such comparison is "extremely useful for (…) the development of one's legal system", as by raising the researcher "above mere technical specialization it leads to legal thinking at a higher and more general level, and it offers the mind thus induced to be critical a world-wide 'supply of solutions'."[52]

This observation highlights the usefulness of comparative law to the specific research question addressed in this thesis. Because the mitigation

---

[49] Vivian Grosswald Curran, 'Comparative Law and Language' in Reinhard Zimmermann and Mattias Reimann (eds), *The Oxford Handbook of Comparative Law* (OUP 2006) 3.

[50] Jan Kleinheisterkamp, 'Development of Comparative Law in Latin America' in Mathias Reimann and Reinhard Zimmermann (eds), *The Oxford Handbook of Comparative Law* (2nd Edn, OUP 2019) 283. Examples on p. 286.

[51] Edward J. Eberle, 'The Method and Role of Comparative Law' (2009) 8 *Washington University Global Studies Law Review* 451.

[52] Konrad Zweigert and Hein Kötz, *An Introduction to Comparative Law*, (Tony Weir tr, 3rd edn, OUP 1998) 34, 45.

doctrine has been long and deeply discussed in other jurisdictions, with intense debates as to its theoretical nature and actual application as a rule, there is much to be considered from how the doctrine of mitigation is interpreted and applied to factual issues in more experienced jurisdictions. Moreover, as will be seen in Chapter 4, the question of whether, and how, to codify the mitigation doctrine has been confronted in other jurisdictions as well as by the drafters of several transnational instruments. The present study will therefore engage in more than simply commenting on foreign law; it will be digging into its sense, to understand its outcome and approach, in order to reach the best solution for Brazilian law. Therefore, and considering (i) the role comparative law has already played in the transplanting of the mitigation principle to Brazil, (ii) the underdevelopment of the subject matter in Brazil and (iii) Brazilian lack of experience with its application, the comparative methodology appears as probably the most appropriate method to be applied in this study. This will be implemented by taking the experience of other jurisdictions as the initial benchmark, which will then be analysed in light of the specific needs and circumstances of Brazil, in order to develop a solution for the local legal problem at stake. Accordingly, this thesis will engage in a comparative study, focused on similarities and differences between several jurisdictions and legal systems.[53]

One particular challenge in any comparative study concerns the comparability of different legal systems. Legal systems have long been divided into different 'legal families', especially the 'Common Law' and the 'Civil Law' families. This reflects the differences in history (values), nature of sources of law (codes or precedents) and structure of judicial systems (organization) and legal professions (authorities) that have shaped different legal mentalities.[54] This adds complexity to comparative studies

---

[53] Curran (n 18).

[54] See Zweigert and Kötz (n 51) also H. Patrick Glenn, *Legal Traditions of the World: Sustainable diversity in law* (5th edn, OUP 2014); Mathias Siems, *Comparative Law* (2nd edn, Cambridge University Press 2018).

which try to compare legal systems belonging to such different families.[55] That is of particular importance for this study, as Brazil belongs to the Civil Law family,[56] whereas the mitigation doctrine is most developed in legal systems belonging to the Common Law family.[57]

There are also other types of differences which can complicate comparison, such as differences in regional circumstances and in levels of economic development from one jurisdiction to the other. Each legal system has its own legal culture.[58]

> "Conceptual differences in the law, linguistic barriers and different political, socio-economic or cultural parameters will thereby often inhibit a fruitful comparative dialogue between the systems involved in the exchange (...) Further difficulties include the translation of foreign legal language, the technical incorporation of a new rule into the existing corpus of the law (which can necessitate cross-referencing the transplanted provision with other parts of the system not immediately affected by the borrowed rule), the harmonization of substantive rule with the underlying law of procedure, and the subsequent

---

[55] For strong emphasis on the complexity of comparability, see especially the work of Pierre Legrand, 'The impossibility of legal transplants' (1997) 4 *Maastricht J. Eur. & Comp. Law* 111.

[56] Kleinheisterkamp (n 49). Brazil's Civil Law character is further explained in Chapter 2. The general features of Civil Law systems is further discussed in Chapter 4.

[57] This is explained in Chapter 3.

[58] John Bell, 'Comparative Law and Legal Theory' in W Krawietz, N MacCormick & H Von Wright (eds) *Prescriptive Formality and Normative Rationality in Modern Legal Systems* (Duncker & Humblot 1995) 19-31: "A legal culture involves a specific way in which values, practices and concepts are integrated into the operation of legal institutions and interpretation of legal texts".

interpretation of the transplanted rule in a different legal and cultural context."[59]

At the same time, it is often precisely such differences that make the comparison interesting and worthwhile, as it opens up new perspectives. Here it is important to point out that this thesis does not seek to bring about a legal transplantation (as the mitigation principle has already been transplanted into, and taken root in, Brazil), but rather to investigate the difficulties that are being faced in accommodating the transplant in its new soil as well as to identify potential solutions to these. The differences between jurisdictions and legal families should also not be exaggerated – this is especially relevant to the topic of this thesis, as there is growing international similarity in the approach to mitigation.[60]

In order to limit the effect of these difficulties and benefit from its positive aspects, this study adopts a comparative methodology which investigates a range of jurisdictions which cut across these various categories. Thus, all jurisdictions selected for the comparison met one or more of the following criteria adopted to confirm their relevance for the purposes of the study: similarity in regional circumstances (Argentina); legally developed jurisdictions which belong to both the Common Law family (United Kingdom and the United States) and the Civil Law family (Germany and France); transnational instruments harmonizing different legal traditions (including the United Nations Convention on Contracts for the International Sale of Goods (CISG)).[61] By exploring the similarities and differences in the treatment of the mitigation principle in these different jurisdictions, this study will be able to distinguish between features which

---

[59] Jörg Fedtke, 'Legal Transplants', in Jan M. Smits *Elgar Encyclopedia of Comparative Law* (2nd edn, Edward Elgar Publishing 2014), ch. 39.

[60] See Chapter 4.

[61] Further explanation of the selection of jurisdictions for study in provided in Chapters 3 and 4.

are merely local and those which are more fundamental and thus usable in Brazil, and to identify current international trends.

Nevertheless, differences remain. What counts as an issue of mitigation in one legal system, might be described in quite different terminology in another system. This is amplified by the use of different languages, which adds the complexity of translation and the influence of the translator's view. A further complication of comparative studies arises from the 'situatedness' of the analyst or observer. As Legrand points out, "the meaning of a rule is (...) a function of the interpreter's epistemological assumptions which are themselves historically and culturally conditioned".[62]

To overcome these issues, this study will employ the well-established 'functionalist' approach to comparison.[63] Thus, the function of the rule will be taken as the starting-point in the comparison. By this is meant that the methodology will be to compare how different systems deal with the same factual problem, namely the "level of diligence (actions) required from the victim in order to reduce its own losses" – rather than to compare what legal systems themselves call "mitigation". This means that the research will aim to identify and comprehend what is the answer each system gives to the legal question under investigation – to be identified as the empirical problem that the law is meant to resolve – and the rules by which different systems approach, deal with and resolve such similar situations. This will provide a basis for considering whether to transplant their solutions to this factual problem into the Brazilian legal system, specifically in the Civil Code, with the necessary amendments. To that end, terminological differences will be disregarded, and the focus will be directed to the functionality of the rules (that is, in this case: how the law deals with diligence (actions) required from the victim in order to reduce its own losses). However, because the phrase "duty to mitigate" is used widely and in many different jurisdictions, including Brazil,[64] to refer to

---

[62] Legrand (n 54) 114.

[63] See Zweigert and Kötz (n 51).

[64] See the titles of the literature referred to in section 1.3 above.

how the law deals with this factual problem, this thesis will use this phrase as convenient shorthand.

This does not mean that the effects of different legal cultures or of the comparativist's own location in a particular tradition will be entirely eliminated. For that reason, attention will be paid to identifying the aspects of the application of the mitigation principle that are closely tied to the specific feature of a particular tradition (for example, the primacy of damages as a remedy for breach of contract in Common Law systems and the principle of full indemnification in Civil Law systems[65]) and to bearing this in mind when developing the proposal for reforming Brazilian Law. Special attention will also be given to the approaches and solutions developed in Civil Law systems (especially in neighbouring Argentina) and transnational instruments with which Brazil has direct links (the CISG, to which Brazil is a party, and the non-binding Latin American Principles of Contract Law (PLACL)).[66] It must also be acknowledged that a full understanding of several jurisdictions would not be achievable. However, that is not necessary in order to make this comparative study useful to answering the research question identified earlier in this chapter. This thesis does not involve an open-ended comparison of legal systems, but rather takes the specific needs of Brazil as its starting point. Because the aim of the thesis is to resolve particular issues which have arisen in Brazil, it does not reduce the usefulness of this study that the comparison will inevitably be influenced by the author's perspective as a Brazilian lawyer. Nevertheless, the methodological strategies outlined above are designed to limit these effects.

---

[65] See Chapters 3 and 4 respectively.
[66] See Chapters 4 and 5.

CHAPTER 2

27

2.1 Introduction

The previous chapter showed that the duty to mitigate has become firmly established in Brazilian law, is applied by the courts and acknowledged by legal doctrine.[1] This chapter takes the discussion of mitigation in Brazil further by explaining and analysing how this principle has been fitted into the fabric of Brazilian law. In doing so, it will provide an overview and assessment of the main ways in which Brazilian courts and doctrinal writers have used existing concepts and principles in the Civil Code to explain and justify the application of the mitigation principle. This responds to the research question identified in Chapter 1 as to whether there is a gap in current Brazilian legislation and, if so, to identify the tensions this raises. As was explained in Chapter 1, the thesis adopts a functionalist approach to identifying the scope of the study, and thus will focus in this chapter on Brazilian law concerning the "level of diligence (actions) required from the victim in order to reduce its own losses".[2]

The chapter places the Brazilian approach to the mitigation principle in the broader context of its character as a codified Civil Law system. It therefore starts with a discussion of general aspects of codification and of the specific features of the Civil Code currently in force. The relevance of the good faith principle in the existing system will be highlighted, as it prevails over the binding strength of contracts and thus enhances the power of judges. This provides the context for understanding both the adoption of the mitigation principle in Brazil and the strategies that have been followed for fitting this principle into the fabric of the existing law in the absence of an express mitigation provision in the Code. The chapter then analyzes these strategies, setting out the most common approaches in legal doctrine and court decisions, and reflecting critically on their ability to account for the definition and application of the mitigation principle in contractual and non-contractual relations. Overall, the chapter will

---

[1] Chapter 1 Sections 1.1 and 1.3.
[2] See Chapter 1 Section 1.4.

not set out to make comparisons with other jurisdictions nor to focus commentators' opinions (to be done in later chapters regarding mitigation), but rather to evidence the tensions and gaps that arise from the absence of a specific provision regarding mitigation in the Code, and thus show the need for such a provision. In doing so, this chapter will also identify the needs for clarity and harmonization which such a provision will have to fulfil. In this way, it will set an agenda for the comparative research to be conducted in the following two chapters and provide a framework for the development in the final chapter of a proposed new Code article on mitigation.

2.2 The legal landscape

As a Civil Law country, Brazil distils in its Civil Code the rules that regulate private parties' relations.[3] Whatever is not pre-established in its codes and legislation, cannot be enforced, and potentially constitutes (according to its relevance in the legal framework) a gap in legislation that may need to be filled.[4] The former Code, dated 1916, had been notably

---

[3] "The modern codes of civil law countries follow the idea of the Enlightenment to provide an abstract, systematic and self-contained treatment which anticipates as completely as possible all relevant issues in particular branches of law." Mathias Siems, *Comparative Law* (2nd edn, Cambridge University Press 2018) at 53.

[4] Civil Law systems are based on a set of existing codes and rules, applicable in all territories, created by the legislative branch, to which the judicial branch is bound. In theory, all possible situations are accommodated in the legal hypothesis, generating legal predictability. In opposition, Case Law systems are based on precedents, which become the binding rules to upcoming similar situations. This system is deemed to be more unpredictable when compared to the Civil Law, but, at the same time, more dynamic and able to adapt the ruling to each given case. "The role of precedents is different in legal systems from the Common Law tradition and systems from the Civil Law tradition. The former systems employ the rule of stare decisis, which implies that some precedents are binding, while the latter do not, with as a consequence that precedents have at best persuasive force." Jaap Hage, 'Legal Reasoning', in Smits (ed), *Elgar encyclopedia of comparative law* (2nd edn, Edward Elgar Publishing 2014) ch. 42, 529.

influenced by the German Civil Code, with strong traits of liberalism, the interests of the dominant classes, guarantees of property rights and freedom of contracts.[5] With the enactment of the current Constitution, in 1988, the pre-existing project of drafting a new Civil Code was resumed[6] and this resulted in the Civil Code of 2002, which came in force in 2003.

Structurally, the new Code was divided in two parts: the General Part, which deals with People, Goods and Legal Facts; and the Special Part, which deals with Obligations, Corporations, Assets, Family and Succession. The new Code was immediately criticized as outdated, as its original project was developed in the 1970's.[7] With regard to its content, the Code however innovated in comparison to its predecessor by including provisions that allow "the nullification of contract in cases of gross disproportion of the result of the bargain of the parties (...), prohibition of the abuse of rights (...), good faith (...) and protection for weaker parties in contracts of adhesion".[8] The new Code also represented a sensible shift in the orientation of the civil regime when compared to the

[5] Erika Nicodemos, 'Codificação e descodificação: o direito civil e o Código Civil de 2002' (2013) *Boletim Conteúdo Jurídico, Coluna Jurídica* <http://jus.com.br/artigos25559> accessed 31 July 2022. Jan Kleinheisterkamp, "Development of Comparative Law in Latin America" in Mathias Reimann and Reinhard Zimmermann (eds), *The Oxford Handbook of Comparative Law* (2nd Edn, OUP 2019) 272-274 explains that the structure and content of the Brazilian Civil Code was influenced extensively by both German and French Civil Law and scholarship. Nevertheless, already in its original 1916 incarnation, "the Brazilian Code was predominantly an indigenous product: more than a third of its provisions are based on the pre-existing law, and another third are new provisions of original Brazilian pedigree": ibid at 273.
[6] Lucas Abreu Barroso, *Contemporary Legal Theory in Brazilian Civil Law* (Juruá, Curitiba, 2014) 13: "The reasons for putting the bill on the voting agenda again are related to (a) the purpose of diverting attention from political scandals involving the Senate and (b) an attempt to justify the performance of crongressmen who had been accused of negligent conduct in the Chamber of Deputies. Thus, the approval of the law served as a 'smokescreen' to avert the eyes of public opinion."
[7] Nicodemos (n 5) 5; Barroso (n 6) 13: "the new civil code was born already old!"
[8] Luciano Benetti Timm, 'The social function of contract law in Brazilian Civil Code: distributive justice versus efficiency – lessons from the United States' (2008)

former Code. Whilst the Code of 1916 privileged the *pacta sunt servanda* principle – strengthening the binding power of contract terms – the Code of 2002 was orientated on the principle of good faith, as demonstrated in the provisions below:

> "Art. 113. Juridical transactions shall be interpreted in conformity with good faith and the practice of the place in which they are made" (original version: Os negócios jurídicos devem ser interpretados conforme a boa-fé e os usos do lugar de sua celebração).
>
> (...)
>
> Art. 422. The contracting parties are bound to observe the principles of probity and good faith, both in entering into the contract and in its performance" (original version: Os contratantes são obrigados a guardar, assim na conclusão do contrato, como em sua execução, os princípios de probidade e boa-fé)."

In the words of Barroso, "The amplitude given to objective good faith by the new codification clearly demonstrates the ethical conduct desired by the spirit of the civil legislative body."[9] This orientation, given in a broad and general way, drives the whole Code and has been absorbed throughout legislation, as the same concepts – especially good faith – are replicated in other provisions that are part of the system.[10] This evidences the power of

---

Latin American and Caribbean Law and Economics Association (ALACDE) Annual Papers <http://escholarship.org/uc/item/29x696kf> accessed 31 July 2022.

[9] Barroso (n 6) 17.

[10] The Consumer Code (Federal Law no. 8.078/1990 – available at <http://www.planalto.gov.br/ccivil_03/leis/l8078compilado.htm>), for instance, makes special provision for (i) acquisitions that take place outside stores, allowing consumers to "regret" for 7 days (art. 49); and (ii) clauses that do not observe good faith, which are void null (art. 51).

judges and courts, grounded in subjective concepts such as context and good faith (as decisions are based on the interpretation given by judges):

> "The Civil Code of 2002 favours several types of general clauses and vague concepts, without substantive guidelines to identify or clarify such concepts, which end up being fulfilled according to personal convictions of each judge." (original version: O Código Civil de 2002 prestigia diversos tipos de cláusulas gerais e conceitos vagos, sem que haja qualquer tipo de diretriz material para identificação ou esclarecimento desses conceitos, que acabam sendo preenchidos de acordo com concepções pessoais de cada julgador).[11]

In another example of how this subjective orientation impacts the system and grants power to judges, the Civil Code also expressly stipulates situations in which contracts can be altered by courts, due to unforeseen events which affect them, allowing parties to claim for contract dissolution whenever "the consideration of one party becomes excessively onerous". This possibility of judicial readjustment – which affects the very foundation of contracts – is found in articles 317, 478, 479 and 480, all of which deal with such situations by granting judges the power to modify the contract to what he or she considers equitable, or to simply dissolve it:

> "Art. 317. When, for reasons that could not be foreseen, the value of the obligation owed and its value when it is performed becomes manifestly disproportionate, the judge may correct this, at the request of the party, in such a way as to ensure, as far as possible, the real value of the obligation" (original version: Quando, por motivos imprevisíveis, sobrevier desproporção manifesta entre o

---

[11] Nicodemos (n 5) 5.

valor da prestação devida e o do momento de sua execução, poderá o juiz corrigi-lo, a pedido da parte, de modo que assegure, quanto possível, o valor real da prestação).

(...)

Art. 478. In contracts with continuing or deferred performance, if the obligation of one of the parties becomes excessively onerous, with extreme advantage for the other, by virtue of extraordinary or unforeseeable events, the debtor may apply for dissolution of the contract. The effects of the judgment that declares dissolution shall be retroactive to the date of claim" (original version: Nos contratos de execução continuada ou diferida, se a prestação de uma das partes se tornar excessivamente onerosa, com extrema vantagem para a outra, em virtude de acontecimentos extraordinários e imprevisíveis, poderá o devedor pedir a resolução do contrato. Os efeitos da sentença que a decretar retroagirão à data da citação).

Art. 479. Dissolution may be avoided if the defendant offers to modify the conditions of the contract, on an equitable basis" (original version: A resolução poderá ser evitada, oferecendo-se o réu a modificar equitativamente as condições do contrato).

Art. 480. If only one of the parties has obligations under the contract, that party may petition that his obligations be reduced, or that the manner of performing them be altered, so as to avoid excessive onerousness" (original version: Se no contrato as obrigações couberem a apenas uma das partes, poderá ela pleitear que a sua prestação seja

> reduzida, ou alterado o modo de executá-la, a fim de evitar
> a onerosidade excessiva)."

But if the tendency in the early 2000's was to give power to the judges by favouring good faith over *pacta sunt servanda*, new changes implemented by Federal Law no. 13.874/2019, in 2019, brought back some of the rationale that limits judges' powers to interfere in the parties' bargain. A new paragraph was added to article 421 (that is: right before article 422, which makes reference to good faith), stating that:

> "In private contractual relations, the principles of minimum
> intervention and exceptionality of contractual revision
> will prevail" (original version: Nas relações contratuais
> privadas, prevalecerão o princípio da intervenção mínima
> e a excepcionalidade da revisão contratual)."

With this new amendment, legislators made it clear that good faith, as ground for contractual revision (and, eventually, mitigation), is relegated to exceptional situations, meaning that the general rule is (again) to give effect to what parties have negotiated. To the extent that legal doctrine justifies the mitigation principle by reference to the notion of good faith, which will be discussed below, this reduces the room for mitigation if the system (and the parties, in their contracts) insists on not expressing it directly.

The special part of the Code, specifically in Book 1 – which deals with obligations – brings general provisions that apply to both contractual and non-contractual relations. In Titles I to III (articles 233 to 388), the types of obligations are detailed, followed by Title IV (articles 289 to 402) which provides for the consequences of defaulting. Titles V to VIII (articles 421 to 926) detail the different types of contracts and the available remedies, whilst civil liability that arises from defaulting is regulated in Title IX (articles 927 to 954), with no relevant distinction being made between damages that arise from contractual and non-contractual situations.

In respect of both, the Code first states the legal principle which links unlawful conduct (i.e. tort) or breach (in the context of contracts) to the innocent party's losses, and then provides that this gives rise to liability to compensate those losses.

In non-contractual (i.e. tort) liability, the parties need not have a prior relationship. The requisites are unlawful conduct by one party, loss on the part of the other, and a causal connection between the conduct and the loss. This is clear from the following provisions:

"Art. 186. A person who, by voluntary act or omission, negligence or imprudence, violates rights and causes damage to another, even though the damage is exclusively moral, commits an illicit act" (original version: Aquele que, por ação ou omissão voluntária, negligência ou imprudência, violar direito e causar dano a outrem, ainda que exclusivamente moral, comete ato ilícito).

Art. 187. The holder of a right also commits an illict act if, in exercising it, he manifestly exceeds the limits imposed by its economic or social purpose, by good faith or by good conduct" (original version: Também comete ato ilícito o titular de um direito que, ao exercê-lo, excede manifestamente os limites impostos pelo seu fim econômico ou social, pela boa-fé ou pelos bons costumes).

(...)

Art. 927. Anyone who, through an illict act (arts. 186 and 187), causes damage to another, is obligated to repair" (original version: Aquele que, por ato ilícito (arts. 186 e 187), causar dano a outrem, fica obrigado a repará-lo)."

When these requisites are fulfilled, the consequence is full recovery of loss by the innocent party, as established further in the Code:

> "Art. 944. Indemnification is measured by the extent of the loss" (original version: A indenização mede-se pela extensão do dano)."

These requisites and consequences apply likewise to contractual liability (where parties are previously bound by a contract), except for the replacement of "unlawful conduct" by "contractual breach".[12] In this sense, articles 389 and 402, which apply to both unlawful acts (torts) and breach of contract, are quite specific when mentioning the breach, the consequential losses and the measure of recovery the breaching party is deemed to provide:

> "Art. 389. If an obligation is not performed, the debtor is liable for losses and damage, together with interest and inflation adjustment according to officially established index, as well as attorney's fees" (original version: Não cumprida a obrigação, responde o devedor por perdas e danos, mais juros e atualização monetária segundo índices oficiais regularmente estabelecidos, e honorários de advogado).
>
> (...)

---

[12] Legal commentators differentiate contractual and non-contractual relations when analyzing the burden of proof. This burden, however, is not directly related to the issue of a party's responsibility itself and will, therefore, be disregarded for the purpose of this research. In this regard, see Patricia Maria Basseto Avallone, 'The Award of Punitive and Emotional Distress Damages in Breach of Contract Cases: A Comparison Between the American and the Brazilian Legal Systems' (2002) 8 *New Eng. Int'l & Comp. L. Ann.* 253.

Art. 402. Except where otherwise expressly provided for by law, the losses and damages owed to the creditor cover, in addition to what he effectively lost, the profit which he reasonably failed to realize" (original version: Salvo as exceções expressamente previstas em lei, as perdas e danos devidas ao credor abrangem, além do que ele efetivamente perdeu, o que razoavelmente deixou de lucrar)."

With regard to contracts, it is worth mentioning that the innocent party has the discretion of choosing between specific performance of the contract or its resolution – with no preference given to one remedy over the other. In any case, the innocent party has the right to be indemnified for losses and damages (meaning: even if one seeks specific performance, the right of recovery for losses is preserved).

"Art. 475. A party injured by non-performance may apply for dissolution of the contract, if he does not prefer to demand performance of it, and in either case, the injured party has the right to indemnification of losses and damage" (original version: A parte lesada pelo inadimplemento pode pedir a resolução do contrato, se não preferir exigir-lhe o cumprimento, cabendo, em qualquer dos casos, indenização por perdas e danos)."

These provisions place the two situations on common ground when it comes to the consequences of contractual breach and unlawful (tortious) conduct: in both cases, the defaulting party is responsible for ensuring the return of the other party to the situation he or she was in before the default (*status quo*). In other words: in both cases, the principle of full recovery is applied. As Pinheiro explains:

> "(...) the treatment as equivalent is due to the identity of elements to the obligation to indemnify, whether its origin is a contract or results from a generic breach of the principle not to cause damages to another" (original version: (…) o tratamento conjunto deve-se à identidade nos elementos de uma obrigação reparatória, independentemente de estar a sua origem em um negócio jurídico ou resultante da violação genérica de não causa danos a outrem – neminem laedere)[13]

2.3 Limitations to the full recovery principle and the duty to mitigate loss: provisions, opinions and jurisprudence

The full recovery principle is qualified by several other provisions in the Civil Code that end up limiting the innocent party's right of recovery.[14] In this regard, the literature disagrees as to the possible role of the mitigation doctrine in Brazil: whilst some authors understand that the existing limitations represent the proper application of the mitigation doctrine in the Brazilian legal system, and highlight the compatibility – in the sense of equivalence – between the doctrine and the current rules,[15] others are

---

[13] Denise Pinheiro, 'Duty to mitigate loss à brasileira: uma questão além do nexo de causalidade' Proceedings of the XXI Congresso Nacional do CONPEDI/UFF (2012) 324-353 <http://www.publicadireito.com.br/artigos/?cod=3e524bf740dc8cfd> accessed 31 July 2022.

[14] To mention a few: the first paragraph of art 944 allows the judge to reduce indemnification according to the proportion between the contribution and the loss; art. 771 imposes duties for indemnification in the context of insurance; art. 422 determines that both parties to contracts must observe the duty of good faith (from which limitations such as those from the mitigation doctrine may derive); art. 188 lists actions which shall not be deemed unlawful, even if they effectively cause damage to a party.

[15] Daniel Pires Novais Dias, 'O duty to mitigate loss no direito civil brasileiro e o encargo de evitar o próprio dano' (2011) 12 *Revista de Direito Privado*, 89-145, 113; Paulo Nalin and Hugo Sirena, 'A Convenção de Viena de 1980 e a sistemática

in favour of adding to the Brazilian legal system provisions regulating the mitigation doctrine as an additional limitation to the existing rules:[16]

In favour of the sufficiency of current rules:

> "Turning to the reality of the national legal system, although the duty to mitigate loss is not expressly mentioned in the Civil Code of 2002, or in any other legal provision in force, it is certain that a global reading of legislation evidences an undeniable compatibility of its conceptual lines and the guidelines of Brazilian Law" (original version: Voltando-se à realidade do sistema jurídico nacional, ainda que o princípio do duty to mitigate loss não esteja expressamente encartado no Código Civil de 2002, ou em qualquer outro diploma legal vigente, é certo que a leitura global do ordenamento leva a crer a inegável compatibilidade entre seus contornos conceituais e as diretrizes que regem o Direito Brasileiro).[17]

In favour of enacting a specific mitigation provision:

> "Although it has been demonstrated that current Brazilian law already contemplates the mitigation principle, its application could occur more widely and securely if the

---

contratual brasileira: a recepção principiológica do duty to mitigate the loss' (2002) 49 *Revista Trimestral de Direito Civil*, 149.

[16] Pablo Stolze Gagliano, 'Editorial 12 – Duty to mitigate' (2010) <www.pablostolze.com.br> accessed 31 July 2022; Nelson Rosenvald and Cristiano Chaves de Farias, *Direito das obrigações* (3rd ed. Rio de Janeiro, Lumen Juris, 2008) 61-62; Gisele Leite, 'Roteiro sobre o princípio da boa-fé objetiva' (2006) <http://www.ambito-juridico.com.br/site/index.php?n_link=revista_artigos_leitura&artigo_id=1712> accessed 31 July 2022; Flavio Tartuce, 'A boa-fé objetiva e a mitigação do prejuízo pelo credor' (2005) <http://www.flaviotartuce.adv.br/artigos/Tartuce_duty.doc> accessed 31 July 2022.

[17] Nalin and Sirena (n 15) 149.

Legislator expressly established the burden of mitigating in the Civil Code of 2002, such as the German and Italian codes" (original version: Apesar de ter sido demonstrado que o direito brasileiro atual já contempla a norma de mitigação, sua aplicação poderia ocorrer de forma mais ampla e segura se o Legislador tivesse previsto expressamente o ônus de mitigar no diploma civil de 2002, a exemplo das codigicações alemã e italiana).[18]

This difference of opinion reflects the divergence that is found in the arguments used by litigating parties and the conclusions of courts as to the grounds of a legally defined rule to mitigate. The limits and boundaries of mitigation are not clear: courts have applied it to different situations, to limit recovery of, for example: (i) a party that did not act proactively to minimize losses caused by the contractual breach of a company that did not deliver the production-line machinery for a factory in time;[19] (ii) creditors that did not enforce their claim in a timely fashion and, as a result, lost their entitlement to the interest ;[20] and (iii) an airways company that offered the passengers impacted by the delay of a flight food and entertainment during their wait.[21] In all these cases, the expression "duty to mitigate" was expressly used and the recovery limited. However, these decisions are far from representing the majority, and furthermore, differ among each other as to what represents the infringement of said duty. Negligence, wilful misconduct, abusive exercise of rights – among others, to be analysed in the following section – have all been related to the mitigation doctrine. These thus fail to establish a legal standard regarding

---

[18] Christian Sahb Batista Lopes, *Mitigação dos prejuízos no direito contratual* (São Paulo, Editora Saraiva, 2013). This paragraph was excluded from the published version of his doctoraL thesis, but is found in the original version submitted to the degree and duly approved, on page 246.

[19] TJ/RS Appeal 70025267683, 5th Civil Chamber (2009).

[20] TJ/MS Appeal 2009.022658-4/0000-00, 3rd Civil Chamber (2009).

[21] TJ/RS Appeal 7002.813.8113, 12th Civil Chamber (2009).

the criteria that are to be used to evaluate the creditor's conduct. This lack of standardization contributes to the absence of certainty – from the legal perspective – and calls for the intervention proposed in this thesis.

Furthermore, mainly after the publication of Enunciate 169, in 2004 – which spread the idea behind the doctrine, that the innocent party should avoid the aggravation of losses – it has become no hard task to find jurisprudence, all over the country, expressly mentioning the duty to mitigate loss as one of the reasons for the decision. An Enunciate is a non-binding guideline, formulated by researchers, judges and lawyers present in annual meetings, which is acknowledged by the courts as an alternative non-official source of legal reference. This Enunciate states: "The principle of objective good faith requires the creditor to prevent the aggravation of his or her own losses" (original version: O princípio da boa-fé objetiva deve levar o credor a evitar o agravamento do próprio prejuízo). [22]

In addition to the fact that it was considered necessary to adopt an Enunciate asserting the functional equivalent of what is referred to as mitigation in other countries as well as Brazil, the simple fact that the Enunciate is frequently mentioned in court decisions is a sign of the existence of a gap in the legal system: it demonstrates both the desire for a clear legal basis for the duty to mitigate and the need to identify such a legal basis. Because of the non-binding character of the Enunciate, courts typically link it to existing rules in the Code in order to legitimate applying the duty to mitigate loss as a limitation on the full recovery principle, which does have a clear legal basis in the Code. This has become more frequent since April 1st, 2014, when the United Nations Convention on Contracts for the International Sale of Goods (CISG) – to which Brazil is a signatory – came into force in the country. Making direct reference to the principle of mitigation in its article 77,[23] the CISG has further stimulated discussions as to the interpretation and application of this principle.

---

[22] Available at <http://www.cjf.jus.br/enunciados/> accessed 31 July 2022.

[23] CISG Art. 77: A party who relies on a breach of contract must take such measures as are reasonable in the circumstances to mitigate the loss, including loss of profit,

Although very influential, Enunciate 169 has therefore not brought certainty and clarity about the legal basis of the mitigation doctrine in Brazilian law. A diversity of approaches is found in judicial decisions, and in the debates of legal writers, attempting to link the mitigation doctrine to a range of different provisions or principles. These reveal both (i) the search for a legal basis for the duty to mitigate and (ii) the failure to find a single satisfactory basis that covers the full reach of the mitigation doctrine. Because this doctrine has been transplanted into Brazilian law from the Common Law tradition,[24] this is probably not surprising.[25]

The following subsections will critically analyse the most common attempts by writers and courts in Brazil to identify an existing legal concept or principle which can serve as the doctrinal foundation of the courts' application of the duty to mitigate. In each case, we will consider whether the concept or principle provides an adequate legal basis for the mitigation principle. We will then consider whether these concepts or principles provide clear answers to central questions about the application, scope and content of the duty. This will enable us to return, in the concluding section of this chapter, to the question whether the Code needs a new provision expressly regulating the duty to mitigate.

---

resulting from the breach. If he fails to take such measures, the party in breach may claim a reduction in the damages in the amount by which the loss should have been mitigated. For analysis, see Chapter 4 section 4.4.2.

[24] See Gustavo Santos Kulesza, *Princípio da mitigação de danos; evolução no direito contratual* (Curitiba, Juruá, 2015); Regina Coeli Soares Oliveira Veloso and Nathalie Gurgel Vieira, 'Duty to mitigate loss: a Brazilian perspective' (2018) *Revue libre de Droit* 14, 16.

[25] On the difficulties of legal transplantation, see Pierre Legrand, 'The impossibility of legal transplants' (1997) 4 *Maastricht J. Eur. & Comp. Law* 111 and Jörg Fedtke, 'Legal Transplants', in Jan M. Smits *Elgar Encyclopedia of Comparative Law* (2nd edn, Edward Elgar Publishing 2014) ch. 39.

2.3.1 The duty of good faith

The introduction of the duty of good faith into Brazilian legislation with the enactment of the current Civil Code changed the rules applicable to several situations where this element had not previously been applied.[26] As a general principle, it modified rules which could be abusively exercised by parties with no sanction.[27] In addition, it allowed judges to decide by considering matters beyond the contract or existing rules in specific classes of cases brought to courts,[28] when deciding whether the exercise of rights was abusive or against values such as fairness and equity. This shift reflected a development in society in favour of moral values, and impacted the whole legal system, affecting also the burden of proof and rules of judgment.[29] It is therefore not surprising that Enunciate 169 based the duty to mitigate on the duty of good faith.[30]

The duty of good faith is divided by Brazilian doctrine into subjective and objective good faith. The first relates to the party's awareness of the rule or the situation and his or her intention; the second (which Enunciate

---

[26] As demonstrated above and in several other sections of the Civil Code, with the addition of articles or provisions in existing articles such as 113 (good faith in juridical transactions), 187 (illicit acts), 242 (obligations to give a certain thing – possessor in good faith), 286 (assignment of rights – assignee in good faith), 422 (contracts in general), 523 (sale with reservation of ownership), 606 (provision of services), 856 (promise to reward), 878 (payment not owned), 896 (debt instruments), 925 (registered securities), 1.049 (limited partnership), 1.149 (establishments – assignment of debts related), 1.222 (effects of possession), 1.228 (real rights), 1.243 and 1.260 (usucaption), 1.247 (acquisition by registration of instruments of title), 1.255, 1.258 and 1.259 (buildings and plantations), 1.268 (delivery), 1.270 (specification), 1.561 and 1.564 (invalidity of marriage), 1.741 (the exercise of tutorship), 1.817 (those excluded from succession) and 1.827 and 1.828 (claim to inheritance).

[27] The disregarding of legal personality ("lifting the corporate veil") became possible in cases of "abuse of legal personality" – article 50 of the Civil Code.

[28] Contracts of adhesion – article 423 of the Civil Code.

[29] The Consumer Code (Federal Law no. 8.078/1990), in article 6, VIII, provided for the inversion of the burden of proof as a rule of judgment.

[30] See note 22 above.

169 refers to) relates to the adequacy of the party's conduct according to society's principles and standards.

> "(…) subjective good faith analyses the intention of the party, as opposed to bad faith, while objective good faith analyses a behaviour, in respect to what had been agreed, in acting with legal loyalty" (original version: (...) a boa-fé subjetiva é aquela que analisa a intenção do agente, se contrapondo à má-fé, já a boa-fé objetiva a um comportamento, ao respeito à intenção do pactuado ou da promessa, ao agir com lealdade jurídica)[31]

After almost two decades, the legal system and contracting parties have assimilated this principle as a general rule: good faith has become an assumption in all transactions, and interpretation of the rules is done according to the legislative intent.[32] Lopes explains its impact as follows:

> "The use of vague terms allows the integration with values that are external to the legal system, which the judge will seek in the social context, as well as other principles and values supplied by the legal order itself" (original version: O uso de termos vagos permite a integração com valores extrínsecos ao sistema jurídico, que o julgador deverá procurar no próprio contexto social, bem como com os

---

[31] Juliana Evangelista de Almeida, 'A boa-fé no direito obrigacional' (2010) available at <http://www.ambito-juridico.com.br/site/index.php?n_link=revista_artigos_leitura&artigo_id=8041> accessed 31 July 2022.

[32] Jaap Hage, 'Legal Reasoning', in Smits (ed) (n26) ch. 42, 524: "Legal rules are made for a purpose. They can express moral rules, aim to realize values or reflect government policies (…) Legal reasoning is substantive to the extent that it takes recourse to these moral rules, values and policies, which are said to provided us with substantive reasons for legal decisions."

demais princípios e valores fornecidos pela própria ordem jurídica).[33]

However, it is often feared that, in some situations, including the application of the duty to mitigate loss, courts might exceed their role of resolving disputes and start to legislate what is acceptable and what is not, based on personal conviction. There is a danger that a duty of good faith might be an "(...) invitation to judges to abandon the duty of legally reasoned decisions and to produce an unanalytical incantation of personal values".[34]

Such a situation is not unique to the Brazilian legal system. On the contrary: it is always present when the law is open-textured. This important aspect of law is analyzed by a legal philosopher as follows:

> "In fact all systems, in different ways, compromise between two social needs: the need for certain rules which can, over great areas of conduct, safely be applied by private individuals to themselves without fresh official guidance or weighing up of social issues, and the need to leave open, for later settlement by an informed, official choice, issues which can only be properly appreciated and settled when they arise in a concrete case."[35]

The first challenge, then, is to define whether the principle of good faith may be imposed as a strict rule, or if it fits better as a standard for the legal system:

> "We are in a position to make a rule against killing instead of laying down a variable standard ('due respect for human

---

[33] Lopes (n 18) 144.

[34] Michael G. Bridge, 'Does Anglo-Canadian Contract Law Need a Doctrine of Good Faith?' (1984) *Canadian Business Law Journal*, 426, 412.

[35] H. L. A. Hart, *The Concept of Law* (2nd edn, Clarendon Press 1994) 130.

life'), although the circumstances in which human beings kill others are very various: this is so because very few factors appear to us to outweigh or make us revise our estimate of the importance of protecting life. Almost always killing, as it were, dominates the other factors but which it is accompanied, so when we rule it out in advance as 'killing', we are not blindly prejudging issues which require to be weighed against each other."[36]

"(…) there are, indeed, areas of conduct where much must be left to be developed by courts or officials striking a balance, in the light of circumstances, between competing interests which vary in weight from case to case"[37]

It is a fact that personal judgement as to what constitutes good faith in each situation will be present and may vary from one person to the other. Besides, no rule could ever be sufficiently exhaustive so as to predict all possible situations that would require one to act in good faith. Thus, leaving it as a variable standard, to be applied by courts according to the circumstances of each case – as in the case of Brazil – emerges as the most appropriate (and it would not be extreme to state "the only") way to insert the principle of good faith to the system. The challenge, then, is to make sure that some level of legal prediction is made possible through the analysis of precedents.

Turning back the discussion to the subject of this thesis, a significant part of Brazilian doctrine interprets the mitigation doctrine as an extension of the principle of good faith, under the argument that it represents the morally most adequate conduct to be expected from the innocent

---

[36] Hart (n 35) 133.
[37] Hart (n 35) 135.

party.[38] Taking a similar position, Paulo Henrique Helene and Eduardo Hoffman interpret the duty to mitigate as a collateral duty to the good faith principle.[39] In general, the duty to mitigate ends up being related to the principle of good faith as the set of steps a party is expected to take so as not to allow the increase of his or her own losses, thereby limiting the expansion of that party's right of recovery against the other party.

Lopes explains the connection between mitigation and the good faith principle in its objective form as follows:

> "(...) in a society that adopts cooperation as a value, a loyal and correct conduct from the creditor upon the contractual breach will be to place all reasonable efforts to reduce the losses generated by the default and not to let avoidable damages take place (original version: (...) em uma sociedade que adota a cooperação como valor, a conduta leal e correta do credor diante do descumprimento contratual será empregar esforços razoáveis para reduzir os danos decorrentes do inadimplemento e não deixar que prejuízos evitáveis ocorram).[40]

An equivalent understanding is acknowledged by the courts, through reasoning that an express link between the principle of good faith and the duty to mitigate loss imposes an obligation on the innocent party to act in a certain way, supposedly determined by the existing rules. This can be seen in the following two quotations from judgments:

---

[38] Judith Martins-Costa, *A boa-fé no direito privado* (São Paulo, Revista dos Tribunais, 1999); Antonio Menezes Cordeiro, *Da boa-fé no Direito Civil* (Bd. II, Coimbra, Almedina, 1984) 797; Lopes (n 18) 163.

[39] Eduardo Hoffman and Paulo Henrique Helene, 'Duty to mitigate the loss: o dever de mitigar sua própria perda' (2012) < www.publicadireito.com.br/artigos/?cod=de3f712d1a02c5fb> accessed 31 July 2022.

[40] Lopes (n 18) 161.

""Duty to mitigate the loss: the duty to mitigate own losses. The parties must take the possible and necessary measures not to aggravate losses. The creditor shall not deliberately take no action upon loss. Aggravation of own losses, due to inertia of creditor. Infringement to the duties to cooperate and loyalty"" (original version: Duty to mitigate the loss: o dever de mitigar o próprio prejuízo. Os contratantes devem tomar as medidas necessárias e possíveis para que o dano não seja agravado. A parte a que a perda aproveita não pode permanecer deliberadamente inerte diante do dano. Agravamento do prejuízo, em razão da inércia do credor. Infringência aos deveres de cooperação e lealdade)."[41]

""In light of the duty to mitigate the loss (...) the creditor cannot claim for full recovery of losses which, with reasonable effort of his own, he could have taken steps to reduce (...) [and] contrary to mandatory good faith, claim from the defendant losses which could have been avoided" (original version: À luz do dever de mitigação do próprio prejuízo ou duty to mitigate the loss (...) não pode o credor demandar a reparação pela integralidade dos danos sofridos se poderia, com comportamento seu, sem maiores esforços, tomar as providências necessárias a reduzi-los (...) contrariamente à necessária boa-fé, exigir do devedor a reparação por prejuízos que se mostravam evitáveis)."[42]

However, whilst the understandings above do not seem wrong – as there is a definite compatibility between the principle of good faith and the

---

[41] STJ Resp 758.518/PR (2005).
[42] TJ/RJ Civil Appeal 2008.001.45909 (2008).

mitigation doctrine – it does not present a solution to the challenges that the broad application of the duty to mitigate loss brings to the Brazilian system. After all, the basis for expecting certain behaviour from a party cannot be solely a requirement of "good-faith orientated conduct", since this would leave open questions as to the extent of such conduct (should a party take additional risks when acting in good faith?), the situations in which it would apply (must there be a previous breach to trigger this duty to remedy?) and the consequences that might arise (what if the action to mitigate results in additional losses or unexpected gains?) – not to mention the matter of the burden of proof (is mitigating conduct a requirement to receive compensation for the incurred damages or is it an argument of defence; which party has the burden of proving that mitigation measures have or have not been taken?). Therefore, it seems fair and reasonable to doubt that the "open-ended" concept of good faith provides sufficient guidance as to the scope of the duty to mitigate loss, since further regulation will in most cases be required for its practical application. It is probably for this reason that references to the concept of good faith are typically (as will be seen in the following sections) accompanied by references to more circumscribed concepts such as contributory fault, or are displaced by such other concepts.

Besides, the Federal Constitution – the highest law in force –[43] is clear in determining that "no one will be obliged to do or not to do anything except in virtue of law" (original version: ninguém será obrigado a fazer ou deixar de fazer alguma coisa senão em virtude de lei). This provision materializes the so-called "legality principle", according to which no one can be penalized for not doing something that is not established by law.[44]

---

[43] Available at <http://www.planalto.gov.br/ccivil_03/constituicao/constituicao.htm> accessed 13 August 2022.

[44] Based on this principle, the Court of Appeal of Rio de Janeiro nullified the conviction of a member of an association for having personal relationship with a co-worker, on the ground that there was no previous rule imposing such a restriction: TJ/RJ 0007994-66.2007.8.19.0087 (2007).

That leaves room for the argument that loss-mitigating conduct cannot be required from anyone in the absence of a specific rule requiring such conduct. . Due to its vagueness the principle of good faith might not be capable of constituting such a rule by itself, for it would require further elaboration to establish any particular mitigating behaviour as mandatory. Therefore, the lack of specific regulation as to the extent of the mitigating conduct bars the imposition of such a duty on any party in most, if not all, contexts.

In light of these arguments, it is concluded that the existing good faith principle – although totally compatible with the duty to mitigate – is not sufficient, as a legal rule, to regulate or ground the application of the mitigation principle in Brazil.

2.3.2 The causation rule

The causation rule imposes a direct connection between the action of the wrongdoer and the indemnifiable consequence: if consequences are not "direct and immediate", they shall not be subject to recovery. Thus, it adds another clear limitation on the full recovery principle. This rule is expressed in the Civil Code, art. 403, as follows:

> "Art. 403. Even where non-performance results from the debtor's wrongful conduct, losses and damages only include effective losses and lost profit that are the direct and immediate effect of non-performance, without prejudice to the provisions of the legislation governing procedure" (original version: Ainda que a inexecução resulte de dolo do devedor, as perdas e danos só incluem os prejuízos efetivos e os lucros cessantes por efeito dela direto e imediato, sem prejuízo do disposto na lei processual).

Hence, causation has also been used to provide a grounding for the duty to mitigate, as is explained by Denise Pinheiro:

> "The duty to mitigate the loss (...) has been adopted by Brazilian doctrine and jurisprudence to solve conflicts, without the necessary adaptations and filters, confusing it with the exclusion of causation, linked to the behaviour of the victim and the concepts of indirect and remote loss" (original version: O duty to mitigate the loss (...) tem sido invocado para solucionar conflitos pela doutrina e jurisprudência brasileiras, sem as adaptações e os filtros necessários, muitas vezes, confundindo-o com a excludente do nexo de causalidade ligada ao comportamento da vítima e os conceitos de dano indireto e remoto) [45].

However, Pinheiro is correct that the causation rule has no relation to the mitigation principle. It refers to the cause of the "losses and damages", limiting recovery to those that are "immediate" and "direct" consequences of the other party's conduct. As such, this rule provides that if a certain loss results "immediately and directly" from the action of the creditor (i.e. victim of an unlawful act (tort) or a breach of contract), such loss cannot be recovered from the other party. At no point does this rule focus on how and when someone is supposed to act, instead limiting its regulation to the effects of the parties' conduct.

To illustrate this rule, the following situation may be pictured: A is driving to a meeting and stops the car at a gas station to fill the car's tank. The pump injects water, instead of gasoline. The car breaks down two blocks from the gas station. A argues that the cost to repair the car must be recovered, as well as the lost profits expected from the meeting that he or she missed. Interpretation of this situation – according to art. 403 – will

---

[45] Pinheiro (n 13).

lead to the conclusion that the car breaking down is an immediate and direct consequence of the water pumped into its tank; missing the meeting, however, might be considered a consequence of A's choice to go by car (as opposed to taking a cab to get to the meeting) and thus not to have been caused by the pumping of water instead of gasoline.

In the example above, the outcome of the case might be similar whether applying the causation rule or the mitigation doctrine: the failure to take a cab to the meeting could also amount to a failure to mitigate, if this would have been a reasonable action to take once the car had broken down. However, the simple fact that the causation rule does not consider when or how one *should* act, whilst precisely this is the focus of the mitigation principle, creates a difference between the analysis of someone's conduct for the purposes of causation and for the purposes of the mitigation doctrine. The two enquiries might have the same impact on someone's claim, and they might even make reference to the same facts, but they are nevertheless distinct enquiries.

The conceptual difference between the two principles can be clearly outlined: causation focuses on the origination of the resulting loss, while the duty to mitigate focuses on the avoidance or limitation of loss which *has been caused* by the other. Therefore, the former refers to the relevance of the conduct of the party in causing the resulting event, and the latter refers to the conduct of the party in mitigating the consequences of such event. This means that causation and mitigation come from opposite sides – although aiming to the same direction: mitigation does not concern the question whether damage has been caused, but rather whether compensation should be awarded for all the damage that has been caused.

The causation rule also does not resolve the constitutional issue identified in the previous section. The Constitution requires that, in order to attribute a failure to act to the innocent party, the law shall previously establish his or her duty to act.[46] If one is not expressly required to act

---

[46] See (n 43) above.

mitigate his or her own losses, than all of the consequences (losses) caused by the other party ought to be attributed to the other party's unlawful conduct or breach of contract. This confirms the conclusion that the law needs a clear provision creating a duty to mitigate.

2.3.3 The contributory fault rule

Another limitation to the right of full recovery – which is closely related to the causation doctrine – is the rule of contributory fault. It is regulated in the Brazilian legal system in the Civil Code, in article 945:

> "Art. 945. If the victim, by his fault, contributed to the damaging event, the seriousness of his fault in comparison with that of the person who caused the damage shall be taken into account in fixing his indemnification" (original version: Se a vítima tiver concorrido culposamente para o evento danoso, a sua indenização será fixada tendo-se em conta a gravidade de sua culpa em confronto com a do autor do dano) [47].

The hypothesis of this rule is even more narrow than causation; while the latter requires the party to contribute immediately and directly to the damaging event, the contributory fault rule is applied to a situation in which the victim is as much author of the damage as the other party, and stipulates the distribution of the loss in accordance to the proportion of each party's responsibility to the losses occurred (comparatively).

However, in the absence of regulation of the mitigation doctrine in Brazil, judicial arguments such as the following have based the mitigation doctrine on the contributory fault rule:

---

[47] In the opinion of this researcher, article 945 should not require an "unlawful" contribution, nor distribute the recovery according to its proportion; the focus of the rule should be the contribution, whether unlawful or not.

"(...) negligent conduct of the author, then, is a defence against the alleged unlawful conduct from the defendant, applied by the theory of the Duty to Mitigate the Loss, which limits recovery when a victim is able to do so but does not make any efforts to mitigate their own losses, in violation of objective good faith" (original version: (...) conduta omissiva do próprio autor, portanto, afasta a alegação de ilicitude na conduta do réu, aplicando-se a chamada teoria do Duty of to Mitigate the Loss (dever de mitigar o dano ou a perda), a qual propugna pelo afastamento do dever indenizatório quando sendo possível a vítima, esta não despende qualquer desforço para mitigar as próprias perdas, implicando em violação à boa-fé objetiva).[48]

The fundamental distinction between this rule and mitigation lies in the fact that contributory fault concerns situations where the victim contributes to the causing of the harm (including its extent). On the other side, mitigation concerns the different situation where the victim fails to reduce the harm that has been caused (whether by the perpetrator alone or by both the perpetrator and the victim). Therefore, if in the contributory fault case there is an active contribution of the victim to aggravate the loss, in the mitigation case the contribution is negative – in the sense that the victim did not act to reduce losses. Thus it is possible to apply the two concepts side-by-side: a finding of contributory fault on the part of the victim in causing the harm does not yet answer the question whether the victim should have reduced the harm that was so caused. The victim may be guilty of both contributory fault and a failure to mitigate, or of only the one or the other.

Another aspect which shows the difference between both rules is that

---

[48] TJ/RS Appeal 70028036465 (2009).

contributory fault overlaps in time with the fault of the other party, and both cause the loss. The duty to mitigate, however, follows after the breach or unlawful conduct of the other party, appearing at a later moment – after the loss has already been caused, when the victim fails to reduce that loss.

Finally, the contributory fault rule in force requires wrongful conduct on the part of the victim. Such misconduct cannot derive from the mere inertia of the party in a situation where no rule – no mitigation rule – imposes a duty to act. As Christian Sahb Batista Lopes states, "(...) if law does not impose that the creditor acts in a certain way, he or she cannot be blamed for not doing so" (original version: se o direito não impõe ao credor que aja de tal forma, não poderá ele ser culpado de não ter agido de tal maneira).[49] The same constitutional argument, mentioned in the previous sections would apply here: one cannot be required to do what is not prescribed by law. Thus, there is no fault (whether contributory or not) in not acting in such way as to avoid the aggravation of the loss as long as there is no rule requiring someone to act in that way. Therefore, the contributory fault rule cannot take the place of an express provision regarding the mitigation doctrine but highlights the need for such a provision.

2.3.4 *Venire contra factum proprium*

The *venire contra factum proprium* doctrine establishes that one cannot exercise a right in contradiction with prior behaviour. For example: the parties agree on the value of the rent being one hundred pounds; the tenant pays ninety pounds for two years, without any compliant from the landlord; the acceptance of the lower sum by the landlord, for two years, would bar a later claim for the difference. The reason is that the *venire contra factum proprium* rule is based on protecting trust. One cannot act in a certain way which generates reliance by the other party, and later

---

[49] Lopes (n 18) 180.

change his or her conduct – denying the confidence placed on this by the other party.

Courts have based their decisions structured under this doctrine on the good faith principle and the prohibition of abusive exercise of rights. But there is also evidence of courts interpreting this as an old version of the role now played by the mitigation doctrine:

> "The long delay by the creditor requires reference to the duty to mitigate loss; understood as the moral obligation, burden, or notion derived from good faith, in relation to venire contra factum proprium, the creditor acted abusively" (original version: Ou seja, a espera alongada do credor faz devida a remessa ao dever de mitigar o prejuízo, ou duty do mitigate the loss; entende-se que, como obrigação moral (obrigação em sentido lato), como incombance (ônus para consigo próprio), ou como noção derivada da boa-fé, i.é., relativamente ao venire contra factum proprium, o credor adotou comportamento faltoso, conduta abusiva (...)).[50]

Part of the literature is in favour of making such a connection. To Vera Maria Jacob Fradera, "the duty to mitigate the loss should be considered an accessory duty, derived from the principle of good faith, with possible reception based on venire contra factum proprium and the prohibition of abuse of rights" (original version: o duty to mitigate the loss deve ser considerado um dever acessório, derivado do princípio da boa-fé objetiva, podendo, ainda, a recepção fundar-se no venire contra factum proprium e no abuso de direito).[51] Carlos Andre Cassani Siqueira and Paula Soares Campeão state similarly that: "the institutes of venire contra

---

[50] TJ/RS Appeal 70019328889 (2009).

[51] Vera Maria Jacob de Fradera, 'Pode o credor ser instado a diminuir o próprio prejuízo?' (2004) 19 *Revista trimestral de direito civil* 109-119.

factum proprium, abuse of rights, supressio and surrectio, contribute to supporting the sanctioning of the failure by the creditor to mitigate his or her own losses" (original version: os institutos do venire contra factum proprium, abuso de direito, supressio[52] e surrectio[53], apresentam-se como contribuições fundamentadoras dos efeitos sancionatórios decorrentes do descumprimento do dever de mitigar a própria perda pelo credor).[54]

This comparison, however, seems inadequate. Although there seems to be some connection between both doctrines (since in terms of both one who does not act to prevent avoidable losses shall not claim their recovery), their requirements are totally different. The *venire contra factum proprium* doctrine requires two lawful but contradictory behaviours on the part of the same party, the first leading the other party to believe that the second will not occur. The mitigation doctrine, on the other hand, is not based on the trust that the conduct of one party generates in the other party; it is solely based on the presence of loss which can be avoided by the innocent party, depending on his or her conduct. It would be incorrect to state that the innocent party caused a certain loss to the defaulting party because

---

[52] Delay in the exercise of a right which generates an honest expectation by the other party that such right has been waived.

[53] Customary exercise of a right, not previously agreed by the parties, which generates the honest expectation that the right is understood in that way.

[54] Carlos André Cassani Siqueira and Paula Soares Campeão, 'A cessação dos efeitos do Inadimplemento obrigacional por não mitigação da perda pelo Credor' (2011) Paper delivered at the XX Congresso Nacional do CONPEDI, Vitória. In the same sense: Silvano J. G. Flumignan, 'A correlação entre o dano moral, o dano social e o caput do artigo 944 do Código Civil na responsabilidade civil do Estado' (2011) Paper delivered at the XXXVII Congresso Nacional de Procuradores de Estado, Belo Horizonte; Tartuce (n 17); Alessandra Cristina Tufvesson Peixoto, 'Responsabilidade extracontratual – Algumas considerações sobre a participação da vítima na quantificação da indenização' (2008) 44:11 *Revista da Emerj*, 135, 136; Fredie Didier Jr., 'Multa Coercitiva, boa-fé processual e supressio: aplicação do duty to mitigate the loss no processo civil' (2009) *Revista de processo, São Paulo*, n. 171; and Renata Malta Villas-bôas, 'Duty to mitigate the loss no Direito Civil pátrio' (2013) XVI *Âmbito Jurídico, Rio Grande*, n. 111, abr. <http://ambito-juridico.com.br/site/?n_link=revista_artigos_leitura&artigo_id=12702> accessed 31 July 2022.

the latter had been led by the innocent party to count on the innocent party to prevent further losses. For the purposes of the mitigation rule, it does not matter whether the innocent party created any expectation on the side of the guilty party or indeed whether the latter had any beliefs at all about whether the innocent party would take reasonable steps to limit the loss. On the other hand, the doctrine of mitigation, unlike *venire contra factum proprium*, requires that the victim's inertia (their first behaviour) must be a breach of duty.

This means that, although both doctrines might – at some point – limit the extent of recovery by the victim, and the same facts may play a role in both of them (for example, delay by the victim), their requisites are different and they should not be regarded as equivalents.

2.3.5 Abuse of right

The theory of abusive exercise of rights is founded on the harm caused by the abusive exercise of a right. It applies in situations in which someone exercises his or her right abusively, with no legitimate interest other than to deliberately cause loss to the other party.[55] In the words of Carvalho Santos, it arises when two interests are opposed:

> "that of the right holder, and that of the victim of its exercise. It is socially useful and necessary that both are protected. It is socially impossible, however, that both are kept intact. Then there is the need of balancing them. But, if at a given moment, the harm on the victim is more relevant than the restriction on the right holder,

---

[55] Maria Claudia Chaves de Faria Góes, 'Breves considerações acerca da doutrina do abuso do direito' (2014) <http://www.tjrj.jus.br/c/document_library/get_file?uuid=a0ff68c7-4cb0-4d86-b33e-c273865fa54d&groupId=10136> accessed 31 July 2022.

from the social perspective, balance is lost and demands intervention for the victim."[56]

Kulesza has argued that the mitigation doctrine does not require the absence of good faith, but the abuse of a right and consequential losses.[57] Nonetheless, there are also authors who identify an intersection between the principle of good faith and the abuse of rights theory:

> "There is, indeed, an overlapping area between the domains of the two concepts (good faith and abuse of rights). Although structured to apply in different situations, they overlap and interact" (original version: Existe, de fato, uma zona de interseção entre os planos atinentes a cada uma das figuras (boa-fé e abuso do direito). Conquanto tenham sido estruturadas para enfrentar conjunturas diversas, vieram a sobrepor-se, passando, assim, a dialogar).[58]

Judicial decisions reach further, and implicate the failure to mitigate loss as a form of abuse of rights:

---

[56] João Manoel de Carvalho Santos, *Código Civil Brasileiro Interpretado* (vol. III, 4th ed., vol. III, Rio de Janeiro, Livraria Freitas Bastos 1950) 343 (original version: Dois interesses, prossegue, estão em presença: o do sujeito do direito e o da vítima do exercício do direito. É socialmente útil e necessário que ambos sejam protegidos. É socialmente impossível, entretanto, que ambos sejam mantidos intactos. Começa daí a necessidade de se procurar equilibrá-los. Mas, se, em dado momento, a lesão do interesse do prejudicado aparece como mais grave, do ponto de vista social, que a lesão do interesse do sujeito, há ruptura do equilíbrio. Essa ruptura determina a intervenção da justiça em favor do interesse ameaçado).
For an overview in English of this principle and its application in European Civil Law systems, see Annekatrien Lenaerts, 'The General Principle of the Prohibition of Abuse of Rights: A Critical Position on Its Role in a Codified European Contract Law' (2010) 6 *European Review of Private Law* 1121-1154.
[57] Kulesza (n 24) 216-217.
[58] Elena de Carvalho Gomes, *Entre o actus e o factum: os comportamentos contraditórios no direito privado* (Belo Horizonte, Del Rey, 2009) 29. This is also the position in European systems: see Lenaert (n 56).

59

"Through the new reading of the Civil Code, one of the modalities of abuse of right is the creditor's duty to reduce his or her own losses (duty to mitigate the loss) (…) There will also be a case of abuse of right by means of violating the duty to mitigate the loss in the circumstances of where the claimant delays obtaining an injunction from the judge" (original version: Diante da nova leitura do Código Civil, uma das modalidades do abuso do direito é o "dever do credor de minorar as suas próprias perdas" (duty to mitigate the loss) (...) Também será caso de abuso do direito por violação do duty to mitigate the loss a situação de inércia do autor de uma ação que obtém do juiz uma tutela antecipatória)[59].

However, the distinction between the abuse of rights theory and the mitigation doctrine is clear. The first of these aims to prevent a party from exercising his or her rights abusively – which is not what is being done when a claim is lodged to recover losses actually suffered. The second has a different basis: a duty to act reasonably to avoid the aggravation of losses wrongfully caused by the other party. The consequences of the two are also different: in the case of abuse of right, compensation is due to the other party; in the case of mitigation, a limit is placed on the extent of recovery due to the victim of a rights violation. The outcome of a failure to mitigate one's own losses, is simply that one is not permitted to recover the avoidable losses; not because the claim is abusive – to the contrary the claim itself is permitted – but because of the failure to mitigate. In other words, whereas the doctrine of abuse of rights restricts someone's use of their rights in light of the rights of others, the duty to mitigate concerns the effect that someone's failure to take care of their own interests has on their legal remedies. The former limits rights whereas the latter limits remedies.

---

[59] TJ/MG Appeal 1.0145.09.532430-0/003 (2012).

2.3.6 Reasonableness of lost profits

Lost profit refers to profits the party could have made if it were not for the unlawful conduct or contractual breach by the other party. It covers, for example, the situation of a taxi driver who is prevented from using his or her car for several days due to an accident wrongfully caused by the other party. The profits which could have been made during those days constitute the lost profits.

In this regard, it is relevant to note that art. 402 of the Brazilian Civil Code provides that compensation shall cover only profit that the victim "reasonably" failed to realize.[60] That means that if the taxi driver in the example above fails to provide a reasonable estimate of his lost profit or unreasonably delays in taking the car for the necessary repairs, the period of delay shall not count when the lost profit is calculated.

The courts have expressly linked this to the mitigation doctrine:

> "(…) duty on the party that suffered losses: act reasonably, in the context, to mitigate losses. This means: the claimant must prove having taken all measures to avoid the losses. Although it is alleged by claimant that the event caused the loss of profits (…), he should demonstrate that he took measures to avoid the losses, by acquiring an equivalent machine or seeking an alternative supplier" (original version: (...) ônus incumbido à parte que sofreu o dano: agir de forma razoável, dentro da realidade circundante, de modo a mitigar o prejuízo. Ou seja, impõe-se à parte requerente o dever de provar que tomou todas as medidas cabíveis para evitar o prejuízo experimentado. Em que pese a alegação da demandante, no sentido de que o evento

---

[60] Art 402. "Except where otherwise expressly provided for by law, the losses and damages owed to the creditor cover, in addition to what he effectively lost, that which he reasonably failed to profit".

danoso lhe rendeu o loss of profits (...), caberia à autora demonstrar que se acautelou de eventual prejuízo, seja ao adquirir outra máquina que desempenhasse a mesma função, ou mesmo entabular contrato de prestação do referido serviço com outra empresa).[61]

However, the best interpretation of art. 402 is that the reference to reasonableness is directed at the estimate of losses and not the innocent party's conduct. In other words: lost profits must be established on concrete grounds and not freely assessed beyond reason[62] (for example, if the taxi driver's profits average fifty pounds a day, and the car was stuck in repairs for three days, recovery for lost profits should be set at one hundred and fifty pounds). In contrast, when the mitigation doctrine calls for reasonableness, it refers to the action to be taken by the innocent party (in the same example, the taxi driver is not expected to spend an extra two hundred pounds just for the repairs to be finished one day earlier – for this would represent an additional unreasonable loss of one hundred and fifty pounds).

It is true that the two concepts might – at some point – partially overlap: the unreasonable delay by the taxi driver results in unreasonable lost profit (the portion aggravated by the delay). In this case, recovery will be equally limited by both concepts. However, this is only a matter of the results of two rules coinciding, as it is still possible to conduct a separate analysis of the party's conduct and of the losses claimed (was the taxi driver diligent to promptly seek the repairs? Was the lost profit claimed

---

[61] TJ/RS Appeal 70025609579-2008.
[62] Special Appeal 1.655.090/MA: party claiming losses after defendant denied funding construction project. Court stated that, although the denial was not justifiable, the claimant failed to reasonably estimate losses as probable, rather than possible, based on concrete circumstances of fact. The mere estimate supposing an unprecedented profitability does not meet the requirement of art. 402 of the Civil Code.

reasonable?. Therefore, the rule requiring reasonableness of lost profit does not play the same role in the legal system as the mitigation doctrine.

2.3.7 Late exercise of rights

Finally, in several precedents the courts have associated the principle that excessive delay by a creditor in the exercise of their rights which aggravates the debtor's losses can constitute unlawful conduct under article 187 of the Civil Code (i.e. a tort), with the duty to mitigate loss:

> "(…) the absence of action from the creditor is excessive, and aggravates losses of the debtor and – in theory and apparently – his own damages (...) By doing so, an unlawful conduct from the creditor arises, in not mitigating his own damages" (original version: (...) a inação da parte credora é demasiada, e veio a agravar o prejuízo do devedor e – em tese, e aparentemente - o seu próprio dano (...) Em o fazendo, exsurge uma conduta indevida do credor que não providencia no mitigar do seu próprio prejuízo).[63]

However, the late exercise of a right principle is narrower than the mitigation doctrine. Whilst it may be true that – in some situations – a party who aggravates the other party's losses by delaying the exercise of their own rights (for example, delaying to require the upstairs neighbour to repair a water leak, which causes the losses due to the leak to aggravate), the focus here falls on a different point in time, namely at the point when the harm is caused. The reasonable conduct expected by the mitigation doctrine is not limited to this, however: it encompasses the consequences of the claimant's unreasonable act or delay (finding an alternative supplier), its cost (buying a similar product at a similar price) and the risks involved (trying desperately to put out the fire set by the other) – to mention

---

[63] TJ/RS Appeal 70024988883-2008.

only a few of the additional aspects. Thus, even though there might be situations in which the two principles overlap (the prolonged delay of a party to exercise his or her right may aggravate their own loss as well as the other party's loss), the mitigation doctrine is much wider in its reach and, therefore, cannot be replaced in the legal system by the late exercise of rights rule.

2.4 Other uncertainties

As demonstrated above, legal writers and courts invoke the mitigation doctrine as a possible solution to different types of controversies, in both contractual and non-contractual contexts. These constant references in cases and doctrine to the duty to mitigate loss evidence (i) the lack of familiarity of most authorities with the doctrine; but also (ii) how useful its clear definition would be to the Brazilian legal system; and (iii) that the search for one generally acknowledged standard that would allow courts to harmonize its application has not been concluded yet. The inappropriate connections drawn with existing principles and rules further demonstrates the need for a new specific rule detailing the scope of application, the requirements and the effects of such a mitigation requirement.

The reliance by Brazilian lawyers and courts on a variety of existing concepts and principles to justify application of the mitigation principle, even though none of these fits very well with the principle, also means that there are several aspects of mitigation that remain uncertain in Brazilian law.

One such aspect is the nature of the duty to mitigate. It could be a duty in a loose sense of this term, indicating a standard of conduct that is expected of the victim – which, if not observed, would impact their right to recovery – or it could be a genuine obligation, giving rise to an enforceable right for the other party.[64] Another important aspect concerns

---

[64] This issue is raised by the reliance that has been placed on the abuse of rights doctrine (see section 2.3.5 above) as well as on art 187 in relation to the late exercise

the requisites for the application of the mitigation principle: does it require unlawful conduct (i.e. a tort) or breach of contract by the other party, or will it – at some point – simply correspond to what is expected from parties under the duty to cooperate?[65] Further, the standard of behaviour expected of the innocent party – the concept of reasonableness – must be clarified,[66] as each of the various existing concepts and principles that have been relied on so far has its own requirements, and these often differ from each other.[67]

The scope of the mitigation doctrine also needs to be established. Firstly, there is the question whether the duty to mitigate only requires of the victim to avoid aggravating the loss, that is, making things worse or allowing things to become worse through inaction, or whether it also requires of the victim to take steps which would reduce the loss caused by the other party. Concepts such as good faith, causation, contributory fault and abuse of right, to mention only the ones that have been most prominent, do not by themselves indicate whether it is the narrower or the broader conception of the duty that should be applied. Secondly, it has also been stated that: "Amounts spent to avoid the aggravation of loss must be included in the recovery". [68] However, the various concepts and principles

of rights (see section 2.3.7 above).

[65] The duty to cooperate is frequently raised as the feature of good faith that provide foundation for the duty to mitigate (see section 2.3.1 above).

[66] On the importance of victim's reasonableness, see Cristiano de Souza Zanetti, 'A mitigação do dano e alocação da responsabilidade' (2012) *Revista Brasileira de Arbitragem*, nº 35.

[67] For example, contributory fault (section 2.3.3 above) and unlawful late exercise of a right (section 2.3.7 above) both require fault on the part of the victim, whilst the concept of good faith (section 2.3.1 above) employs a broader concept of reasonableness, and the concepts of causation (section 2.3.2 above) and *venire contra factum proprium* (section 2.3.4 above) do not require the assessment of the relevant conduct as unreasonable. See also the discussion of reasonableness of lost profits in section 2.3.6 above.

[68] Francisco Cavalcanti Pontes de Miranda, *Tratado de direito privado: tomo XXII – parte especial* (Campinas, Bookseller, 2003) 231, 311, 312 (original version: Importâncias gastas para evitar o agravamento do dano deverão ser incluídas na indenização).

relied on so far would again point in different directions.[69] Thirdly, there is the question of how a claim for damages should be affected when the innocent party has indeed taken mitigating measures and has reduced the loss caused by the other party. This is an issue especially if the innocent party went beyond the requirements of reasonableness and avoided losses he or she would have been able to recover if they had taken no action. It is not clear what answer the various concepts and principles would provide: is it contrary to good faith or an abuse of rights to recover such avoided losses?[70] Should all mitigating steps actually taken, even ones which were not required by a reasonableness standard, reduce the compensation recoverable by the innocent party?

More generally, the variety of concepts and principles that have been relied on in Brazil to give effect to the mitigation principle creates uncertainty by itself about its impact and/or coexistence with other rules[71] and practical matters such as which side will bear the burden of proof.

2.5 Conclusion

The mitigation principle has been supported in Brazil on both social[72] and economic grounds, with Lopes arguing that:

> "In establishing that there will be no compensation for avoidable damages, the mitigation standard creates an incentive for the creditor to take measures so that society does not permanently lose economic resources" (original

---

[69] Thus, the principle *venire contra factum proprium* (section 2.3.4 above) serves purely to prevent a claim (or part thereof) and does not create scope for increasing the claim. Because such expenditure is at least partly attributable to the unlawful act or breach of contract of the other party, it could in theory be covered by the other concepts and principles, but this would need to be argued.

[70] The doctrine of unjust enrichment may be helpful here – see Arnaldo Rizzardo, *Responsabilidade civil* (5 ed. Rev. e atual., Rio de Janeiro, Forense, 2011) 12.

[71] For example unjust enrichment – see ibid.

[72] Villas-bôas (n 53).

version: Ao estabelecer que não haverá indenização pelos danos evitáveis, a norma de mitigação cria um incentivo para que o credor adote medidas para que a sociedade não perca, de forma definitiva, recursos econômicos).[73]

This rationale fits well with the shift in the 2002 Civil Code away from strict adherence of *pacta sunt servanda* to a more social orientation allowing greater judicial control over parties' choice via the notion of objective good faith. It is therefore not surprising that the mitigation principle, first introduced hesitantly in 1991, has come to be widely adopted by both the courts and legal writers since the enactment of the Code.[74] This trend was reinforced when Brazil joined the Convention on the International Sale of Goods in 2014, which expressly imposes a duty to mitigate. Mitigation is now firmly established as part of the Brazilian legal landscape, as is affirmed by the publication of Enunciate 169, back in 2004.[75]

But the fact remains that the Code does not make express provision for its application, and this creates difficulties in a Civil Law system where the Code is meant to provide a comprehensive statement of the law. Because the mitigation principle contradicts the full recovery principle in art. 402 CC, this has generated, as this chapter has shown, a range of attempts for finding doctrinal justifications in concepts and principles that are already included in the Code. Critical analysis in this chapter of seven such concepts and principles has led to the conclusion that none of them is able to provide an adequate grounding for the mitigation principle. There certainly is compatibility and an overlap between each of these and the mitigation principle, and the same facts will often be relevant to these principles as well as to mitigation and lead to similar outcomes and impacts on a claim for compensation, but each also has its own distinctive features which distinguish it from the mitigation principle. This may

---

[73] Lopes (n 18) 265.
[74] For details, see Chapter 1 section 1.1 and 1.3.
[75] See note 22 above.

explain why the courts and the legal literature have not been able to settle on a single legal basis for mitigation: none of them covers exactly and in full all aspects of the mitigation principle. Moreover, the analysis in this chapter also showed that none of these existing concepts and principles is able to provide clear answers to questions about the application of the duty to mitigate, its scope or its content. The result is a lack of clarity in Brazilian law about the most important aspects of the mitigation doctrine.

One significant reason for the inadequacy of current concepts and principles lies, as was explained, in Art. 5, II of the Federal Constitution, which provides that, "no one will be obliged to do or not to do anything except in virtue of law". As was explained, this makes the absence of an express legislative duty to mitigate problematic also for attempts to base this duty in the existing principles of good faith, contributory fault and abuse of rights. This indicates the direction in which to find the solution for the legislative gap and lack of clarity: the inclusion of an express mitigation principle in the Civil Code.

In this regard, the legal literature is not unanimous. On one side, Lopes states that such a provision is "necessary to give content to the requirements flowing from the general good faith clause with regard to mitigation".[76] Dias, on the other hand, states that although a party cannot be prevented from aggravating his or her own losses, there is sufficient law concerning the impact of the victim's actions or inaction on the amount that is recoverable.[77] Valdesoiro also argues against a new provision on the basis that the causation rule plays the same role as the mitigation doctrine.[78] In this controversy, the conclusions reached in this chapter

---

[76] Lopes (n 18) 193. (original version: necessário preencher o conteúdo do comando dado pela cláusula geral de boa-fé no que diz respeito à mitigação).

[77] Dias (n 15) 50.

[78] Gabriella Michetti Mora Valdesoiro, 'O instituto do duty to mitigate the loss e seu conteúdo eficacional no direito brasileiro em case da causalidade cumulativa do artigo 945 do Código Civil' <https://repositorio.ufsc.br/bitstream/handle/123456789/114922/TCC%20-%20FINAL%20-%20REPOSIT%C3%93RIO%20-%20TERMO%20DE%20APROVA%C3%87%C3%83O%20-%20PDF%20A.

provide firm support for the position taken by Lopes. None of the existing limitations to the full recovery principle has the same reach or embraces the same situations as the mitigation doctrine. Therefore, a new provision would not disrupt the system; instead, it would complement the existing principles and rules, filling the gaps identified in this chapter.

This conclusion gives rise to a new question: how should the gap be filled? This question raises issues of two kinds, each of which in turn raises a series of sub-questions. The first type of issue concerns what one can call issues of substance: what should the content of such a provision be in terms of the application, scope and content of the mitigation principle? How should it answer the questions about these matters that were outlined in this chapter? The second kind of issue could be called issues of legislative style and approach: where should such a provision be located in the Code and how should it be drafted? Should it be presented as a qualification of the full recovery principle in art. 403, as Lopes proposes, or form part of the contributory fault rule in art. 945, as is proposed by Comino?[79]

The next chapters are devoted to developing answers to both types of issues through a comparative study of the development and application of the mitigation principle in other legal systems. Chapter 3 focuses on common law systems, where the duty originated, which therefore have rich experience in relation to the application, scope and content of the mitigation principle. The aim is not to find a single formulation that can be transplanted, but to learn from their experience, both good and bad. Because they lack Civil Codes, these systems are not best suited for exploring answers to the second type of issue. For that reason, and also because there are important differences between Common Law and Civil

---

pdf?sequence=1&isAllowed=y> accessed 31 July 2022. See also notes 17 and 19 above.

[79] See Lopes (n 18) 266 and Tomas Barros Martins Comino, 'As desaventuras do duty to mitigate the loss no Brasil' Dissertation for the degree of Mestrado Profissional em Direito dos Negócios Aplicado e Direito Tributário Aplicado, Fundação Getúlio Vargas, São Paulo (2015) available at <https://bibliotecadigital.fgv.br/dspace/handle/10438/13610?show=full> accessed 31 July 2022.

Law approaches to remedies,[80] Chapter 4 examines a selection of Civil Law systems, as well as official and unofficial transnational codifications. This chapter will explore how Civil Law systems and transnational instruments are dealing with the duty to mitigate, providing further insights about the appropriate application, scope and content of the mitigation principle. This will enable a comparison between Common Law and Civil Law approaches that will make it possible to identify which answers are most suitable to Brazil's legal landscape, and it will also provide information on the different ways in which such a provision may be drafted and located in the Code. Chapter 5 will draw all this together, presenting a proposal for filling the legislative gap which draws on the results of this comparative study.

---

[80] See Siems (n 3) 72-73.

CHAPTER 3

3.1 Introduction

The duty to mitigate loss originated in Common Law jurisdictions.[1] According to Anne Michaud, this is due to "historical and juridical circumstances that may have caused Common Law to attain higher levels of generality and of abstraction than Civil Law with regard to the issue of mitigation."[2] The duty to mitigate is well established in all common law jurisdictions. Although developed by the courts through the doctrine of precedent, the mitigation doctrine has also been acknowledged and supported by statutory law in several Common Law countries.[3] In the United States, where it is usually referred to as "the avoidable consequences" rule or doctrine, it is incorporated in the Restatement (Second) of Contracts,[4] as well as the Restatement (Second) of Torts.[5]

This chapter focuses on the development and application of the mitigation doctrine in the Common Law jurisdictions as part of the

---

[1] Tomas Barros Martins Comino, 'As desaventuras do duty to mitigate the loss no Brasil', (2015) Dissertation for the degree of Mestrado Profissional em Direito dos Negócios Aplicado e Direito Tributário Aplicado, Fundação Getúlio Vargas, São Paulo, 18 available at <https://bibliotecadigital.fgv.br/dspace/handle/10438/13610?show=full> accessed 31 July 2022.

[2] Anne Michaud. 'Mitigation of Damage in the Context of Remedies for Breach of Contract' (1984) 15 Rev. Gen. de Droit, 295 and 339.

[3] Common law jurisdictions which statutory law supports the mitigation principle: Sale of Goods Act, 1979, c. 54, §§ 50(3), 51(3) in England, Sale of Goods Act, C.C.S.M. c. S10 § 51(3) in Canada, Sale of Goods Act 1895, § 50(3) in Australia. These provisions require substitute transactions in the event of a breach. For their relationship to the mitigation rule, see section 3.2.2 below.

[4] Section 350(1): "Damages are not recoverable for loss that the injured party could have avoided without undue risk, burden or humiliation".

[5] Section 918(1): "[O]ne injured by the tort of another is not entitled to recover damages for any harm that he could have avoided by the use of reasonable effort or expenditure after the commission of the tort." The Restatement of the Law is a set of treatises on legal subjects, published by the American Law Institute, intended to inform judges and lawyers about general principles of common law. Produced by experts, it is one of the most respected and widely used secondary sources of law in the USA.

investigation in this thesis into the question whether Brazil should introduce a specific mitigation provision into its Civil Code. In doing this, it answers the research question posed in chapter 1 as to what lessons can be learnt from Common Law jurisdictions that regulate the duty to mitigate. The aim of this chapter is to obtain insight into the operation of the mitigation principle by investigating the experience of the legal systems which have the longest history of expressly recognizing and applying this principle. This chapter therefore does not seek to provide a complete detailed description of all aspects of mitigation in Common Law systems; rather, it focuses on aspects of the Common Law experience that hold lessons that are relevant to finding a solution to the current gaps and uncertainties in Brazilian law that were identified in Chapter 2. These concern especially the scope of application of the mitigation principle, its content and practical application, and its relationship with related legal doctrines.

The Chapter therefore starts with an overview of the mitigation doctrine, including a brief account of the history of its express recognition. It then moves on to the practical operation of the doctrine, investigating first the scope of its operation and then various aspects of its practical operation. Regarding the latter, specific attention is paid to the content of the principle, namely the taking of reasonable mitigating steps, and to how this is applied to require of the innocent party to make substitute arrangements where appropriate. This is followed by a discussion of how the law deals with the benefits gained as well as any costs incurred as a result of mitigating steps. Part of the aim of this investigation of the practical operation of the doctrine is to identify tensions and divergences which may hold lessons for Brazil. The Chapter then explores theoretical analyses of the mitigation principle in Common Law systems. It identifies and discusses two levels of such analyses: firstly, debates about the grounds and justification of the principle, and secondly, debates about the relationship between mitigation and related legal doctrines. Taken together, the topics discussed in this Chapter provide important insights and lessons for both the question whether Brazil ought to adopt a specific mitigation provision and regarding the content of such a provision.

Finally, it should be pointed out that this Chapter takes the law of England and Wales as the starting point and basic framework for its discussion of the Common Law position, but also refers to cases and writers from other Common Law jurisdictions such as Canada and the United States. This reflects the fact that the Common Law tradition – and the mitigation doctrine – developed in England, but also contains considerable diversity.[6] This will enable comparison among different approaches and emphases to the mitigation doctrine within the Common Law tradition.

3.1.1 The principle and its development

The mitigation principle "comprises various rules concerned with avoidable and avoided losses."[7] Although it is perhaps most prominent in contract law, it also applies to damages for torts.[8] The leading text describes the principle as comprising "three different, although closely interrelated, rules",[9] as follows:

(i) "[T]he claimant must take all reasonable steps to mitigate their loss consequent upon the defendant's wrong and cannot recover

---

[6] See Mathias Siems, *Comparative Law* (2nd edn, Cambridge University Press 2018), Chapters 3 and 4.

[7] Michael G. Bridge, 'Mitigation of damages in contract and the meaning of avoidable loss' (1989) 105 Law Quarterly Review 398, 400.

[8] *The Liverpool (No. 2)* [1963] P 63 at 77-78. Harvey McGregor, James Edelman, Jason Varuhas and Simon Colton (general eds), *McGregor on Damages* (21st Ed., London, Sweet & Maxwell, 2020) Chapter 9, par 9-002, 9-005. This chapter is the leading and most comprehensive text on mitigation of loss in English law (and other common law jurisdictions).

[9] McGregor (n 8) 9-003. All three rules were also endorsed by Leggatt J in *Thai Airways International Public Co Ltd v KI Holdings Co Ltd* [2015] EWHC 1250 (Comm); [2016] 1 All E.R. (Comm) 675 at [32]. In *Sainsbury's Supermarkets Ltd v Visa Europe Services LLC* [2020] UKSC 24 at [212], [214], the UK Supreme Court endorsed the first and the third rule.

damages for any such loss which they failed, through unreasonable action or inaction, to avoid".[10]

(ii) "[W]here the claimant does take reasonable steps to mitigate the loss to them consequent upon the defendant's wrong they can recover for loss incurred in so doing". [11]

(iii) "[T]he claimant cannot generally recover for avoided loss".[12]

The second rule can be seen as already implicit in the first rule,[13] and therefore arguably does not need to be listed separately.[14] Michaud explains that the principle has a "positive" aspect and a "negative one", which coincide with the first and the third rule above:

"The positive aspect is concerned with cases where an aggrieved party has reacted to a wrong in such a way that his loss has been reduced; the issue is whether this actual reduction of damage ought to be taken into account. The negative aspect of mitigation provides that a plaintiff's failure to act when he could have avoided some loss must be taken into account in measuring what damage counts for compensation. Since the eitheenth [sic] century this negative aspect of mitigation has gradually taken the lead over the positive aspect; it now constitutes

---

[10] McGregor (n 8) 9-004.

[11] McGregor (n 8) 9-005.

[12] McGregor (n 8) 9-006.

[13] Thus McGregor (n 8) 9-005 describes the second rule as "the corollary" of the first and the UKSC found it sufficient to endorse the first and the third rules only in *Sainsbury's Supermarkets Ltd v Visa Europe Services LLC* (n 9).

[14] Andrew Dyson and Adam Kramer, 'There is no 'Breach Date Rule': mitigation, difference in value and date of assessment' (2014) 130 Law Quarterly Review, 259 at 263 believe that the mitigation principle "is better expressed using just one: damages are assessed as if the claimant acted reasonably, if in fact it did not act reasonably". This compresses rules one and two, and reflects their rejection of McGregor's broad formulation of the third rule. The latter point is discussed below.

the basic principle of the modern doctrine of mitigation in Common Law. Thus, the rule on avoidable losses is primary, that on losses avoided is subsidiary."[15]

McGregor also describes the first rule as "the most important".[16]

Although it is common to refer to the duty to mitigate loss,[17] there "is not strictly a 'duty' to mitigate, but rather a restriction on the damages recoverable, which will be calculated as if the claimant had acted reasonably to minimize his loss."[18] There is strictly speaking no duty because if the victim "wishes to adopt the more expensive ... [option], he is at liberty to do so and by doing so he commits no wrong against the defendant or anyone else".[19] Thus, "mitigation takes effect as a rule for the assessment of damages and not as a prescriptive guide to the claimant's post-breach conduct".[20] In other words, while in a loose sense the mitigation principle expects of parties to act so as to minimize the total costs for providing the equivalent of performing a contract, and provides them with a strong incentive for doing so,[21] in a practical sense, "the failure to mitigate merely

---

[15] Michaud (n 2) 296.

[16] McGregor (n 8) 9-004.

[17] Indeed, Viscount Haldane did so in his classic formulation in *British Westinghouse Electric & Manufacturing Co Ltd v Underground Electric Railways Co of London Ltd* (1912) AC 673, 690 (quoted below).

[18] Joseph Chitty and H. G. Beale, *Chitty on Contracts* (33rd Ed. Incorporating Second Supplement, London, Sweet & Maxwell, 2020) 26-079. Also McGregor (n 8) 9-018; Ewan McKendrick, *Contract Law* (11th edn, Palgrave Macmillan 2015) 357.

[19] *Darbishire v Warran* [1963] 1 WLR. 1067 CA at 1075. The same point was made by Lord Toulson in *Bunge SA v Nidera BV* [2015] UKSC 43; [2015] 3 All E.R. 1082 at [81].

[20] Andrew Dyson, 'British Westinghouse Revisited' (2012) 3 *Lloyd's Maritime and Commercial Law Quarterly* 412, 420.

[21] Ewan McKendrick, *Contract law: Text, cases, and materials* (6th edn, Oxford University Press 2014) 887.

'disables' the injured party from recovering avoidable losses."[22] More precisely,

> "The Common Law rule is that the promisee cannot recover expenses that were unreasonably incurred, and the promisor's liability is capped at the loss that would have arisen had the promisee acted reasonably in bringing about the promised state of affairs"[23]

The expression "duty to mitigate" is however familiar, convenient and in widespread use, and this does not do any harm as long as the above is borne in mind. It will therefore be used in this chapter as well as the remainder of the thesis.

A final important general point is that "it is the loss that has to be avoided and not the wrong itself".[24] The duty to mitigate can only apply to acts or omissions after the breach of contract or the tort.[25] Acts or omissions enabling or contributing to the wrong itself are dealt with via a different concept, contributory negligence/fault.

According to Farnsworth, [26] the first precedent demonstrating the application of the duty to mitigate dates from 1677, in the case *Vertue v*

---

[22] Charles J. Goetz and Robert E. Scott, 'The Mitigation Principle: Toward a General Theory of Contractual Obligation' (1983) 69 *Virginia Law Review* 967. According to Lord Bingham, mitigation imposes an "assumption" that the claimant acted reasonably "whether in fact the injured party acts in that way or, for whatever reason, does not" (*Golden Strait Corpn v Nippon Yusen Kubishika Kaisha ("The Golden Victory")* [2007] UKHL 12; [2007] 2 AC 353 at [10]).

[23] George Letsas and Prince Saprai, 'Mitigation, Fairness and Contract Law', in Klass, G., Letsas, G., and Saprai, P. (eds), *Philosophical foundations of contract law* (Oxford University Press 2015) 333. Letsas and Saprai observe that: "The promisee is morally free to sit back and not to seek alternatives. All that he is prevented from doing is to claim damages for losses he could have easily avoided."

[24] McGregor (n 8) 9-001.

[25] Adam Kramer, *The Law of Contract Damages* (2nd ed. Hart Publishing 2017) 349.

[26] E. Allan Farnsworth, *Contracts* (4th edn, Aspen Publishers, 2004) 778.

Bird.[27] In this case, the claimant had been hired to deliver goods in the city of Ipswich, at a location to be determined by the defendant. The defendant took longer than expected to indicate the precise location, and the horses of the claimant (which were carrying the cargo) died of exhaustion, giving rise to the claim for damages. The court, however, decided that the loss was attributed to the claimant's own action upon the defendant's breach (the defendant's breach: not indicating place of delivery; the claimant's action: keeping horses standing loaded for hours) and, thus, the claim was denied. Although the defendant was in breach, it was due to the claimant's voluntary (in)action that the horses were kept loaded for longer than they could endure. Reasonable conduct, which was within claimant's reach, would have spared the horses from such additional and fatal effort, and such loss would – therefore – have been avoided.

However, it is more usual to trace the origins of this principle to the eighteenth century.[28] Patrick Atiyah has observed that: "Because questions of damages were almost entirely a matter for the jury until late in the eighteenth century, little is known for certain about the origin about the mitigation rule".[29] Still, according to Atiyah, the position in the last thirty years of that century was that an attempt to mitigate (like reselling a product that was refused) could disable performance and bar the right to recover damages. The stages that represent the subsequent development of the mitigation principle were: first, when the claimant was permitted to seek performance elsewhere and sue for the difference; the next stage (which Atiyah admits is a speculative one), took place when juries would award damages on a similar basis, had the claimant mitigated or not; the

---

[27] 84 Eng. Rep. 1000, 85 Eng. Rep. 200 (K.B. 1677)

[28] E.g. Michaud (n 2): "Mitigation of damage in Common Law is a concept which came into existence during the eighteenth century, when damages for breach of contract became more strictly controlled by the courts."

[29] Patrick S. Atiyah, *The rise and fall of freedom of contract* (first published 1979, Clarendon Press 1985) 425. Also, Gustavo Santos Kulesza, *Princípio da mitigação de danos; evolução no direito contratual* (Curitiba, Juruá, 2015), 131

final stage taking place when mitigation became a must for the claimant and juries limited the award of damages.[30]

In the latter context, in *Gainsford v Carroll*,[31] the seller failed to deliver products and the buyer sued for the increase in the market price after the breach. Recovery was granted, but limited to the difference between the price on the date of the contract and on the date of the breach. Nowadays, this limitation on the damages recoverable is thought of as based on the notion that the victim of the breach should mitigate his losses by purchasing a substitute as soon as reasonably possible after the breach.[32] Despite a few other cases that applied the same reasoning, Atiyah found that it was only "by the mid-nineteenth century [that] the mitigation rule was generally established".[33] An example is *Beckham v Drake*,[34] where it was held that the dismissed employee was under an obligation to obtain work elsewhere, as an action to mitigate loss, and entitled to recover damages only to the difference in salary.

The case that is still today acknowledged as the leading case on mitigation – *British Westinghouse v Underground Railways*[35] – was decided in the early twentieth century. The parties had entered into contract for the production and delivery of turbines. The turbines produced insufficient power, causing London Underground Railways – in order to prevent additional losses – to buy substitute turbines, which turned out to be more effective than those supplied by Westinghouse. London Underground sued to recover the price of the new turbines, but the Court considered that savings and gains from the new turbines exceeded their cost, and no recovery was granted. The House of Lords, through Viscount Haldane, stated the mitigation rule as one "which imposes on a plaintiff the duty of

---

[30] Atiyah (n 29) 425-426.
[31] *Gainsford v Carroll* [1824] 2 B & C 624, 107 E.R. 516.
[32] See section 3.2.3, below.
[33] Atiyah (n 29) 426.
[34] *Beckham v Drake* [1849] 2 HLC 579, 9 E.R. 1213.
[35] *British Westinghouse Electric & Manufacturing Co Ltd v Underground Electric Railways Co of London Ltd* (n 17).

taking all reasonable steps to mitigate the loss consequent upon the breach, and debars him from claiming any part of the damage which is due to his neglect to take such steps."[36] As to the steps to be taken by the innocent party, it was held that the "claimant is not required to take any step which a reasonable and prudent man would not ordinarily take (...)."[37] Further, the Court clarified the assumption of reasonable step as "one which a reasonable and prudent person might in the ordinary conduct of business properly have taken".[38] On the facts, the House of Lords concluded that the claimant had acted reasonably to mitigate the losses, in such an effective manner that no residual losses resulted from the breach – and thus no recovery was due.

Although this case is well-established as the most important precedent on the principle of mitigation, there has been some debate about what exactly was decided. In the view of Andrew Dyson, "the House of Lords' decision in *British Westinghouse* has been widely mischaracterized in support of the so-called 'avoided loss rule'".[39] This is the third of the rules in McGregor's analysis referred to above. Importantly, this rule denies recovery of damages for *all* losses which the claimant in fact avoided by taking mitigating steps, including where such mitigating steps went beyond the reasonable steps required under the first rule.[40] In Dyson's view, the basis for the decision in this case was narrower: "[I]t is not necessary or plausible to explain *British Westinghouse* as an application of the rule that 'claimants cannot recover for an avoided loss'. Instead, the case merely exemplifies the rule that benefits resulting from reasonable conduct in mitigation are taken into account in the assessment of damages."[41]

---

[36] Ibid, 689.
[37] Ibid.
[38] Ibid, 690.
[39] Dyson (n 20) 425.
[40] McGregor (n 8) 9-110.
[41] Dyson (n 39) 412.

However, Viscount Haldane's statement of the principle in *British Westinghouse* leaves no doubt that he supported the avoided loss rule:

> "When in the course of his business he [the claimant] has taken action arising out of the transaction, which action has diminished his loss, the effect in actual diminution of the loss he has suffered may be taken into account even though there was no duty on him to act."

Dyson's analysis of the case sees the *ratio decidendi* of the case as narrower than the proposition in this statement. According, to Dyson, the replacement of the Westinghouse turbines was in fact what Westinghouse was reasonably required to do in the circumstances.[42] For that reason, he concludes that: "There was therefore no need to invoke the avoided loss rule ... in order to justify the result that the House of Lords reached."[43] To him, "*British Westinghouse* is a good—albeit complicated—illustration of the reasonable expenses rule",[44] i.e. McGregor's second rule referred to above.

Nevertheless, the broader avoided loss rule is applied by the courts,[45] and, with one possible exception,[46] endorsed by the judges of the highest court in England.[47] Moreover, Dyson's argument appears to confuse two questions that are in fact distinct: whether the loss-avoiding steps in fact

---

[42] Ibid, 423.

[43] Ibid.

[44] Ibid.

[45] See generally the cases cited in McGregor (n 8) 9-121 – 9-131; and especially, *Koch Marine Inc v D'Amica Societa di Navigazione Arl (The Elena D'Amico)* [1980] 1 Lloyd's Rep 75 (Goff J) at 89; *Thai Airways International Public Co Ltd v KI Holdings Co Ltd* (n 9); [2016] 1 All E.R. (Comm) 675 endorsing all three rules at [32].

[46] In *Dimond v Lovell* [2002] 1 AC 384 (HL) at 401–2 Lord Hoffmann referred to "the rule that requires additional benefits obtained as a result of taking reasonable steps to mitigate loss to be brought into account in the calculation of damages'".

[47] *Dimond v Lovell* [2002] 1 AC 384 (HL) Lord Hobhouse at 406; In *Sainsbury's Supermarkets Ltd v Visa Europe* (n 9) 214.

taken were reasonable steps, and whether these steps were required. These are distinct because loss-avoiding steps may be reasonable even though they go beyond what is required by the law under McGregor's first rule. Thus, the reasonableness of replacing the Westinghouse turbines does not indicate that their replacement was required as mitigating action (under McGregor's first rule): replacing them may well have been more than the law required but nevertheless reasonable. Dyson confuses the avoidable loss rule (McGregor's first rule), which concerns the question whether losses which were in fact suffered *should* have been avoided, and the avoided loss rule (McGregor's third rule) which concerns the different question of how the law should respond where the losses *were* in fact avoided. His interpretation of *British Westinghouse* must therefore be rejected.

Indeed, there is good reason for the broader avoided loss rule, as formulated by Viscount Haldane and reflected in McGregor's third rule. It is not necessary to limit the avoided loss rule to only the losses that were reasonably avoided,[48] because the application of this rule serves only to benefit the defendant, never to increase the damages. Whilst it makes sense to limit recovery of mitigation expenses under McGregor's second rule to only reasonable expenses because application of this rule can increase the liability of the defendant,[49] who thus is in need of protection, this need does not exist in case of the avoided loss rule. If the actual mitigating steps taken by the claimant go beyond what is reasonable, then the claimant only is disadvantaged and has only himself to blame. The very same reason why damages are reduced when a claimant takes steps that are reasonable but go beyond what the law required (as may have happened in *British*

---

[48] In their co-authored article Dyson and Kramer (n 14) at 263, and also Kramer on his own (n 25) at 359 – 360, express the view that only reasonable mitigating action should be taken into account. This does not involve the same mistake as is made in Dyson's sole-authored article analysed above.

[49] Lord Scott identified this danger clearly in a Tort case, *Lagden v O'Connor* [2004] 1 AC 1067 (HL) at para [78]. It is illustrated in the context of breach of contract by *Banco de Portugal v Waterlow & Sons Ltd* [1932] AC 452 (HL) at 507. See further section 3.2.4.2 below.

Westinghouse) also support reducing the recoverable damages when the claimant goes further, beyond even what reasonableness requires. This reason is that the claimant voluntarily took the steps which reduced the loss: the claimant *chose* to mitigate his loss and this has actually reduced his loss. On Dyson's approach, the claimant would be able to recover more than his actual loss, and that is contrary to the most basic principle of liability in both contract law and tort law.

The law concerning mitigation has developed significantly since the *Westinghouse* decision was handed down more than 100 years ago. In the most recent edition of *McGregor on Damages*, the current authors of this leading work make the following remarks about the issue just discussed, which apply equally to the principle as a whole:

> "When this text was initially compiled in the late 1950s
> the matter was not well worked out in the authorities and
> all that could be done was to sketch what the law probably
> was. Over the intervening years a formidable body of case
> law has gradually appeared and today hardly a year goes
> by without a difficult decision on this issue facing the
> courts (…([B]y the start of the 21st century the time ha[s]
> come (…) to get the cases into line."

As this quotation suggests, this remains a developing area of law where the courts continue to be faced with new issues, and where the answers to some questions remain debatable. The discussion in the remainder of this chapter will reflect this, and seek to highlight those issues and uncertainties that hold lessons for the overall aims of this thesis.

3.2 Practical operation

3.2.1 Scope of application

As pointed out in the previous section, mitigation works similarly in contract law and tort law.[50]

Further, in contract law, it can apply to all sorts of contracts – provided the facts allow the court to identify a situation in which the innocent party could have acted reasonably to mitigate their own losses: "In certain cases of personal service it may be unreasonable to expect a claimant to consider an offer from the other party who has grossly injured him; but in commercial contracts it is generally reasonable to accept an offer from the party in default. However, it is always a question of fact. About the law there is no difficulty."[51]

Finally, it is worth clarifying that even when the mitigation of losses is totally successful, that is, even when all losses that could have arisen from the breach have been prevented by mitigating measures and no losses at all occur, contractual penalties for breach might still be due, for the trigger can be the breach itself (and not the losses) and its amount can exceed the compensation of losses.[52]

In principle, the duty to mitigate is only applied when someone claims damages.[53] Nevertheless, a specific issue which has arisen in the law of

---

[50] *McAuley v London Transport Executive* [1957] 2 Lloyds Rep 500.

[51] Klass, Letsas and Saprai (n 23) 331.

[52] For the most recent decisive case on contractual penalty clauses, see the UK Supreme Court decision in the combined appeals of *Cavendish Square Holdings BV v Talal El Makdessi* [2015] UKSC 67 and *ParkingEye Ltd. V Beavis* [2015] UKSC 67, in which allegedly penal clauses were held enforceable as considered a secondary contractual obligation. According to *ParkingEye*, a contractual penalty is enforceable as long as it serves a legitimate purpose and does so proportionately – on the facts of this case, the party enforcing the penalty did not suffer any loss as a result of the breach.

[53] Andrew Tettenborn, 'Damages, Causation Mitigation and the Conduct of the Claimant' in Neil Andrews, Malcolm Clarke, Andrew Tettenborn and Graham Virgo, *Contractual Duties: Performance, Breach, Termination and Remedies* 2nd

contract about the scope of application of the mitigation principle, is whether it affects only claims for damages or also any rights the innocent party has to insist on performance of the contract. Can the innocent party insist on performance even when the losses would be mitigated if the contract were terminated and that party received damages only? This is worth examining more closely, as different common law jurisdictions and different writers disagree about this.

3.2.1.1 Performance and the duty to mitigate

In contrast with Brazil, where the victim of a breach of contract has a right to enforce the contract if they so wish,[54] it is a basic feature of all common law systems that the victim of a breach of contract does not have a right to a court order that instructs the party in breach to perform the contract. Instead, this remedy, which is referred to as "specific performance", lies in the discretion of the court and generally functions as a secondary remedy that is awarded only if damages would be an inadequate remedy in the circumstances of the case and it would be equitable to order specific performance.[55] Only damages is available as of right and in all cases of breach of contract.

The practical effect of this is that the mitigation principle operates automatically, and silently, in relation to specific performance: this remedy (performance) will only be available in cases which damages would not compensate the claimant's losses adequately. Moreover, the primacy of damages as a remedy ensures that a contracting party, as claimant, cannot refrain from being subject to the application of the mitigation principle

---

ed (Sweet & Maxwell Ltd 2012) 508; Janet O'Sullivan, 'Mitigation and Specific Performance in the Canadian Supreme Court' (2013) 72 *Cambridge Law Journal* 253 at 253.

[54] Chapter 2 section 2.2 above.

[55] *Co-operative Insurance Society Ltd v Argyll Stores (Holdings) Ltd* [1997] 2 WLR 898. See Andrews, N., *Contract Law* 2nd ed (Cambridge University Press 2015) 524-529; McKendrick (n 18) 924-944.

in his claim for damages by instead choosing specific performance. This can be seen clearly in the Canadian case *Southcott Estates Inc. v Toronto Catholic District School.*[56]

The claimant was a single purpose company – a property developer – which wished to buy vacant land from the defendant. The agreement entered by the parties established that the deal was "conditional upon the Board obtaining the appropriate planning severance and which also gave the claimant a further thirty days in which to exercise due diligence to ensure that it could successfully develop the land into residential building lots."[57] The claimant realized, after a number of extensions of time by the Board, that it would never secure severance, and sued for breach of contract, claiming defendant failed to use best efforts to secure the planning approval. Additionally, the claimant requested specific performance. In the trial court, the Board's breach was recognized but specific performance was not granted for the reason that the court held that damages was an adequate remedy. Applying existing Canadian precedent, the court came to this conclusion because the claimant was only interested in the land as a development opportunity, which meant that it was not unique but could be substituted.[58] Substantial damages were awarded instead. The Ontario Court of Appeal however reduced the award to nominal damages only (one dollar), as the Court held that Southcott should have mitigated its loss in full by purchasing an equivalent investment property. The refusal

---

[56] *Southcott Estates Inc. v Toronto Catholic District School* 2012 SCC 51.

[57] Jeff Berryman, 'Mitigation, Specific Performance and the Property Developer: Southcott Estates Inc. v Toronto Catholic District School Board' (2013) 51 *Alberta Law Review* 165.

[58] *Semelhago v Paramadevan* [1996] 2 S.C.R. 415. English law, in contrast, treats land as always unique, so that specific performance is normally available in respect of contracts for the sale of land: Janet O'Sullivan, 'Mitigation and Specific Performance in the Canadian Supreme Court' (2013) 72 *The Cambridge Law Journal* 254; and Andrews and McKendrick in the passages cited above (n 55). On the facts of this case, the question of mitigation would therefore not have arisen in England; however it would have arisen outside the specific context of contracts for the sale of land. For this reason the case is of general importance.

of specific performance was not considered, since Southcott did not appeal against this.

Finally, the Supreme Court of Canada – by a majority (6:1) – dismissed Southcott's appeal against the reduction of the damages award by upholding the decision that the claimant should have acted reasonably in order to mitigate its losses by buying alternative property instead of only pursuing performance of the contract by the Board. This was justified on the basis of a precedent which had held that the mitigation principle will not reduce the damages of an innocent party who fails to limit his losses by pursuing specific performance if "circumstances reveal a substantial and legitimate interest in seeking specific performance as opposed to damages". [59] The majority held that In the context of the case, the claimant should mitigate unless he or she has a substantial and legitimate interest in receiving actual performance, and this would be so if damages would be an inadequate remedy because the property possesses a "peculiar and special value" (the hypothesis of unique land).[60] As this was not the case on the facts and the claimant could have made the same profit from another property development – that is, could have reduced his loss to zero by taking reasonable mitigating steps – recovery was limited to only nominal damages. The dissenting judge held that on the facts Southcott did have the necessary substantial interest to pursue specific performance.

As O'Sullivan has observed, "all members of the [Supreme] court in *Southcott* appeared to accept that a purchaser of land, faced with a breach of contract by the vendor, is immediately required to mitigate its loss even if he also seeks specific performance, the only live question therefore being whether he actually has mitigated, in other words whether he has acted reasonably to keep his loss to a minimum."[61] The effect of this approach is that "[se]eking specific performance will rarely be accepted as an excuse for failure to mitigate. Indeed a plaintiff who fails to mitigate may, as

---

[59] *Asamera Oil Corp v Sea Oil & General Corp* [1979] 1 S.C.R. 633.
[60] *Southcott* (n 56) par 41.
[61] O'Sullivan (n 58) 254-255.

Southcott demonstrates, be left without a remedy"[62] but still incur in the costs of litigating.

Berryman points out that: "The plaintiff is always protected by a residual damages claim for any deficiency between what has been obtained in mitigation and that which was contracted."[63] However, the approach applied in *Southcott* creates a disincentive against seeking specific performance. Because the purchaser will only be able to obtain specific performance if they manage to persuade a court that the land had "peculiar and special value" (the hypothesis of unique land)[64] – which the claimant tried but failed to do in this case – the "purchaser has little choice but to accept a vendor's breach, discharge the agreement, mitigate its losses, and claim any remaining damages."[65] Besides, pursuing performance carries a double risk: "the factors that lead a court to deny the order almost certainly will also lead to the conclusion that the failure to mitigate was unreasonable. The plaintiff consequently will be left with nothing."[66]

This decision has attracted considerable criticism. Friedmann rejects the reference to alternative transactions in situations where performance is claimed, for the two courses of action are contradictory: "The claimant who seeks performance cannot be expected to make an alternative transaction. In fact, if he makes another similar transaction, he may be entitled to claim that this is an additional transaction and not one made in substitution to the original transaction."[67] To Hall, the decision in "*Southcott* represents a triumph of theory over commercial reality and is a troubling decision as

---

[62] Richard J Olson, 'Who Mourns for Specific Performance?' (2013) 71 *Advocate Vancouver* 860.

[63] Berryman (n 57), 175.

[64] *Southcott* (n 56) par 41.

[65] Mitchell McInnes, 'Specific performance in the Supreme Court of Canada' (2013) 129 Law Quarterly Review, 165, 168.

[66] McInnes (n 65) 3.

[67] Daniel Friedmann, 'Economic Aspects of Damages and Specific Performance Compared', in Djakhongir Saidov and Ralph Cunnington (eds), *Contract Damages: Domestic and International Perspectives* (Hart Publishing 2008) 87.

a result"[68], for the court did not consider that the nominal claimant was a single-purpose company with a project for that specific piece of land. According to O'Sullivan, it fails to protect the contractual performance interest, because "*Southcott* ... involves the court giving its blessing to the re-writing of the contract by the party in breach, effectively inserting a unilateral right to alter the transaction, to the detriment of the innocent party."[69]

These appear to be well-made criticisms, but it should be pointed out that they appear to turn on how the courts' discretionary power over specific performance was applied on the facts of the case rather than on the existence of that discretion, which is long established in common law systems. Berryman makes the important observation that (in common law systems):

> "The issue of the availability of specific performance cannot be divorced entirely from the obligation to mitigate. If specific performance is available, the obligation to mitigate is suspended because the innocent party is entitled to keep the contract alive and does not have to accept the defendant's breach. The obligation to mitigate is suspended but will reemerge whenever specific performance becomes impossible, or where the innocent party does later accept the defendant's breach"[70]

Perhaps the Canadian courts were too willing to find that damages was an adequate substitute on the facts in *Southcott* and that it would therefore have been reasonable for the claimant to pursue alternative

---

[68] George Hall, 'Contract Law, Coherent Legal Theory, and Sound Commercial Practice: the Need for a Balance' (2013) 2 *Commercial Litigation and Arbitration Review* 1, 3.

[69] O'Sullivan (n 58) 256.

[70] Berryman (n 57) 174.

investment opportunities.[71] However, the general approach applied in this case does protect the mitigation principle by preventing the innocent party from avoiding its application by pursuing specific performance. In this sense, the mitigation principle here prevails over the innocent party's performance interest. Interestingly, the court adopted a broad description of the mitigation principle which does not tie it to a specific remedy: "Mitigation is a doctrine based on fairness and common sense, which seeks to do justice between the parties in the particular circumstances of the case."[72]

The question of whether the victim has a right to insist on performance of the contract can also arise outside the context of orders for specific performance. For example, if the breach consists of a failure to pay the victim an agreed sum (i.e. when someone fails to pay the price for goods or services), then the victim has a right to a court order to enforce payment – this remedy is not discretionary or secondary because the common law distinguishes between monetary remedies and specific performance. The mitigation principle does not apply to such debt claims.[73] Nevertheless, the question has arisen whether such a claim should be subject to the duty to mitigate so as to restrict the victim's right to payment. How this question arises, and its practical significance, can be seen in a couple of American cases in which the mitigation principle was indeed applied to restrict the victims' rights to payment.

In *Clark v Marsiglia*,[74] the defendant continued to clean and repair the claimant's paintings after the claimant had repudiated their agreement. The issue was whether a party can recover the agreed payment for services rendered after a contract has been repudiated, or whether the victim *must* accept the repudiation so that the one who repudiates the contract

---

[71] This question of the reasonable steps required by the mitigation doctrine is discussed below in section 3.2.2.

[72] *Southcott* (n 56) par 25.

[73] Tettenborn (n 53) 508-509.

[74] *Clark v Marsiglia* (1845) Denio 1 (N.Y.) 317, 43 Am. Dec. 670.

need only compensate the other party for the performance rendered prior to repudiation and anticipated loss in regard to the unexecuted portion (accordingly lost profits minus cost avoided). If the victim rendered no or little performance prior to repudiation, their costs would be limited, so that compensation will normally be a smaller sum than the full contract price. The court applied the mitigation principle and awarded compensation rather than the full contract price:

> "The defendant, by requiring the plaintiff to stop work upon the paintings, violated his contract, and thereby incurred a liability to pay such damages as the plaintiff should sustain. Such damages would include a recompense for the labor done and materials used, and such further sum in damages as might, upon legal principles, be assessed for the breach of the contract; but the plaintiff had no right, by obstinately persisting in the work, to make the penalty upon the defendant greater than it would otherwise have been."[75]

A similar outcome was reached in *Rockingham County v Luten Bridge Co.*[76] In this case, the claimant hired the defendant to construct a bridge. Later, the County Commission voted not to continue with the construction. Despite being aware of this fact, Luten Bridge continued the work and sued to recover damages from the breach. The court decided that the non-breaching party has no right to increase the breaching party's damages.[77] That is, the court recognized the innocent party's duty to mitigate upon the other party's breach and that this limited the entitlement of the defendant to insist on the performance of the contract. As such, the additional damages incurred by the innocent party – who choose

---

[75] *Clark* (n 74) 318.
[76] *Rockingham County v Luten Bridge Co.* 35 F. 2d 301 (4th Cir. 1929)
[77] Ibid, 307.

to continue performance, instead of preventing further loss — were not granted:

> "The measure of plaintiff's damage, upon its appearing that notice was duly given not to build the bridge, is an amount sufficient to compensate plaintiff for labor and materials expended and expense incurred in the part performance of the contract, prior to its repudiation, plus the profit which would have been realized if it had been carried out in accordance with its terms."[78]

The English courts have adopted a different approach, however. The leading case is *White & Carter (Councils) Ltd. v McGregor.*[79] The parties had entered a 156-week contract for advertisements by McGregor to be displayed on certain litter receptacles in Clydebank by White & Carter. When the contract was about to expire, a representative of McGregor renewed it for an additional 156 weeks. On the same day, McGregor himself contacted White & Carter arguing the representative that had renewed the contract had no authority to do so, and repudiated the new contract before performance began. White & Carter did not accept the repudiation and argued that no substitute transaction would fit and posted the advertisement. Further, based on Condition 8 of the Contract,[80] White & Carter sued for the price. The Court allowed the claimant to recover the price, under the right to perform, holding that the victim may choose to insist on performance even if accepting the repudiation would have limited their losses.

---

[78] Ibid, 308.

[79] *White & Carter (Councils) Ltd. V McGregor* [1962] A.C. 413.

[80] This read: "In the event of an instalment or part thereof being due for payment, and remaining unpaid for a period of four weeks or in the event of the advertiser being in any way in breach of this contract then the whole amount due for the 156 weeks or such part of the said 156 weeks as the advertiser shall not yet have paid shall immediately become due and payable."

As Tettenborn points out, "[a]lthough the case strictly did not turn on mitigation (concentrating instead on establishing that clients' unaccepted repudiation could not take away the advertisers' contractual rights), the essence of the clients' argument was that the advertisers had failed to mitigate, and it is implicit in the result".[81]

The decision was split with strong arguments on both sides. The majority, formed by Lords Reid, Hodson and Tucker, granted the action for the agreed sum. Lord Reid affirmed performance as the "general rule" for English Common Law, and argued that:

> "If one party to a contract repudiates it in the sense of making it clear to the other party that he refuses or will refuse to carry out his part of the contract, the other party, the innocent party, has an option. He may accept that repudiation and sue for damages for breach of contract, whether or not the time for performance has come; or he may if he chooses disregard or refuse to accept it and then the contract remains in full effect."[82]

> "It is, in my judgement, impossible to say that the appellants should be deprived of their right to claim the contract price merely because the benefit to them, as against claiming damages and re-letting the advertising space, might be small in comparison with the loss to the respondent (...)"[83]

As Chitty points out,[84] Lord Reid "introduced a qualification, to the effect that the plaintiff could not insist on completing performance so as to

---

[81] Tettenborn (n 53) 509.
[82] *White & Carter* (n 79) 427.
[83] Ibid, 431.
[84] Chitty (n 18) 26-116.

be able to claim the agreed price as a debt, if he had 'no legitimate interest, financial or otherwise, in performing the contract rather than claiming for damages.'[85] Lord Tucker simply agreed with Lord Reid, whereas Lord Hodson added that: "When the assistance of the court is not required the innocent party can choose whether he will accept repudiation and sue for damages for anticipatory breach or await the date of performance by the guilty party. Then, if there is failure in performance, his rights are preserved."[86]

Dissenting Lords Morton and Keith both argued that the claimant should have mitigated losses once aware of repudiation, instead of its "unreasonable and oppressive" course of action. Lord Morton considered White & Carter was "bound to take steps to minimise their loss", and argued that:

> "[H]aving incurred no expense at the date of the repudiation, they made no attempt to procure another advertiser, but deliberately went on to incur expense and perform unwanted services with the intention of creating a money debt which did not exist at the date of the repudiation."[87]

In the words of Lord Keith, "a repudiation can never be said to be accepted by the other party except in the sense that he acquiesces in it and does not propose to take any action. Otherwise he founds on it as a cause of action. (…) I know of no authority for saying that the offended party can go quietly on as if the contract still continued to be fully operative between both parties."[88] As to condition 8 of the Contract, Lord Keith considered it

---

[85] *White & Carter* (n 79) 431.
[86] Ibid, 445.
[87] Ibid, 433.
[88] Ibid, 437-439.

was "only intended to take effect after the contract comes into operation",[89] which was not the case due to its repudiation.

The majority of the court therefore adopted an approach that is the opposite of the American one: "If the innocent party chooses not to accept the repudiation of a contract, he is under no duty to mitigate the damages or reduce the loss."[90] This is supported by Tettenborn, who argues that:

> "The duty to mitigate is regarded as arising in response to
> a breach of contract by the defendant, or at the very least
> in response to an accepted repudiation. It follows that a
> claimant cannot be under any such duty unless and until
> the defendant is in fact in breach."

Another English case with a similar outcome is *Strutt v Whitnell*.[91] The case concerns a vendor that promised to sell a house with vacant possession, but conveyed it with a tenant in occupation (which made the property much less valuable). Vendor offered to accept re-conveyance and return the current price. The court, however, decided that buyer/claimant was not to be obliged to give up its right to keep the property and claim for damages or to give up its ownership. In both cases, the innocent party's interest in performance prevailed over the mitigation principle.

However, the qualification introduced by Lord Reid (and applied in subsequent cases),[92] does limit the innocent party's right to enforce their performance interest in a way that is arguably similar to the mitigation

---

89 Ibid, 443.
90 Ibid, 420.
91 *Stutt v Whitnell* [1975] 1 WLR 870 (CA).
92 For example, *Clea Shipping Corp v Bulk Oil International Ltd (The Alaskan Trader)* (No 2) [1984] 1 All ER 129. For a survey of cases seeking to apply this qualification, and the difficulties to which it gives rise, see J W Carter, "*White and Carter v McGregor* – How Unreasonable?" (2012) 128 Law Quarterly Review, 490 and McGregor (n 8) 9-026 – 9-035.

principle although it does not go quite as far.[93] O'Sullivan has critically noted the similarity between Lord Reid's qualification and the approach followed by the Canadian Supreme Court in *Southcott*,[94] discussed above.[95] She further points out that "the claimant will have a legitimate financial interest in *virtually all* cases, *other than* in exceptional circumstances where it would be utterly unreasonable for the claimant to insist on keeping the contract alive."[96] Besides, she argues, "there was no attempt to consider what W&C measure of damages would have been if it had accepted McGregor's repudiation at the outset."[97] She insists that:

> "A claimant who opts to keep the contract alive has already shown, by its choice, what is in its interests. To

---

[93] Qiao Liu, "The *White & Carter* Principle: A Restatement" (2011) 74 *MLR* 171, 186, who nevertheless rejects "the suggestion that the distinction between the two should be removed entirely and the mitigation principle should be applied to a victim who chooses to continue to perform".

[94] *Southcott* (n 56).

[95] "*Southcott*, and Lord Reid's dictum in *White & Carter*, involve the court giving its blessing to the re-writing of
the contract by the party in breach, effectively inserting a unilateral right to alter the transaction, to the
detriment of the innocent party. So much for the common law's commitment to protect the contractual
performance interest." – O'Sullivan (n 58) at 256. There is however a difference in language noted by Angela Swann and Jacub Adamski, 'Specific Performance, Mitigation, and Corporate Groups: A Comment on Southcott Estates Inc v Toronto Catholic District School Board' (2014) 56 *Canadian Business Law Journal* 118: this seems to indicate that Canadian courts apply a test (substantial and legitimate interest) that is stricter than the one adopted by Lord Reid in *White and Carter* and subsequently applied by English Courts (legitimate interest), since the expression "substantial" indicates claimant must evidence the loss to which he or she will be subject in the absence of performance. Given this, the Canadian approach appears to lie between the American and the English approaches.

[96] Janet O'Sullivan, 'Repudiation: Keeping the Contract Alive', in Graham Virgo and Sarah Worhington (eds), *Commercial Remedies Resolving Controversies* (Cambridge University Press, 2017) 52.

[97] Ibid, 55.

acknowledge this involves nothing more controversial than upholding freedom of contract and respecting the sanctity of the bargain, in the face of a repudiatory breach by the defendant."[98]

There is, however, also support for the English approach of favouring performance in cases in which there is legitimate interest to reject contract repudiation. Barry Adler considers that "the current limitation of the mitigation obligation might be the better rule after all, at least as a default".[99] He points out that "the victim need not accept substitute performance unless that performance is fungible with that promised under the contract".[100] He recognizes however that the residual application of the mitigation doctrine may compromise the results expected from its enforcement: "There is a cost, of course, in that a weak mitigation doctrine will in some setting yield an insufficient incentive to mitigate. But this tradeoff may be sensible".[101]

Some authors disagree more strongly with O'Sullivan. They consider that the English approach is too timid, and prefer one that is more in line with the American approach outlined above. Thus Mark Gergen remarks that "none of the opinions in *White & Carter* speaks to why the pursuer thought it in its interest to perform and sue for the price, rather than to bring an action for lost profit."[102] In response to Gergen, David Campbell refers to a Scottish Law Commission Report to endorse the opinion that the election of either remedy (mitigation or performance) ought to "be

---

[98] Ibid, 74.

[99] Barry E. Adler, 'Efficient breach theory through the looking glass' (2008) vol 83 New York University Law Review 1679-1725.

[100] Ibid, 1723.

[101] Ibid, 1725.

[102] Mark P. Gergen, 'The Right to Perform after Repudiation and Recover the Contract Price in Anglo-American Law', in Larry Dimatteo and Martin Hogg (eds), *Comparative Contract Law* (Oxford University Press 2016) 332.

reasonable"[103] – which could potentially reverse the outcome of the case. Whether this requirement of reasonableness would in practice dilute the performance of the contract as is feared by O'Sullivan is open to doubt, for, as Campbell argues: "Had the defender [in *White and Carter*] known the response it would get from the pursuer, it would never had repudiated."[104]

Jonathan Morgan goes further and favours the full-blown application of the mitigation principle in cases like *White and Carter*:

> "The mitigation principle holds that the claimant cannot recover losses which it could easily have avoided, or which it has unreasonably increased. This is the best default rule for the law of contract to adopt."[105]

Morgan argues that applying the mitigation doctrine fits with commercial expectations and benefits all parties:

> "[T]his will reduce the overall cost of performance, which will therefore reduce prices. Evidently this is to the benefit of all parties. (…) Its contribution to the reduction of the parties' joint costs (and so the maximization of their joint profits) seem beyond realistic doubt – rather unusually in the law and economics field."[106]

This is also the position endorsed by the authors of *McGregor on Damages*, who describe the American approach as "salutary" and consider it "economic waste to allow a contracting party, when it is of no benefit

---

[103] David Campbell, 'Reply to Mark P. Gergen, 'The Right to Perform after Repudiation and Recover the Contract Price in Anglo-American Law', in Dimatteo and Hogg (eds) ibid, 341.
[104] Ibid, 341.
[105] Jonathan Morgan, 'Smuggling Mitigation in White & Carter v McGregor: Time to Come Clean?' (2015) *Lloyds Maritime and Commercial Law Quarterly* 575, 591.
[106] Ibid, 592.

to them, to carry through a performance unwanted by the other party",[107] as happened in *White and Carter.*[108] Qiao Liu has proposed a test which, while accepting that the duty to mitigate is strictly speaking not suitable for this context, nevertheless applies its underlying rationale: "whether, in the particular circumstances of the case, the wastefulness of the victim's continuing performance outweighs its performance interest in earning the contract price".[109]

This academic debate, along with the cases discussed above, shows that there is a tension in Common Law systems about the extent to which the mitigation principle should have an impact beyond the calculation of damages and also affect performance-directed remedies. Morgan's remarks as well as the reasoning of the Supreme Court of Canada in *Southcott* demonstrate that a broad understanding of the mitigation principle and its rationale tends to pull in favour of applying it in ways which impact on the innocent party's right to performance of the contract. On the other hand, the criticisms of *Southcott,* especially by O'Sullivan, as well as her criticisms of *White and Carter,* and the fact that only the American courts have gone so far as to use the principle to expressly limit the innocent party's right to insist on performance, shows that there is also a strong counter-tendency which sees mitigation as applying only to claims for damages.

For the purposes of this thesis, the survey above has revealed three important facts. The first is that the experience in these countries also indicates that there is a potential tension between mitigation and performance, and that legal systems may have to choose whether to prefer one to the other or to try to balance these competing priorities by giving the innocent party a choice which is restricted or limited. Secondly, there

---

[107] McGregor (n 8) 9-035.

[108] Similarly, Lord Sumption, in a dissenting judgment in *Societe Generale, London Branch v Geys* [2012] UKSC 63 at par [137], described the outcome in *White and Carter* as producing the "unattractive consequence" of "a waste of resources which could have been avoided if the parties had been left to their remedy in damages" and forced to mitigate.

[109] Liu (n 93) 192.

is no single approach in Common Law systems; instead, a variety of approaches are compatible with the adoption of the mitigation principle. And thirdly, the tensions and choices made in Common Law systems are closely connected to the discretionary and secondary nature of specific performance in those systems and the associated primacy of damages as a remedy for breach of contract. This creates a space for considering mitigation, and makes mitigation the normal, standard, expectation.

All this indicates that, whilst it will be important for this thesis to consider what the relationship should be between mitigation and performance, Brazil, which recognizes the right of the innocent party to enforce performance,[110] may well want to make a different choice and insist strictly, like some of the English commentators,[111] on limiting the mitigation principle to claims for damages only.[112]

3.2.2 Reasonable steps

When the duty to mitigate applies in respect of a breach of contract or tort, the claimant is required to "take all reasonable steps to mitigate their loss".[113] One of the most important aspects of the practical operation of the doctrine is therefore to determine what actions constitute the reasonable steps innocent parties are supposed to take. In fact, it is not always easy to define whether someone has acted reasonably or not, because "[w]hether the claimant has acted reasonably is in every case a question of fact, not of law".[114] The lack of specific guidance that this provides has been criticized:

"The constant emphasis on fact and reasonableness, so characteristic of a Common Law that is concerned with

---

[110] See Civil Code Art. 475, discussed in Chapter 2 section 2.2 above.
[111] Particularly Tettenborn (n 53) 508-509 and O'Sullivan (n 58) 253.
[112] This is considered in Chapter 5 section 5.3.2.
[113] McGregor (n 8) at 9-004.
[114] McGregor (n 8) at 9-079.

the need for retaining flexibility, has served the law badly in this section of mitigation."[115]

However, "a number of indications as to what is likely to be regarded as reasonable in particular circumstances can be found in the case law",[116] and examples of this will be discussed below. Thus the interpretation and application of this requirement by the courts over time has brought considerable clarity as to what is required, whilst at the same time allowing the specific circumstances of each case to be taken into account.

The notion of reasonableness is connected to the judgement of a reasonable and prudent person; this means that the innocent party is not expected to take risks when acting to mitigate. Professor Waddams explains the approach that is followed:

> "Furthermore, it has been said that the reasonableness of
> the plaintiff's decision is not to be judged too rigorously
> for it is the defendant's breach that occasions it, and it
> lies ill in the mouth of the contract breacher to criticize
> the making of a difficult decision necessitated by the
> breach"[117]

This is reflected in the following statement in a leading precedent on mitigation (which according to McGregor applies equally to torts):[118]

> "Where the sufferer from a breach of contract finds
> himself in consequence of that breach placed in a position
> of embarrassment the measures which he may be driven
> to adopt in order to extricate himself ought not to be

---

[115] Bridge (n 7) 20.
[116] Tettenborn (n 53) 512. An extensive discussion of examples is provided by McGregor (n 8) 9-079 – 9-101.
[117] Stephen M. Waddams, *The Law of Contracts* (7th edn, Thomson Reuters 2017) 762.
[118] McGregor (n 8) 9-079.

weighed in nice scales at the instance of the party whose breach of contract has occasioned the difficulty. It is often easy after an emergency has passed to criticize the steps which have been taken to meet it, but such criticism does not come well from those who have themselves created the emergency. The law is satisfied if the party placed in a difficult situation by reason of the breach of a duty owed to him has acted reasonably in the adoption of remedial measures".[119]

This means that, "in the commercial context the standard expected of the victim of breach is not put excessively high. In particular, he will not be penalized for failing to take measures that would be unusually difficult or troublesome (…) Outside commercial contract, the standards expected of a claimant are, if anything, even lower".[120]

For a court to conclude whether someone was reasonable and prudent or not is easier because the final outcome is known. The challenge for contracting parties is to take actions which later will be considered reasonable and prudent. For this reason, the judgment on whether someone acted reasonably and prudently or not should not only consider the result of the action (which comes later), but also the information the party had at the time of action, how much the actions which were taken are justifiable on the grounds of mitigation (namely altruism, fairness and avoidance of waste), and how effective (and low-risk) such actions seemed for preventing the aggravation of losses. Only after going through these aspects – and verifying the outcome (whether losses are avoided or aggravated) – can someone's action be evaluated as reasonable or not, in order to be covered by mitigation.

As mentioned, judicial decisions over time have produced examples of situations which are considered to go beyond what is reasonable and

---

[119] *Banco de Portugal v Waterlow & Sons Ltd* (n 49).
[120] Andrews (n 55) 512-513.

which, therefore, are not required from innocent parties. For example, these may exclude from the list of reasonable mitigating steps: (i) incurring unreasonable expenses or unreasonable personal risks,[121] (ii) engaging in litigation,[122] (iii) taking risk of jeopardizing commercial reputation,[123] and (iv) accepting alternative employment in cases of wrongful dismissal or (sometimes) personal injury.[124]

Unreasonable expenses are those which are not proportional to the amount of loss that is being mitigated or which can financially compromise the innocent party: "The buyer should not be called on to risk his capital in the service of diminishing the seller's liability."[125] As Berryman explains: "The plaintiff is not required to take extraordinary efforts or serious business gambles to reduce his losses. The test is an objective one, but it is also cognizant of the realities and circumstances facing the claimant at the time of the breach."[126] In *Evra Corp. v Swiss Bank Corp.*,[127] the claimant sued the defendant for the negligent failure to wire transfer an installment payment, causing the cancellation of a ship charter. The defendant's argument was that the claimant should have mitigated by entering into another charter. The court considered that by such action the plaintiff would assume "substantial additional risk", which it considered to be unreasonable – and, therefore, not required.

In the tort context especially, the question can arise whether a claimant should incur the personal risks involved in undergoing an operation in order to mitigate the effects of an injury caused by the defendant. It has been held that refusing to undergo a dangerous and risky surgical operation, or even one where medical evidence is evenly balanced or unavailable, does not constitute a failure to mitigate; but it would be

---

[121] McGregor (n 8) 9-087 – 9-089.
[122] Ibid, 9-090 – 9-093.
[123] IBID, 9-097.
[124] Ibid, 9-060 – 9-063 and 9-065; Tettenborn (n 53) 514-515.
[125] Bridge (n 7) 3.
[126] Berryman (n 63) 174.
[127] *Evra Corp. v Swiss Bank Corp.* 673 F.2d 951 (7th Cir. 1982).

one to refuse an operation that would not be regarded as a risky one by reasonable persons.[128]

Litigation normally implicates risk, time and cost. Unless it is a legally obvious claim, with a predictable outcome, litigation will not be required as a reasonable step: "Normally, 'reasonable steps' do not require a claimant to engage in litigation, unless that course is exceptionally predictable and risk-free. Certainly, the claimant is not required to sue third parties if this will injure its commercial reputation."[129] The leading case is *Pilkington v Wood* where the claimant sued his solicitor for professional negligence in failing to discover in a property transaction that the seller's title to the property was defective.[130] The court rejected the solicitor's argument that the claimant should first have sued the seller for breach of contract (implied covenant of title) because "the so-called duty to mitigate does not go so far as to oblige the injured party, even under an indemnity, to embark on a complicated and difficult piece of litigation against a third party."[131] In *Bishopsgate Investment Management Ltd v Maxwell*,[132] a case in which the plaintiff brought action against the director of a trustee company for breach of fiduciary duty, defendant argued that claimant could have sued the third party who benefited from the breach. The court, however, stated that "it had no duty to engage in doubtful litigation for the purpose of minimizing the loss" for the defendant.

As to commercial reputation, it is accepted that innocent parties need not take any action that conflicts with their commercial interests. In *James Finlay & Co., Ltd. v N.V. Kwik Hoo Tong Handel Maatschappij*,[133] the claimant had bought products for the purpose of resale. As delivery was late and the market fell, the claimant brought a claim for damages. The

---

[128] McGregor (n 8) 9-088.

[129] Andrews (n 55) 511.

[130] *Pilkington v Wood* [1953] Ch. 770.

[131] At 777.

[132] *Bishopsgate Investment Management Ltd v Maxwell* [1993] BCLC 814.

[133] *James Finlay & Co., Ltd. V N.V. Kwik Hoo Tong Handel Maatschappij* [1929] 1 K.B. 400 CA.

claimant had in fact resold the goods before this delivery had taken place and could have forced their sub-buyers to take the goods. The defendant argued that the claimants should have mitigated their loss in this way. The Court, however, considered it to be unreasonable to require a claimant to take steps which were likely to "injure its commercial reputation" – by forcing an overpriced sale onto the sub-buyer – in mitigation of damages.

Where employment is lost, the innocent party should act – first and foremost – driven by his or her own interests. It was stated in *Forshaw v Aluminex Extrusions Ltd.,*[134] that: "The duty to 'act reasonably', in seeking and accepting alternate employment, cannot be a duty to take such steps as will reduce the claim against the defaulting former employer, but must be a duty to take such steps as a reasonable person in the dismissed employee's position would take in his own interests – to maintain his income and his position in his industry, trade or profession." Subject to this, an employee who is wrongfully dismissed should seek alternative employment,[135] and this may require accepting an offer of re-employment with the defendant,[136] but it will not be a failure to mitigate if the employee refuses to accept an offer which involves a demotion.[137] Moreover:

> "There may be cases where as matter of fact it would be unreasonable to expect a plaintiff to consider any offer made in view of the treatment he has received from the defendant. If he had been rendering personal services and had been dismissed after being accused in presence of others of being a thief, and if after that his employer had offered to take him back into his service, most persons would think he was justified in refusing the offer, and that

[134] *Forshaw v Aluminex Extrusions Ltd.* 39 B.C.L.R. (2d) 140, 1989 CanLII 234 (BCCA) 6.
[135] Andrews (n 55) 512.
[136] *Brace v Calder* [1895] 2 KB 253 CA.
[137] *Shindler v Northern Raincoat Co. Ltd* [1960] 1 WLR 1038.

it would be unreasonable to ask him in this way to mitigate the damages in an action of wrongful dismissal."[138]

Where the defendant's tort caused the claimant personal injuries which prevent them from continuing in their existing employment, the obvious mitigating step is to take up such other employment as they are now capable of doing. But what the claimant has to do will depend on what is reasonable. Thus it has been held not to be a failure to mitigate where someone decides after an injury to retrain for a job (taxi driver) that is less well paid than the one he could no longer do (mechanic).[139]

These employment cases are applications of the general expectation that someone will enter into alternative contractual arrangements to limit their loss where it is reasonable to do so. For example, someone whose car is damaged is normally expected to hire a substitute at a reasonable price for the duration of repairs, and what is reasonable will depend on the circumstances of the claimant.[140] The next section will look in more detail at the need to enter into substitute transactions in cases of breach of contract. Here it is important to note that (especially) in commercial cases this may well require of the innocent party to accept an alternative offered by the guilty party. This course of action is very common in situations which involve late delivery, alternative cargos at lower rate, or a seller who agrees to give credit and then refuses to deliver except for cash: "Sometimes the injured party will be required to mitigate by accepting from the party in breach a performance which differs in some way from that originally bargained for."[141]

Thus in *Payzu v Saunders* it was held that the claimant should have mitigated his loss by accepting an offer by the defendant for late delivery

---

[138] *Payzu v Saunders* [1919] 2 K.B. 581 CA.
[139] *Conner v Bradman & Co* [2007] EWHC 2789 (QB).
[140] *Lagden v O'Connor* [2004] 1 A.C. 1067.
[141] Guenter H. Treitel, *Remedies for Breach of Contract: A Comparative Account* (Oxford University Press 1988) 1064.

of goods the latter had sold to the claimant but had previously, in breach of contract, refused to deliver.[142] Going even further, in *The Solholt* it was held that buyers of a ship who had exercised a contractual right to cancel the contract when delivery was a day late (in breach of contract), were not entitled to recover damages to compensate them for the difference between the contract price and the actual (higher) value on the delivery date because they should have mitigated their loss by offering to repurchase the ship at the original contract price.[143] These two decisions have been strongly criticized.[144] However, there are also cases showing that, "while failure to accept offers from the guilty party may constitute a failure to mitigate, in practice it very frequently will not."[145] For example, where defective goods or services were supplied by the defendant and the claimant has reason to mistrust the defendant's competence, the claimant is not obliged to accept an offer from the defendant.[146]

What we can conclude from this discussion is that the broad and general requirement that mitigation involves taking "reasonable steps" achieves a balance between flexibility and predictability. On the one hand, it enables the courts to engage in a thorough analysis of the facts (what aspects were available for the mitigating party to consider at the time of action) in order to come to a solution that is appropriate to the circumstances of the case. Moreover, the openness of this test allows the variety of considerations which provide the grounds for this doctrine (such as fairness and avoidance of waste – discussed below in 3.3.2) to shape the outcome of the court's decision. On the other hand, precedents serve as guidance for future cases and enable a degree of predictability as to how certain issues will be dealt with. The concept of reasonableness appears to

---

[142] Above n 138.

[143] *The Solholt* [1983] 1 Lloyd's Rep. 605 CA

[144] Bridge (n 7) 412-423.

[145] Tettenborn (n 53) 514.

[146] See *Manton Hire & Sales Ltd v Ash Manor Cheese Co Ltd* [2013] EWCA Civ 548; Tettenborn ibid.

be concrete enough to enable the courts to decide how the innocent party should have acted – which is perhaps not surprising because this concept is used widely in the law. It is of course worth noticing that there are still issues that are controversial despite the relatively long period during which Common Law courts have been applying the mitigation doctrine, but this must be balanced against the benefits of having a flexible test that can be adapted to the specific needs of different circumstances. This holds an important lesson for how a new mitigation provision for Brazil should be drafted.

3.2.3 Substitute transactions

Substitute transactions often serve as an effective manner to mitigate, and the failure to enter into a substitute transaction is perhaps the most common cause for reduction of damages. The following is a simple illustration: A, the owner of a property rents it for the holiday to B. B repudiates the contract just a few days before. In order to mitigate his own loss, A manages to rent the house to C, though at a lower price. Recovery will be limited to the difference between the price B should have paid and the price C actually paid – thanks to the substitute transaction A agreed with C.

The case of *Southcott Estates*,[147] which was discussed in a previous section, provides a clear illustration of how this works in practice. Here the Supreme Court of Canada upheld a decision by the Ontario Court of Appeal which had reduced the claimant's damages for breach of contract to the nominal sum of one dollar. As we saw, the reason for this was that the defendant could have reduced his losses to zero by entering into an alternative transaction. The claimant was a property developer, who could

---

[147] *Southcott Estates Inc. v Toronto Catholic District School Board* (n 56).

have pursued alternative investment opportunities after the defendant seller of land had breached the contract. [148]

In short: the claimant is supposed to search for alternative solutions for the breach, seeking substitute transactions which minimize the effect of the breach and bring about the promised state of affairs, as if the other party had performed as agreed: "Where there is an available market in which the innocent party can obtain what has not been supplied to him, he is normally expected to go into that market to obtain it."[149] These aspects of the mitigation principle are reflected in the fact that it is usual for courts to award damages equivalent to the difference between the cost of the original contract and the cost of the substitute operation:

> "Where an available market exists, that is, where reasonably close substitutes can be purchased, it is usual to award damages equal to the difference between the contract price and the cost of performing the contract 'on the defendant's behalf' at the market price at the time of breach. No allowance is made for the possibility that the contracted-for quantity may no longer be the most efficient use of the plaintiff's resources given the new circumstances. Only if the price of the alternative is so high that there is held to be no 'available market' is the plaintiff assumed to adjust the contractual quantity – that is, he is assumed to buy nothing and his damages

---

[148] Similarly, in *100 Main Street Ltd. V W.B Sullivan Construction Ltd.* (1978) 88 DLR (3d) (Ont. CA Can), the vendor of the land was granted the difference between the contract price and the price that the land could have been sold at the time buyer repudiated the acquisition.

[149] Chitty (n 18) 3. The same sense is conveyed by the following statement made by Andrews (n 55) 512: "*Sale of goods: failures to supply or purchase*. The assumption is that the innocent party can resell to a third party or repurchase from a third party, thereby mitigating his loss, provided there is an 'available market' for such goods."

are calculated in terms of the whole loss of profits on the contract (as in *O'Hanlan v Great Western Railway*)."[150]

This aspect of the mitigation principle is so well established, that the market price rule is also reflected in statutory law which makes the market price the normal measure of damages in contracts for the sale of goods:

> "This mitigating step was incorporated in the normal measure of damages by section 51(3) of the Sale of Goods Act 1893 (now the Sale of Goods Act 1979), which states that for a seller's breach by non-delivery the prima facie measure of damages, where there is an available market, is the difference between the contract price and the market price at the time the goods should have been delivered or, if no such time is fixed, at the time of refusal to deliver."[151]

The market price rule has important practical consequences. For example, it means that if the market is such that the demand for the goods sold exceeds supply, so that the seller could always find a purchaser for every item he could offer for sale, then the seller will only receive nominal damages where a buyer in breach of contract refuses to accept goods which he has agreed to buy.[152] In the opposite situation, where the buyer can easily obtain substitute goods at the original price (or below), the buyer will likewise be limited to nominal damages.

As the authors of Chitty point out, the market price rule "assumes that the buyer should be able to finance the purchase of substitute goods at the time of the breach, even though he may not receive the damages until much later. (...) But the buyer's lack of financial resources could prevent his

---

[150] Paul Fenn, 'Mitigation and the Correct Measure of Damage' (1981) 1 *Int. J. of Law and Econ*, 225.

[151] Harvey McGregor, 'The Role of Mitigation in the Assessment of Damages', in Saidov and Cunnington (n 67), 329-346.

[152] *Charter v Sullivan* [1957] 2 Q.B. 117; Chitty (n 18) 26-099.

purchase of a substitute if he had paid the price (or a substantial deposit) in advance, or if the rise in price [since the sale] has been substantial."[153] Thus the rule can arguably sometimes produce an unfair result; however, these factors have not so far has prevented its application.[154]

This market price rule, reflecting the application of the mitigation doctrine in some situations, must be distinguished from the principle according to which someone who speculates that the market will rise or fall should not be allowed to transfer the results of a misjudgment onto the shoulders of the other party: "the loss of a buyer who accepts the seller's repudiation is crystalised on the date that he should have bought in."[155] If the innocent party speculates on the market, he or she will do so at their own risk: "The buyer is not allowed to enjoy a one-way bet at the seller's expense."[156]

This can be seen in the outcome of *Kaines (UK) Ltd v Österreichische Warenhandelsgesellschaft Austrowaren GmbH*.[157] The case arose from the sale of oil for US$18.48 per barrel. Seller repudiated and buyer accepted seller's repudiation on 18 June. However, the buyer obtained a substitute only on 29 June. In a market that is as volatile as the oil market, such a delay can be consequential and may be due to an attempt to speculate. On the facts of this case, the delay increased the buyer's loss: on 18 June the market price was $18.72, it was still $18.74 on 19 June, but had risen to $19.23 on 29 June. It was held that the buyer could not recover his full loss but only the difference between contract price and market price on 19 June, as a reasonable buyer of oil would have bought a substitute no later than on 19 June.

---

[153] Chitty (n 18) 26-098.
[154] Ibid.
[155] Michael G. Bridge, 'Market damages in sale of goods cases – anticipatory repudiation and mitigation' (1994) *Journal of Business Law*, 204, 2.
[156] Michael G. Bridge, 'Market and damages in sale of goods cases' (2016) Law Quarterly Review, 404, 410.
[157] *Kaines (UK) Ltd v Österreichische Warenhandelsgesellschaft Austrowaren GmbH* [1993] 2 Lloyd's Rep 1 (CA).

As a result, the mitigation principle may make it necessary for the victim of a repudiatory breach to obtain a substitute already before the date of performance. This was made clear by Lord Sumption in the UK Supreme Court:

> "Normally ... the injured party will be required to mitigate his loss by going into the market for a substitute contract as soon as is reasonable after the original contract was terminated. Damages will then be assessed by reference to the price which he obtained. If he chooses not to do so, damages will generally be assessed by reference to the market price at the time when he should have done".[158]

It is also important to bear in mind, however, that limitations apply to the requirement to enter substitute transactions.[159] These flow from the reasonableness standard analysed in the previous section. Buyers are not always required to accept goods of inferior quality, as substitutes to the ones originally ordered, in case they do not fit the original purpose.[160] After all, a "victim need not accept substitute performance unless that performance is fungible with that promised under the contract."[161] The general principle is that the innocent party only needs to take "reasonable commercial steps" to limit the loss.[162]

In the context of this thesis, the incorporation of the mitigation principle into the normal measure of damages via the market price rule holds an important lesson: it shows that this principle can be given effect through means other than an express general mitigation rule. On the other hand, the market price rule is just one way in which the possibility

---

[158] *Bunge SA v Nidera BV* [2015] UKSC 43, [2015] 3 All ER 1082 at [16].

[159] Treitel (n 141) 1064.

[160] *Heaven & Kesterton Ltd v Etablissements Francois Albiac et Cie* (1956) 2 Lloyd's Rep. 316.

[161] Adler (n 99) 1722.

[162] *The Golden Victory* (n 22) at [10].

of alternative transactions affects the recoverable damages. As we saw in the previous section, the innocent party may sometimes be required to accept offers from the counterparty who breached the contract. A legal system which only has the market price rule will therefore lack this broader application of the mitigation principle.

3.2.4 Treatment of extra benefits and losses

Descriptions of the mitigation doctrine tend to focus on the actions required of the innocent party to lessen the amount of losses caused to them by the other party. But the practical consequences of someone's mitigating conduct may go beyond the prevention of his or her own losses, also impacting on the outcome for the party in breach or default. Seen in this way, mitigation addresses not only the innocent party's damages, but also – and equally importantly – the breaching party's losses.

As such, any attempt to apply the mitigation doctrine must deal with at least four possible outcomes that might follow: (i) the innocent party did not act to mitigate and suffered the full loss; (ii) the innocent party acted to mitigate and successfully prevented part or all of the losses; (iii) the innocent party acted to mitigate and ended up better off than expected in the promised state of affairs; and (iv) the innocent party acted to mitigate but ended up aggravating the losses.

The outcome of the first situation is clear: no recovery will be awarded for the part of the loss which could have been prevented by reasonable action.[163] So is the outcome of the second situation: no recovery will be awarded for the part of the loss which was in fact prevented.[164] These situations have already been discussed in this Chapter. But the third and fourth situations require additional attention: how are extra losses and unexpected gains to be treated when they result from the mitigating conduct?

---

[163] This is McGregor's first rule – see section 3.1.1 above.
[164] This is McGregor's third rule – see section 3.1.1 above.

The answers arrived at in Common Law systems are investigated below. This discussion will show that the mitigation principle is able to provide answers that ensure that the outcomes in the four situations outlined above are consistent and thus form a coherent whole. As will be shown, in relation to both benefits and burdens, the basic test is whether they were caused by the claimant's reasonable efforts to mitigate or by external causes.

3.2.4.1 Benefits gained

Let us take, again, the example of landlord A and tenant B, who repudiated the rental a few days before the holiday. Acting to mitigate, A succeeded in renting the property to C, at a higher amount. This means that, at the end of the rental period, A will have received more from C than he or she expected to receive from B, incurring no loss, but in fact obtaining a gain. Such gain will reduce or even eliminate the damages payable by B, but not benefit B beyond that, so that the positive balance between the two transactions will favor A, who diligently and successfully acted to mitigate. That is what happened in the leading case *British Westinghouse Electric and Manufacturing Co Ltd v Underground Electric Railways Co of London Ltd*.[165] This is because the mitigation principle only requires that the "Innocent party must offset against his damages any benefits which in fact accrue to him as a result of steps taken by him in response to the relevant breach".[166]

When referring to *British Westinghouse*, commentators have pointed out that "benefits gained after the breach are to be taken into account to the extent that a subsequent transaction, giving rise to such benefits, arises as a consequence of the breach and is not an independent or disconnected

---

[165] For details of the case: (n 35). Viscount Haldane confirmed in *The Liverpool (No. 2)* (n 8) at 77-78 that this also applies in respect of tort claims. Examples of tort cases applying this are provided by McGregor (n 8) 9-125 –9-128.

[166] Andrews (n 127) 514 – interpreting *British Westinghouse* (n 20).

transaction".[167] Thus the only benefits to be offset are those which arise as a consequence of the breach and the successful attempt to mitigate.[168] This can be seen clearly in the UK Supreme Court decision in *Globalia Business Travel S.A.U. (formerly TravelPlan S.A.U.) of Spain v Fulton Shipping Inc of Panama, the New Flamenco*,[169] where the court did not take into account the gains made by the shipowner from the early sale of the vessel in a falling market after the charterer had terminated the charter early in breach of contract. According to the court, there was no relevant causal link between the sale and the termination: "The sale of the vessel was not itself an act of mitigation because it was incapable of mitigating the loss of the income stream" which the charter would have provided to the owner.[170]

This means – returning to the example above – that if the new rental to C takes place in a building still more than half vacant, and evidence showed that C would have rented another part of the building if B were not in default, then there would be no gain to be offset against A's losses.[171] In such a case: "The defendant's breach is the occasion but not the cause of the plaintiff's profit".[172] The same applies if the claimant sells goods for profit, buyer breaches and does not pay the price and seller sells to someone else with profit. The sale to the new buyer is regarded as an independent transaction.[173] Likewise, where the claimant is a buyer who obtained the goods more cheaply after the defendant seller repudiated the contract, the buyer's saving is not taken into account, because the buyer's decision whether or not to enter the market again after the breach "is an

---

[167] Djakhongir Saidov and Ralph Cunnington, 'Current Themes in the Law of Contract Damages: Introductory Remarks', in Saidov and Cunnington (n 67) 19-32.
[168] McGregor (n 8) 9-120 states that, "the basic rule is that the benefit to the claimant, if it is to be taken into account in mitigation of damage, must arise out of the act of mitigation itself".
[169] *Globalia Business Travel S.A.U. (formerly TravelPlan S.A.U.) of Spain v Fulton Shipping Inc of Panama, the New Flamenco* [2017] UKSC 43.
[170] Ibid para 34.
[171] *APECO of Canada Ltd. V Windmill Place* [1978] 82 DRL (3d) I.
[172] Waddams (n 117) 765.
[173] McGregor (n 8) 9-135.

independent decision, independent of the breach, made by the buyer on his assessment of the market".[174]

Gratuitous assistance by a third party which reduces or wipes out the claimant's loss is also not taken into account in mitigation of their damages. Thus it has been long established that where, for example, family members or employers assist the victim of a personal injury by covering their needs or their expenses, no deduction will be made from the claimant's damages.[175] This principle has also been applied beyond this, for example, to a claim for professional negligence against a solicitor.[176] The proceeds of an insurance policy covering personal injury will also not reduce the damages recoverable by the claimant, on the ground that "the fruits of the claimant's thrift and foresight should in fairness enure to their advantage and not to that of the defendant".[177] Insurance payments are also not taken into account in respect of other claims, such as those arising from damages to property or financial losses, but here the reason is that the insurance contract is made on an indemnity basis so that the claimant must pay any damages received to the insurer.[178]

There is a residual controversy on whether unemployment insurance is to reduce damages for wrongful dismissal. The English courts say yes,[179] whilst Canadian courts say no (holding wrongdoer should not benefit by the unemployment insurance scheme).[180] The answer, apparently, depends on the foundation of the unemployment insurance: if it aims to provide additional support to the employee, this payment should accrue to damages

[174] *Koch Marine Inc v D'Amica Società di Navigatione, The Elena d'Amico* [1980] 1 Lloyd's Rep. 75 at 89.
[175] *Liffen v Watson* [1940] 1 K.B. 556 CA; *Dennis v L.P.T.B.* [1948] 1 All E.R. 779; *Cunningham v Harrison* [1973] Q.B. 942 CA; *Redpath v Belfast and County Down Railways* [1947] N.I. 167.
[176] *Hamilton-Jones v David & Snape* [2004] 1 W.L.R. 924.
[177] McGregor (n 8) 9-167. This has been the position since the 19th Century: see *Bradburn v Great Western Railways* (1874) L.R. 10 Ex. 1.
[178] McGregor (n 8) 9-169.
[179] *Nabi v British Leyland (UK) Ltd.* [1980] 1 WLR 529 (CA).
[180] *Jack Cewe Ltd. V Jorgenson* [1980] 111 DLR (3d) 577.

owed due to wrongful dismissal and be suspended once a replacement job in obtained. On the other side, if it is paid as compensation for the dismissal, the employer – who, in most systems, collects for the scheme – should offset the insurance payment to his debt in favor of the employee.

3.2.4.2 Losses incurred

On the opposite side, there are cases in which the innocent party acts to reduce losses, but ends up aggravating them: "It is possible for steps taken in performance of the duty to mitigate to be reasonable, but actually to increase the loss".[181] That would be the case, for instance, if, in the example above, A – upon B's repudiation of the rental – advertised his property but found no tenant in time for the holiday. The expenses of taking such an apparently reasonable step as advertising the property would add to the losses that derived from B's breach. However, the innocent party acted with the aim to reduce his or her own loss to the benefit of the party in default. As such, the result of the innocent party's action – provided such action is reasonable – will be borne by the party in default, whether to reduce or add to the losses he or she is liable for.[182] After all, "the defendant was the party who created the need to mitigate in the first place by his breach".[183]

This can be seen in *Thai Airways International Public Co Ltd v KI Holdings Co Ltd*.[184] The case concerned a claim for damages resulting from the defendant's breach of contract through the late delivery and failure to deliver aircraft seats to Thai Airways for use in new aircraft which they had purchased. To overcome the resulting shortage of aircraft to perform its planned services, Thai Airways leased three aircraft to cover the temporary gap in capacity and ordered replacement seats for its

---

[181] Treitel (n 141) 1062, citing *Choil Trading S.A. v Sahara Energy Resources Ltda* [2010] EWHC 374 (Comm).

[182] McGregor (n 8) 9-102 – 9-108; Waddams (n 117) 760; Andrews (n 55) 513.

[183] Katy Barnett, 'Substitutive damages and mitigation in contract law – Tensions between two competing norms' [2016] 28 SacLJ 808.

[184] *Thai Airways International Public Co Ltd v KI Holdings Co Ltd.* (n 9) 675.

new aircraft from another supplier. Its claim for damages included the costs which it incurred in mitigating its loss by of leasing the replacement aircraft. Leggatt J held that Thai Airways was entitled to recover the costs of leasing the replacement aircraft for two years.

In *Metelmann & Co v NBR*,[185] defendant repudiated a contract to buy sugar from claimant. Aiming to mitigate, in response to defendant's repudiation, claimant sold the product before the date fixed for acceptance at a low market price. However, on the fixed date, the market had recovered – prices were higher – and claimant's attempt to mitigate ended up causing losses corresponding to the price difference. The Court of Appeal held claimant was entitled to be compensated for such damages.[186]

As Stephen Waddams points out, "This rule, though it may aggravate damages, appears to be a necessary corollary of the 'duty to mitigate', for if the claimant must attempt to mitigate on pain of diminution of the right to damages, the cost of the unsuccessful attempt is attributable to the defendant's breach."[187] Again, the same argument applies: the burden to act was placed on the innocent party by the other party's breach. And, besides, the actions taken to mitigate serve the breaching party's interest. Therefore, so long as the actions are reasonable, it is the breaching party who will suffer the positive or negative effects of the actions taken to mitigate.

Another relevant case decided with this rationale is *Banco de Portugal v Waterlow & Sons Ltd.*[188] Defendant had printed forged bank notes which were passed into general circulation. When claimant became aware of such breach, it withdrew the entire affected class of banknotes and traded them for genuine notes in exchange to the forged ones. The claim for recovery included the face value of the notes and was granted by the court, based on

---

[185] *Metelmann & Co v NBR* [1984] 1 Lloyd's Rep 614 (CA).

[186] McGregor (n 151) 329-346: "Losses incurred in the attempt to mitigate were higher than if sellers had done nothing. Court of Appeal held sellers were entitled to be compensated for the additional damage".

[187] Waddams (n 117) 762.

[188] *Banco de Portugal v Waterlow & Sons Ltd* (n 49).

the understanding that the extra cost incurred by the bank was intended to prevent further losses. Lord Macmillan stated that:

> "The law is satisfied if the party placed in a difficult position by reason of the breach of a duty owed to him has acted reasonably in the adoption of remedial measures and he will not be held disentitled to recover the cost of such measures merely because the party in breach can suggest that other measures less burdensome to him might have been taken".[189]

A further issue here is whether there is any limit on the amount of loss which may be incurred by the innocent party's mitigating actions. Courts have stated that a claim for losses cannot exceed the value of the deal, for in such case recovery would be greater than what was at stake – the price paid. That was the case in *Grant v Dawkins and Others*.[190] The promisor contracted to sell a house free of encumbrances, but the house was sold with two mortgages. The buyer claimed damages to compensate him for the cost of removing those encumbrances himself; the court capped the compensation to the value of the house. After all, it was buyer's choice to keep the deal (through a specific performance claim) despite the encumbrances. Hence, the vendor could not be held liable to pay more than what he had received, for it would exceed the value of the deal.[191] From that point on, any additional voluntary loss would result from the buyer's choice to keep the deal, conduct that would not be reasonable under

---

[189] Ibid, 456.

[190] *Grant v Dawkins and Others* [1973] 3 All ER 897.

[191] As interpreted by Letsas and Saprai (n 23) 334: "Responsibility for loss caused by the broken promise is shared when the prromise takes action to secure the promised state of affairs, in this case the costs of discharging the mortgages, the costs of which exceed the loss that would have been suffered by the promise had the promise done nothing, in this case that loss is represented by the value of the house".

the efficient use of resources rationale, and therefore would not be covered by the mitigation doctrine.

A different outcome, in which the value-of-the-deal limitation gave room to "the loss truly suffered by the promisee" (yet, inferior to the value of the deal) can be found in *Ruxley Electronics v Forsyth*.[192] In this case, the cost for the promisor to cure a defect in the performance of building contract (depth of the pool was six feet, and not the promised and expected seven feet, six inches) was contrary to common sense and unreasonable. Thus the claimant was awarded loss of "amenity" for the breach of contract, which was inferior to the value of the deal but deemed to be sufficient to compensate his frustration.

Still, there might be cases in which such limitation is rejected; in exceptional cases, the cost of securing the promised performance exceeded the market value of the good. That was the outcome in *O'Grady v Westminster Scaffolding Ltd.*[193] The repair of the claimant's car – considered to be unique by reason of some of its features – exceeded the market value of the car. The claim was granted because the uniqueness of car was acknowledged: "the market value of the good in question does not exhaust the value of that good to the claimant, or the loss that the claimant would suffer if the state of affairs to which he is entitled does not materialize."[194] Thus, the limit imposed on the loss recoverable – including in claims in which mitigation is argued – is the value of the deal, which can exceptionally be higher than the market value.

As demonstrated, the value of the deal, which must be perceived by both parties, is used to determine what will constitute reasonable steps and additional expenses covered by the mitigation doctrine.

---

[192] *Ruxley Electronics v Forsyth* [1996] A.C. 344.
[193] *O'Grady v Westminster Scaffolding Ltd.* [1962] 2 Lloyd's Rep. 238.
[194] Letsas and Saprai (n 23) 335.

3.2.5 Burden of proof

Another relevant aspect to the application of the mitigation doctrine is the burden of proof. As to this matter, courts have established and legal writers have agreed that it is the defendant who must demonstrate that the claimant has not acted as reasonably expected to minimize his or her own losses:[195]

> "[T]he burden is squarely on the defendant to show that the claimant has failed to take reasonable steps to mitigate."[196]

In *Lombard North Central v Automobile World (UK) Ltd.*,[197] the claimant had sold a vehicle to the defendant, whose price would be paid in installments. As the defendant defaulted, the claimant repossessed the vehicle and proceeded with a forced sale of the vehicle, suing the defendant for the difference between the agreed price and the price of the subsequent sale. To deny the defendant's argument that the claimant had failed to mitigate, the court asserted that: "It is well recognised that the duty to mitigate is not a demanding one... it is the party in breach which has placed the other party in a difficult situation. The burden of proof is therefore on the party in breach to demonstrate a failure to mitigate. The other party only has to do what is reasonable in the circumstances."[198]

Nevertheless, the claimant does have to prove that they suffered the loss being claimed. Thus someone who claims the cost of hiring a replacement where their own car was damaged by the defendant's tort,

---

[195] *Sainsbury's Supermarkets Ltd v Visa Europe Services LLC* (n 9) 211; See McGregor (n 8) 9-020; Waddams (n 117) 762; Chitty (n 18) 3.

[196] Tettenborn (n 53) 518. .

[197] *Lombard North Central v Automobile World (UK) Ltd* (2010) EWCA Civ 20.

[198] Ibid, 72: "The burden of proof is therefore on the party in breach to demonstrate a failure to mitigate. The other party only has to do what is reasonable in the circumstances."

must establish that they needed to hire the replacement and cannot require of the defendant to prove that it was not needed.[199] The UK Supreme Court has also held that a claimant which is in possession of the evidence regarding how the loss could have been avoided has a heavy "evidentiary burden" to "produce that evidence in order to forestall adverse inferences being taken against it by the court which seeks to apply the compensatory principle".[200]

3.3 Theoretical matters: the foundations of mitigation and its relationship to other limits on recoverability

As was pointed out in Chapter 2, the mitigation doctrine is not the only rule to limit the right of recovery of the innocent party.[201] Anne Michaud has described the relationship between mitigation and these other doctrines in the following way:

> "Mitigation appears to be very closely related to other doctrines which also play a role in measuring the extent of recoverable losses, namely causation, contributory negligence and remoteness, but mitigation possesses certain particular attributes that differentiate it from these other doctrines. These attributes are mainly found in its legal foundations, considerations of policy such as the avoidance of waste and the efficacy of transactions."[202]

Michael Bridge indicates that all three of these have been identified by some as providing the juridical basis of mitigation in the common law.[203] This requires investigation because it is plainly relevant to the research

---

[199] *Singh v Yaqubi* [2013] EWCA Civ 23 CA.

[200] *Sainsbury's Supermarkets Ltd v Visa Europe Services LLC* (n 9) 216.

[201] See section 2.4.

[202] Michaud (n 2) 309.

[203] Bridge (n 7) 400-405.

question investigated in this thesis: if, contrary to Michaud's claim in this quotation, mitigation does *not* "possess certain particular attributes that differentiate it from these other doctrines", it may not need its own provision in the Civil Code of Brazil.

The following two sections will therefore investigate the two issues touched on in this quotation: firstly, what Michaud calls the "legal foundations" or "considerations of policy", in other words its grounds and justifications, and secondly, how mitigation relates to the doctrines of causation, remoteness and contributory negligence. The aim will be to determine whether these foundations to serve to differentiate mitigation from these other doctrines.

3.3.1 Grounds and justifications of the mitigation doctrine

A clear perception that derives from the discussion above is that the mitigation doctrine targets the conduct of the innocent party, to the benefit of the breaching party. As a result, legal commentators often describe the mitigation doctrine as imposing a burden on the innocent party. For example:

> "The main mitigation rule is that an innocent party is
> expected to take reasonable steps to reduce or eliminate
> the loss caused by, or likely to ensure from, the other
> party's breach of contract (or tortious misconduct)."[204]

> "Plaintiffs must be encouraged to contribute to the effort
> of re-establishment of the original equilibrium disturbed
> by the breach of contract."[205]

Professor Seana Shifrin considers it unacceptable to place this additional burden on the innocent party as a result of the other party's

---

[204] Andrews (n 55) 511.
[205] Michaud (n 2) 299.

wrongdoing: "It is morally distasteful to expect the promisee to do work that could be done by the promisor when the occasion for the work is the promisor's own wrongdoing."[206]

Authors also express concern that the mitigation doctrine might weaken the binding force of contracts:

> "The rules inevitably give some incentive to the defendant deliberately to break his contractual undertaking whenever he finds a better opportunity for the resources he intended to use in performing the contract: if he makes a higher profit on a new contract, he may be better off even after paying damages to compensate the original promise (because these damages may be relatively low whenever substitute performance is readily available)."[207]

But these objections would only be valid if the doctrine served no value or purpose which could justify these consequences. However, as Fried points out, "promising is not all there is to morality",[208] and enforcing contracts is also not necessarily the only objective of contract law. Many authors have identified possible justifications of the doctrine. The main responses to these objections will be analysed in the next two subsections. These arguments reach beyond one party's interest and justify the mitigation doctrine on the basis of duties owed to others (altruism), the interests of both parties (fairness), and the interests of society in general (avoiding waste). The analysis shows that while the objections reflect valid concerns, they have been successfully addressed by defenders of the mitigation doctrine. Michaud is right to state that the foundations

---

[206] Seana V Shiffrin 'The divergence of contract and promise', (2007) 120 *Harvard Law Review* 724-725.

[207] Chitty (n 18) 2.

[208] Charles Fried, 'The convergence of contract and promise', (2009) *Harvard Law Review* 7.

of the mitigation doctrine lie in the basic policies of the Common Law, "particularly in the objectives of avoidance of waste of human and material resources, commercial efficiency and also fairness to the wrongdoer."[209]

3.3.1.1 Imposition of a burden on the innocent party

While it is true that the innocent party will be expected to act, it is not only in the mitigation context that a person capable of preventing someone else's harm will be expected to do so:

> "There are a number of relationships where the responsibility of one party for the care of the other is recognized as giving rise to an affirmative duty to prevent harm."[210]

From the duty of parents to safeguard their children and the doctors' duty of care for patients – applicable to specific to people, in their own capacities – to the limited duty to disclose information during pre-contractual negotiations,[211] there are several situations in which there is a legal obligation to act.[212] In all of such cases, there is a special relationship between the parties, there is a specific assumption of responsibility or there is a specific responsibility to protect. And just as in the mitigation context – where the victim of a breach of contract, whose actions can affect the size of the loss and therefore the amount of compensation payable by the other party, has the fate of the latter in his hands – those on whom the

---

[209] Michaud (n 105) 309.
[210] Michael A. Jones, Anthony M. Dugdale and Mark Simpson, *Clerk & Lindsell on Torts* (22nd Ed, Sweet & Maxwell Ltd 2017) 8-52.
[211] See *Brownlie v Campbell* [1880] 5 AC 925 and *Davies v London and Provincial Marine Insurance Co* [1878] 8 Ch. D469, in which silence that meant to induce the other party in error was considered unlawful misrepresentation.
[212] Clerk & Lindsell (n 210) 8-52 mention the cases of "an employer, who owes an affirmative duty to take care to prevent harm to his employees as does a carrier to a passenger, a parent or school to a child a custodial authority to a detainee".

law imposes a duty to assist or protect others have the fate of those others in their hands.

Taking their cue from this, several authors have justified the mitigation doctrine on the basis of duties owed to others. Daniel Friedman has stated in broad terms that "the aggrieved party should at least to some extent take the interest of the other party into account and that he ought not to impose on the party in breach expenses that do not serve the interest of the aggrieved party."[213]

Authors have provided different justifications for the existence of this duty. To Eisenberg, the duty to mitigate is a contextualized expression of the duty to rescue: "the duty to rescue in contract law has not been explicitly recognized as such, but it is instantiated in more specific principles and rules that apply in a variety of contract-law setting, including mitigation (...)".[214] He argues that "a duty to rescue is congruent with other areas of law" and cites admiralty law and the law of restitution.[215] Charles Fried bases the mitigation principle on altruism, arguing that morality would recognize "the duty to save another from serious loss when the actor can do so with little trouble", pointing out that:

> "Normative economics is about furthering human goods. Morality too is a human enterprise, and its special case, promising, underwrites human cooperation in furthering human goods, but on terms of equality, trust and mutual respect."[216]

Fried insists that "it is a duty without cost, since the victim of the breach is never worse off for having mitigated (...). And if the victim of a

---

[213] Friedmann (n 67) 88.

[214] Melvin A. Eisenberg, 'The duty to rescue in Contract Law' (2002) *Fordham L. Rev.* 647, 654.

[215] Eisenberg (n 214) 693.

[216] Fried (n 213) 9.

breach fails in his duty the only penalty he suffers is the proportional loss of his own remedial rights."[217]

However, there is reason to doubt that reliance on a duty to rescue or altruism can provide a genuinely successful defence of the mitigation principle. This is because, as we saw when the principle was outlined in section 3.1.1, there is in fact no real "duty to mitigate" – the principle merely limits the losses for which the claimant can recover compensation. The consequence is that, as Letsas and Saprai point out that, altruism (and, one may add, Eisenberg's duty to rescue) is ruled out as justification for the mitigation doctrine, since altruism would require a duty to avoid losses rather than merely an inability to claim losses that could have been avoided. In their view, the principle of fairness instead provides the foundation for the doctrine:

"The principle of fairness bars the promisee from blaming the promisor for those easily avoidable losses or claiming compensation for them, at the same time as extinguishing the promisor's responsibility for them, the promisee has no right to claim these losses and, correlatively, the promisor is not responsible for them. This is so even though the promisee was under no duty to minimize or not to exacerbate losses".[218]

This justification does fit with the most basic features of the mitigation principle outlined above, namely that it is concerned with determining what losses are recoverable and that it focuses on whether the claimant acted in a reasonable manner in the circumstances of the case. Moreover, as was seen in section 3.2.2 above, the "duty to mitigate" is not a stringent one, as the courts take a benevolent approach which takes into account

---

[217] Charles Fried, *Contract as Promise: A Theory of Contractual Obligation* (Harvard University Press 1981) 131.
[218] Klass, Letsas and Saprai (n 23) 326, 327.

the pressure under which the innocent party is acting. As Kimmel points out, the expectation to mitigate exists only where the harm "can easily be avoided by the innocent party".[219] The mitigation doctrine as applied in practice therefore reflects concern for *both* parties. As Peter Alces explains:

> "[I]t would be an error to conclude that the doctrine is overindulgent of those who do not fulfill their obligations. Though non-breaching parties' duty to mitigate operates to avoid waste, contract's provision of consequential damages assures that the non-breaching party will realize the full benefit of her bargain, the expectation measure of damages."[220]

3.3.1.2 Encouragement of breaches of contract

The objection that the mitigation doctrine encourages deliberate breaches[221] of contract because it frees the guilty party of full responsibility for all the losses caused by the breach, has been met by arguments which draw attention to the limited availability of resources and the importance of their efficient use.

Indeed, "many writers on law-and-economics to argue that mitigation supports 'efficient' breaches of contract (*viz* breaches which will leave society as a whole better off, while the original promisee is left no worse off)."[222] The argument advanced by such writers is based on the idea that in a world with limited availability of resources it is appropriate to permit breaches that result in savings of such resources: If a buyer finds the

---

[219] Dori Kimel, *From Promise To Contract: Towards A Liberal Theory Of Contract* (Hart Publishing 2003) 110.

[220] Peter A. Alces, *A Theory of Contract Law: Empirical Insights and Moral Psychology* (Oxford University Press, 2011) 224.

[221] Also referred to as "efficient breaches", in which the party in breach accepts the allowance of expectation damages for it represent less than his or her cost to perform.

[222] Chitty (n 18) 4.

same product at a lower price, and the difference economically justifies repudiation of the original contract – and its consequences – the breach is deemed to be efficient and the amount saved by buyer would best be spent elsewhere. As Friedman explains: "If the outcome of this calculation is less than the loss that the defendants would have suffered from their performance of the contract, then the performance of the contract with the defendants became wasteful and should not have been carried out."[223]

Thus Hillman argues that the main purpose of the mitigation doctrine is to ensure the economic use of resources and, consequently, avoid economic waste: "The avoidable consequences doctrine provides that damages caused by a breach of contract which could be avoided by taking reasonable steps are not recoverable in an action for the breach. The main purpose of the doctrine is to avoid economic waste (…)."[224] As Barnett explains, "The law provides incentives via the doctrine of mitigation to encourage a rational plaintiff to fix the breach herself where this is appropriate and possible."[225] Barnett argues that in doing this the law reflects society's common interest:

> "A dominant concern is community welfare: it is suggested that our contract law reflects a policy that is economically efficient (and therefore for the benefit of society as a whole) if those who suffer from contractual breaches help themselves when they are better placed to do so than the court or the unwilling defendant."[226]

This argument can be applied equally to the context of tort law: here

---

[223] Friedmann (n 67) 88.
[224] Robert A. Hillman, 'Keeping the Deal Together after Material Breach – Common Law Mitigation Rules, the UCC, and the Restatement (Second) of Contracts' (1976) 47 *U. of Col. L. R.*, 558.
[225] Barnett (n 183) 795.
[226] Barnett (n 183) 806.

also the mitigation principle encourages a rational claimant to limit her losses because it prevents her from recovering compensation for losses which she could have limited.

This explanation and justification of mitigation is very prominent in the literature. It is the most common explanation in American literature,[227] and is also supported by Waddams (Canadian) [228] and McKendrick (British).[229] The argument of economic efficiency is criticized, however, for this cannot be the only principle, as some contracts are less efficient are still binding on the parties:

> "In general, then, damages awarded by the courts following breach of contract take account of optimal quantity adjustment only in a very rough and discontinuous way: either the contracted-for quantity is bought or sold in mitigation, or nothing is bought or sold. The reasonableness of pursuing the former rather than the latter form of mitigation is assessed in relation to ordinary business practice in the light of the available price. As a result, there is little incentive for plaintiffs to reduce their losses by partial quantity adjustment, and consequently defendants are bearing some 'avoidable' losses. In other words, as a result of damages which are 'too high', some contracts are being performed when it would be economically efficient for them to be broken."[230]

In other words: as much as efficient breaches are beneficial in light of

---

[227] See the citations in Bridge (n 9) at 404 n 41.

[228] Waddams (n 117) 758: "Behind this principle there lie two notions, one of causation, that the defendant's breach does not cause losses that were reasonably avoidable, the other of the desirability of avoiding economic waste".

[229] McKendrick (n 18) 357: "The aim of the doctrine of mitigation is to prevent the avoidable waste of resources".

[230] Fenn (n 150) 225.

the limited availability of resources, they also threaten the binding force of contracts and leave the promisee a hostage of the promisor's economic interest over his moral duty. That the law does not give full effect to the economic argument can be seen, for example, in *The Hansa Nord* case,[231] for it restricts a party's right to terminate to cases in which there is either a substantial breach or the breach of a contractual condition (if both are absent, the party will be left with the option to claim for damages). Therefore, the efficient breach theory can only provide limited support to the doctrine of mitigation, as it does not – by itself – overrule the binding force of contracts.

Moreover, like the justifications based on altruism and a duty to rescue, this rationale would require a genuine duty to mitigate, for only such a duty would serve as an incentive for victims of breach to minimize economic waste. It is therefore subject to the same objection as those two justifications: the mitigation doctrine, as we saw, does not in fact impose a duty but merely reduces the compensation recoverable. This does not mean that waste prevention should be rejected completely as a rationale for mitigation, because the inability to recover full compensation may well serve as an incentive to avoid losses for which no compensation will be available. But it does provide support for Bridge's statement that, "while the idea of economic waste may help explain certain workings of the duty to mitigate, it hardly amounts to a universal explanation".[232] It is therefore probably best to treat the avoidance of waste as resting only "partly on a policy of avoiding economic waste".[233]

---

[231] *The Hansa Nord* [1976] QB 44 (*Cehave NV v Bremer Handels GmbH*): defendant was supposed to deliver goods and shipment was "to be made in good condition" Claimant rejected the goods under the argument that not all of them were shipped in "good conditions". Court held the goods were usable for the same intended purposes and that claimant could not reject the entire shipment, but only claim for damages. In the same sense, see *Hongkong Fir Shipping Co. Ltd. V Kawasaki Kisen Kaisha Ltd.* [1962] 2 QB 26 (CA).

[232] Bridge (n 7) 405.

[233] Stephen M. Waddams, *The Law on Damages* (Canada Law Book 2004) 15-3.

Nevertheless, even if encouraging efficient use of resources does not on its own provide a complete justification for mitigation and needs to be supplemented, the arguments which focus on this do provide an answer to the objection that the mitigation principle encourages breach of contract. They show that enforcing contracts is not the only legitimate consideration for contract law – it can and should also take account of the social interest in avoiding waste. Mitigation promotes a sense of collective solidarity between the parties and society – as a whole – that sometimes calls for care, cooperation and avoidance of waste.

This survey of the debate in Common Law systems about the justifiability of the mitigation doctrine suggests that it is grounded in the coexistence of the values of fairness and the economic use of resources. Fairness is focused on the relationship between the parties, while the avoidance of waste focuses on the relationship that the parties have to the broader society. This suggests that the mitigation principle has a complex rationale which cannot be reduced to a single dimension. That has important implications for the matters discussed in the next section, and also for the thesis as a whole, for it suggests that it is unlikely that mitigation is simply an application of one of the other limits on recoverability.

3.3.2 The relationship between mitigation and other limits on recoverability

According to Bridge, the "most common explanation" of the juridical basis of the mitigation doctrine "is that a plaintiff's loss is not in fact caused by the defendant when it stems from the plaintiff's failure to mitigate".[234] This appears to have been the position taken by Viscount Haldane in the *British Westinghouse* case,[235] and has also more recently been supported

---

[234] Bridge (n 7) 400
[235] *British Westinghouse Electric & Manufacturing Co Ltd v Underground Electric Railways Co of London Ltd* (n 17) 689: failure to mitigate "debars him from claiming any part of the *damage which is due to his neglect* to take such steps" (emphasis added).

by Legatt J in *Thai Airways* when he described the three mitigation rules identified by McGregor as having an underlying unity in that they "are all aspects of the principle of causation".[236] This echoes the words of Robert Goff J in *Koch Marine Inc v D'Amica Società di Navigatione, The Elena d'Amico*:[237]

> "[T]hese three aspects of mitigation are all really aspects
> of a wider principle which is that, subject to the rules of
> remoteness, the plaintiff can recover, but can only recover,
> in respect of damage suffered by him which has been
> caused by the defendant's legal wrong. In other words,
> they are aspects of the principle of causation."

In the UK Supreme Court case of *Lagden v O'Connor*,[238] Lord Walker described mitigation as "an aspect (or category) of the larger principle of causation". Academic support for this position is provided by Dyson and Kramer in their joint article, in which they state that "the rule of mitigation displaces the factual assessment of the claimant's breach position and replaces it with the position that the claimant would have been in if it had acted reasonably. Any costs and benefits that would have arisen if the claimant had acted reasonably are considered; any other actual costs and benefits are ignored."[239] By that these commentators mean that losses will be measured by considering not only the defendant's conduct, but also the impact that reasonable action by the claimant would have had to the outcome of the situation (thus, both are causes to the measure of losses). Waddams also supports this connection between causation and mitigation, stating that the later "rests partly on the principle of causation: losses that

---

[236] *Thai Airways International Public Co Ltd v KI Holdings Co Ltd* (n 9) 33.
[237] *Koch Marine Inc v D'Amica Società di Navigatione, The Elena d'Amico* [1980] 1 Lloyd's Rep. 75 at 88.
[238] *Lagden v O'Connor* [2004] 1 A.C. 1067 at 99–100.
[239] Dyson and Kramer (n 14).

could reasonably have been avoided are caused by the plaintiff's inaction rather than by the defendant's wrong and partly on a policy of avoiding economic waste". [240]

Michaud, on the other hand, disagrees with the analysis according to which mitigation derives from causation by stating that "the rule on avoidable consequences exists by itself, and not only as a reflection of the doctrine of causation."[241] This indicates that both doctrines may be applied separately in the same case, when recoverability is reduced because the claimant both caused part of the loss (causation) and, at another point, took no action to avoid its aggravation (failure to mitigate).[242] In *Uzinterimpex Jsc v Standard Bank Plc*,[243] Lord Justice Moore-Bick L.J also questions the utility of explaining mitigation through the prism of causation, as the tests for each are distinct as to the level of interference in claimant's action in the result: "If one analyses a failure to mitigate in terms of a new event which breaks the chain of causation between the wrongful act and the subsequent loss, it is necessary to recognise that the way in which the test of a new supervening cause has traditionally been formulated must be adapted or applied so as to take into account the relatively undemanding level of the duty to mitigate which the law imposes on the victim of a wrongful act."

There is no doubt that the aspect of the mitigation rule which deals with the effects of claimant's action (or inaction) on his own losses correspond to the application of the causation rule when proportionally attributing liability. But the mitigation rule goes beyond this aspect, as it also deals with matters such as the reasonableness of the claimant's action (risks and costs taken) and the context in which the situation occurred (availability of market and/or substitutive operations). Therefore, whilst causation seeks

---

[240] Waddams (n 233) 591.

[241] Michaud (n 2) 301.

[242] Example: the claimant took no preventive measures to avoid consequences of fire set by defendant to his or her property (did not install fire extinguishers – causation) and, once fire was lit, chose not to call the fire brigade(which would be the reasonable action to prevent the aggravation – failure to mitigate).

[243] *Uzinterimpex Jsc v Standard Bank Plc* [2008] EWCA Civ 819 at 56.

to identify the loss as the effect of one's action or inaction, focusing on identifying what has caused the loss to then proportionally distribute the right of recovery (with a more demanding level-of-interference test), mitigation, on the other hand, targets what action one could reasonably take to avoid aggravation of loss, and limits the right of recovery to the loss that could not have been avoided with such action. McGregor supports this position by stating that:

> "What must be ascertained is whether the claimant has or has not acted, or failed to act, reasonably. This, as we have seen, is a question of fact and one that is capable of resolution by an examination of the circumstances of the particular case. Adding causation into the mix gives no assistance. There is indeed a danger here, as elsewhere, of using causation as a disguise for the real ground of a decision. It is significant that the cases on the avoidable loss aspect of mitigation are not full of references to causation."[244]

When detailing the relationship between mitigation and other rules of damages assessment, Waddams refers to the "basic rules of assessment of damages in sale cases, whereby the buyer is entitled to recover the difference between the contract price and the market value."[245] Beyond that, some legal commentators also relate mitigation to the doctrine of remoteness (sometimes called legal causation). In terms of this doctrine, the claim is limited to the losses that are not "too remote" consequences of the breach, as it would be unfair to consider defendant liable for losses

---

[244] McGregor (n 8) 401 also differentiates both principles by exemplifying cases of "sale of goods, whose governing Act contains rules for calculating damages according to the market price at the due date of performance."
[245] Waddams (n 233) 15.100.

which are not the expected effect of the breach.[246] The application of this doctrine is a question of law, and rests on the potential losses that are contemplated by hypothetical prediction of the consequences of a possible future breach.[247] Simply put, losses are too remote if they are not within the reasonable contemplation of the parties at the time of entry into the contract.[248] Its connection to the mitigation doctrine is supported by Furmston, who argues that "In relation to the computation of damages, mitigation is substantially an aspect of remoteness, since it is within the contemplation of the parties that the plaintiff will take reasonable steps to mitigate his loss."[249] But Waddams disagrees with this, arguing that "little would be gained by such a formulation since the basic principle of mitigation does not depend on the defendant's actual knowledge, contemplation, or foresight, and it is clearer, therefore, to treat mitigation as a separate rule".[250] Bridge agrees:

> "remoteness is concerned with a hypothetical prediction *ex ante* of the consequences of a future breach of a contract, and is a question of law. Questions of mitigation, on the other hand, are invariably converned with a factual assessment of the qualifty of the plaintiff's behavior in the circumstances in which he was placed."[251]

However, the practical application of the two doctrines will not always

[246] "The general test is that the claimant can only recover in respect of losses which were within the reasonable contemplation of the parties at the time of entry into the contract" – Michaud (n 2) 303-304.
[247] Bridge (n 7) 401.
[248] McGregor (n 8) ch. 8.
[249] MP Furmston, *Cheshire, Fifoot, and Furmston's Law of Contract* (Oxford University Press, 17th edn) 777. In the same sense: McGregor on Damages 19th ed §297 and Katy Barnett, 'Mitigation and Remoteness in Contract: Policy and Principle' (2019) 36(1) *Journal of Contract Law* 5.
[250] Waddams (n 233) 15.110.
[251] Bridge (n 7) 403.

produce the same result. It makes no difference for the limitation proposed by the remoteness doctrine if the loss could have been avoided or not; if it is remote (not within reasonable contemplation of the parties), it shall not be recoverable. According to the mitigation doctrine, however, regardless of whether part of the loss is considered remote or not, it will not be recoverable if the duty to mitigate is not complied with by the innocent party. In other words: if reasonable action from the claimant could have avoided the loss but was not taken – and that is a question of fact – no recovery will be available to that portion of the loss even if it had been in the contemplation of the parties when they entered into the contract. Thus, although both doctrines deal with limitation of recoverability, the reasons for applying them are different:

> "There is certainly a close relationship between the doctrines of remoteness and mitigation, which is not surprising since they are both used for the same purpose, that of ascertaining the limits of the plaintiff's loss that must be made good by the defendant. (…) the results of the rules of mitigation have some effect on the measure of the plaintiff's damage; but losses which remain uncompensated because they could have been avoided do not become too remote from the breach for that reason."[252]

A practical example can be given to illustrate this. In a hypothetical situation in which someone buys a bus ticket to travel to another city and the arrival at the destination is delayed due to malfunctioning of the bus, so that the passenger misses the deadline for recovering his lottery prize due to this delay, the bus company, as the defendant in a claim for losses, could raise two arguments. One is that the lottery prize was beyond its contemplation when the ticket was sold to the passenger; the other is that

---

[252] Michaud (n 2) 303-304.

the passenger could have left the bus and taken a taxi to his destination, thereby avoiding the delay and consequential loss. In this situation, both doctrines could be argued by the defendant against the claim for losses, based on completely different arguments. The first of these would be a remoteness argument and the second a mitigation argument. This shows how both can be easily differentiated, even in cases when both lead to the same result. Likewise, there might be situations in which one doctrine applies, and the other does not.

Thus, remoteness and the mitigation doctrine are two different – but totally compatible – rules that limit recovery: one does that under the argument that part of the loss is too remote from the breaching party's action (and, therefore, not directly connected); the other because such part of the loss – remote or not, directly connected or not – was within the reach of the innocent party to mitigate. This allows mitigation to reach further than remoteness, for it might also cover losses that are not clearly within the contemplation of the parties.

Contributory negligence also overlaps with the mitigation doctrine, for in many situations both might apply to the same facts and lead to the same outcome. This is so because the mitigation doctrine limits recovery for someone who failed to act reasonably to avoid the aggravation of losses, and contributory negligence apportions distribution of liability according to how much one's inertia has contributed to cause his own losses. They are similar to the extent that "(...) the defendant's wrongdoing and the plaintiff's failure to mitigate are both active and substantial factors in the occurrence of the unmitigated part of the loss: they are both *contributory causes* of this loss."[253] Nonetheless, there are many aspects that differentiate the one from the other.

At first, it may be argued that the distinction between them relies on the time of inaction and application: contributory negligence being simultaneous to the default, most commonly in tort claims, whilst failure

---

[253] Michaud (n 2) 299.

to mitigate would arise subsequently to the breach, most commonly in contractual relations.[254] But this division is more theoretical than functional, with commentators still admitting a correlation between both doctrines:

> "There is no fundamental difference between the doctrines of contributory negligence and of the failure to mitigate the loss. The difference is only in their relative importance. So it should not matter whether the creditor's contributory negligence relates to the materialization of the damage or to the later mitigation of its effect. Both doctrines are founded on an appropriate care for one's own interests. This is not a legal duty or an obligation that can be enforced by law, rather it indicates that the liability of someone else does not absolve the aggrieved party of the responsibility to take care of its own interests."[255]

But though they might be considered similar in meaning and effects currently, it is important to highlight that the two doctrines have had an independent evolution over time. Contributory negligence, for a long period, was a complete defense to claims for compensation, until legislation provided it should instead result only in apportionment of damages.[256] Moreover these rules apply only to torts, and not to claims based on breach of contract (except where there is a complete overlap between contract and tort liability).[257]

---

[254] Waddams (n 233) even discusses mitigation under the heading "Plaintiff's Conduct after the Wrong".

[255] Anne Keirse, 'Why the Proposed Optional Common European Sales Law Has Not, But Should Have, Abandoned the Principle of All or Nothing: A Guide to How to Sanction the Duty to Mitigate the Loss' (2011) 19 *European Review of Private Law*, 961.

[256] Law Reform (Contributory Negligence) Act 1945.

[257] See *Barclays Bank plc v Fairclough Building Ltd (No 1)* [1995] QB 214 (CA).

But most importantly, the fundamental practical difference between the two doctrines (as they have developed in the common law) is that under contributory negligence any loss that the victim could have avoided is apportioned between the victim and the wrongdoer. In contrast, under the doctrine of mitigation, a victim cannot recover for any element of loss that could have been avoided by taking reasonable steps. As Keirse explains, "the legal consequence of a breach of the duty to mitigate the loss is not an apportionment of the loss between the parties but rather an exclusion of the liability of the wrongdoer for the additional loss."[258] Briefly speaking: mitigation concerns questions of assessment of compensation, and contributory negligence questions of apportionment of responsibility for a loss. The two doctrines are different in scope and application. In this sense, Tettenborn sums this up as follows:

> "The doctrine of mitigation involves conduct by one who, faced with a loss for which someone else is liable, culpably fails to minimize the consequences of that loss. Contributory negligence, by contrast, involves culpable failure to prevent a loss being suffered in the first place."[259]

All the different doctrines discussed in this section limit recoverability. Causation seeks to identify the cause of the loss; remoteness concerns how much of such loss is sufficiently closely connected to the contract or tort; and contributory negligence aims to apportion responsibility for the loss between the parties. Mitigation also limits recoverability, but clearly does so on distinct grounds, has a distinct content, and a distinctive scope of application. Even when the same fact calls for the application of more than one doctrine, or when different facts lead to the same result, mitigation remains distinguishable from the other principles and should be analysed as an independent principle. The mitigation doctrine might play a similar

---

[258] Keirse (n 255) 968.
[259] Tettenborn (n 53) 519.

role in as much as it also has the effect of limiting recoverability, but it does so in its own way, which in some situations is not covered by any of the other doctrines. Treating mitigation as distinct also represents the most up-to-date legal tendency in more recent national and transnational statutes, as will be seen in the next Chapter. Therefore, despite the admitted overlaps between mitigation and the other principles limiting compensation, mitigation should be available in a legal system as one of the possible limits on the recoverability of damages.

3.4 Conclusion

The study of the mitigation doctrine in Common Law jurisdictions shows that the principle of mitigation is not strictly a duty, but a standard of conduct expected from the innocent party that will impact on the recoverability available. It places on the innocent party a burden of reasonable action, based on ideals of fairness, and in the interest of the broader benefit of preventing the waste of resources (or at least encouraging the innocent party to do so). Placing both the burden of proof of failure to mitigate and the risk of liability for extra losses incurred in reasonable attempts to mitigate on the shoulders of the party who benefits from the duty, namely the party in breach or default, serves to balance the parties' relations.

This study identified that the law has evolved to allow the mitigation doctrine to be applied to commercial and private relations, in tort or contract claims. This is because whenever the party that suffered the losses can act to avoid further losses, mitigation rules will be useful to prevent the aggravation of the situation and the waste of resources, as a complement to existing rules like causation, contributory negligence and remoteness.

The study of different common law jurisdictions showed how the principle developed differently in each jurisdiction, perhaps reflecting different local values. The case law analysed provided a clear view of the structure of the rule, and of how it deals with losses avoided, losses incurred and gains earned as result of mitigation. Losses avoided are given the same treatment as losses that could have been avoided by reasonable action, and cannot be claimed for; losses incurred in reasonable attempt to mitigate and gains earned in mitigating will increase or reduce recovery, respectively.

Conceptually, the mitigation doctrine plays an important role in affirming parties' duty to cooperate with each other and stimulates the innocent parties to act reasonably in order to save resources that should not be wasted. On the other hand, the doctrine gives space to efficient breaches (in which one party voluntarily chooses to breach, for it might cost less than keeping the contract), requires substitute transactions (especially when an alternative market is available), challenges specific performance in some situations and adds obligations and burdens that might go beyond what the parties have contracted for. The result is to place reasonableness and prudence on the part of the parties, fairness, and the effective use of resources, as leading factors in the legal resolution of the consequences when obligations have not been met. The effect, therefore, is to preserve some of the force of contracts, and also to add a cooperative spirit with a financial incentive.

The measure of reasonableness, on which the application of the mitigation doctrine inevitably depends, remains a matter of fact, subject to the court's judgment of the situation, and affected by local culture (therefore, adaptable from place to place), of how a prudent and reasonable person would act. The court's evaluation of this goes beyond the effectiveness of the actions taken to mitigate, and considers the party's judgment with the information available at the time of action. Still, this will always be an aspect subject to considerations relevant to each specific case, no matter how many opportunities a legal system might have for defining reasonable actions. The experience of the common law systems examined in this chapter indicates that a broadly formulated mitigation principle can be used by courts to achieve an appropriate balance between the necessary flexibility and reasonable predictability of outcomes.

Another point of tension identified is the co-existence of the mitigation doctrine and the remedy of specific performance. Different approaches were identified in different Common Law jurisdictions – whether preferring the specific performance remedy (English and Canadian Courts) or the right to terminate combined with the duty to mitigate (American Courts) – with strong arguments on both sides, making it clear that the default rule in each reflects the evolution of the mitigation doctrine over years and through diverse cases. Thus different approaches in different jurisdictions have demonstrated alternative ways in which the doctrine can be introduced to a new legal system. But, most of all, these differences indicate how much the background of a jurisdiction must be considered in order for mitigation to fit into a legal system. In the case of Brazil, the victim's right to choose between specific performance or claiming for losses has to be taken into account. This reduces the potential field for application of the mitigation doctrine compared to common law systems, but also means that the tension observed in common law systems will not be a practical problem in Brazil.

Finally, besides these practical aspects concerned with its implementation, the mitigation doctrine was compared to other doctrines that have a similar role in limiting recoverability. The arguments examined – from legal commentators and court precedents – evidenced the distinctiveness of this doctrine, and its importance in the context of a legal system to complement other limiting rules and its potential to bring a fair, economically efficient and legally up-to-date approach to countries, like Brazil, that have not yet adopted it. The analysis presented in this chapter has demonstrated how causation, remoteness and contributory negligence can and should coexist with the mitigation doctrine, for it stands on its own grounds, applies to some different situations and complements these other reasons for limiting the recoverability of compensation.

The next chapter will explore and examine selected Civil Law systems and transnational instruments, to identify how the mitigation doctrine has been treated in civil codes and similar legal instruments. This will enable a comparison to be made between the different formulations of the rule, and provide up-to-date information to be considered in developing the best formulation for Brazil. Finally, building on relevant lessons from both Common and Civil Law systems, Chapter 5 will come up with a proposal on how to expressly regulate the duty to mitigate loss in Brazil.

CHAPTER 4

4.1 Introduction

This chapter seeks to examine how the principle of mitigation is dealt with in Civil Law systems. It answers the research question posed in Chapter 1 to investigate what can be extracted from the experience of Civil Law jurisdictions which have notably influenced Brazilian law or with which Brazilian law has a cultural or geographical connection. As explained in Chapter 1, Brazil belongs to the Civil Law family of legal systems. The purpose of this chapter is therefore to examine the treatment of the principle of mitigation in systems that are more closely related to Brazil than the Common Law systems examined in Chapter 3. The overall aim is to see if and how such countries regulate and apply mitigation rules, and whether there are any positive or negative lessons to be learnt from these jurisdictions for the purposes of developing a proposal, in Chapter 5, for the reform of the Civil Code of Brazil.

This chapter accordingly starts with an introductory overview which summarizes the broad trends in Civil Law systems and relates these to the position in Common Law systems. This section of the chapter also explains the reasons for the choice of the individual jurisdictions examined in the following sections: Germany, France, Argentina, and group of transnational instruments. The chapter will conclude by drawing together the lessons to be learnt from this comparative exercise.

4.1.1 Families of the Civil Law system and the regulation of the mitigation doctrine

The Civil Law tradition of legal systems relies on statutes and codified sets of rules as the main source of law. [1] This tendency to rely on a pre-established standardized solution is reflected in the remedies for contractual breaches: while Common Law systems tend to accept the breach and

---

[1] See Jaap Hage, 'Legal Reasoning', in Smits (ed), *Elgar Encyclopedia Of Comparative Law* (2nd edn, Edward Elgar Publishing 2014) ch. 42, 521-537.

favour compensation (as best applied to each case), in the Civil Law approach the emphasis is in favoring specific performance of the contract as the immediate remedy (that is: the pre-established solution/contractual commitment agreed by the parties).[2] This approach (less focused on the damages and their compensation, and more focused on the obligations of each party), over time, has left more limited room for the mitigation doctrine to develop in Civil Law jurisdictions. Consequently, Michaud observes that, in contrast with the position in Common Law systems, "in Civil Law mitigation has not reached the status of a legal principle; it is simply an element to be taken into account in the practical implementation of certain legal principles to which it is related."[3] Lopes likewise contrasts the "autonomous principle" of Common Law systems with Civil Law countries where, he writes, "mitigation is a mere application of the fault or causation principles" (original version: a mitigação aparece como mera aplicação do conceito de culpa ou de causalidade).[4]

Still, when dealing with the duty to mitigate loss, jurisdictions that follow the Civil Law tradition of legal systems can be classified into two main variants: those which have no specific provision and leave it all for courts to decide, and those which have some specific provision on the duty to mitigate, typically as part of the contributory negligence or causation rules. The jurisdictions considered in this Chapter represent both variants,

---

[2] Guenter H. Treitel, *Remedies for Breach of Contract: A Comparative Account* (Oxford University Press 1988) par 41: "the availability of enforced performance is limited in all the legal systems under discussion. Three main approaches may be distinguished. Under the first, the general principle of enforced performance is accepted, subject to certain exceptions; under the second enforced performance is available in respect of obligations of a certain content but not (in principle) in respect of others; and under the third enforced performance is regarded as an exceptional, discretionary remedy. These may be called respectively the German, French and COMMON LAW approaches."

[3] Anne Michaud. 'Mitigation of Damage in the Context of Remedies for Breach of Contract' (1984) 15 *Rev. Gen. de Droit*, 336.

[4] Christian Sahb Batista Lopes, *Mitigação dos prejuízos no direito contratual* (São Paulo, Editora Saraiva, 2013) 54.

and have been selected by criteria of relevance in the global legal scene or their potential similarity with the Brazilian context. The Civil Law family is often divided into the Germanic and French/Romanistic traditions, as the Civil Codes of Germany and France represent distinct approaches to codification and have each served as a model for subsequent codifications of Civil Law in other countries.[5] Their status as archetypes of civilian systems therefore makes it necessary to examine both of these, also taking into account that the structure and content of the Brazilian Civil Code was influenced extensively by both German and French Civil Law and scholarship.[6] At least as importantly, the Germanic tradition represents the second of the two variants distinguished above, since, as Dias points out, in Germany (as well as Italy, Greece, Switzerland and Portugal), "[c]ontributory negligence is the path taken (...) to resolve situations in which the victim does not act to avoid or reduce own losses".[7] The French tradition, on the other hand, has long represented the first variant as a result of the broader and less detailed drafting style of the Napoleonic Code compared with its German equivalent,[8] although France (as we shall see below, in section 4.2.2.1) is notably at the present moment undergoing a project of law reform which deals specifically with the duty to mitigate. The latter development clearly adds a further reason for investigating the

---

[5] Konrad Zweigert and Hein Kotz, *Introduction to Comparative Law* (Tony Weir tr, 3rd edn, OUP 1998) 1B.

[6] Jan Kleinheisterkamp, 'Development of Comparative Law in Latin America' in Mathias Reimann and Reinhard Zimmermann (eds), *The Oxford Handbook of Comparative Law* (2nd Edn, OUP 2019) 272-274. On the legal system of Brazil, see also Chapter 2 above.

[7] Daniel Pires Novais Dias, 'O duty to mitigate loss no direito civil brasileiro e o encargo de evitar o próprio dano' (2011) 12 *Revista de Direito Privado*, 89, 108 (original version: culpa da vítima é a via utilizada (...) para resolver as situações em que a vítima de um dano não adota conduta para evitar ou minorar o próprio prejuízo).

[8] Zweigert and Kotz (n 5) 1B7; also H. Patrick Glenn, *Legal Traditions of the World: Sustainable diversity in law* (5th edn, Oxford University Press 2014) 148; Mathias Siems, *Comparative Law* (2nd edn, Cambridge University Press 2018) 51; Thomas M. Leonard, *Encyclopedia of the Developing World* (Routledge 2013) 951.

legal position in France in a thesis exploring the need for and possibility of amending the Civil Code of Brazil. The same is true in Argentina. It is examined in this chapter not only due to its proximity, as a South American jurisdiction, to the Brazilian reality and culture, but also because it has recently enacted a new Civil Code, which brought the duty to mitigate expressly to the scene. The analysis of such jurisdictions (from historical, ruling and practical perspectives) and of how courts have applied the principles and provisions will provide lessons as to how the mitigation doctrine could be properly regulated in Brazil.

Finally, the treatment of mitigation in several transnational initiatives which try to harmonize principles and rules for different countries, by presenting instruments with uniform provisions that are intended to be widely accepted and applicable – will be analyzed. Representing recent efforts to learn from both Common Law and Civil Law systems, and to formulate principles in a code-like instrument, these might also represent useful material for the purpose of formulating a proposal for the most adequate approach for the duty to mitigate loss in Brazil.

4.2 Application of the duty to mitigate loss in European Civil Law jurisdictions

4.2.1 Germany

The German Civil Code (*Bürgerliches Gesetzbuch* – BGB) "was first drafted in 1881, ratified in 1896, and formally took effect on January 1, 1900".[9] As much as the then-existing codes of Prussia, France and Austria, which "intended to satisfy the desire for territorial legal unity",[10] the German Code served as the one instrument to rule the different territories

---

[9] Nicole Sotelo, 'German Civil Code (Bürgerliches Gesetzbuch, BGB) (1900)' available at <http://hist259.web.unc.edu/german-civil-code-burgerliches-gesetzbuch-bgb-1900/> accessed on 7 August 2022.

[10] Reinhard Zimmermann, *The New German Law of Obligations: Historical and Comparative Perspectives* (Oxford University Press 2005) 6.

Germany had been divided into up to that time. It is divided into five parts, each regulating a different aspect of the law: the general part, the law of obligations, property law, family law and inheritance. [11] Like other codes from the Civil Law traditions, one of the main characteristics of the BGB is abstraction instead of case-specific law, and a precise and coherent legal terminology. The style in which it is written is however very different from the older French Civil Code: it is much more 'technical', detailed and prescriptive in approach.[12] It also has a very deliberate architecture: general principles and common elements are consolidated and put in front.[13] The BGB underwent significant modernization in 2002, including reform of the remedies for breach of contract.[14]

The BGB sets the full recovery principle as the standard rule, as stated in article 249 (1): "A person who is liable in damages must restore the position that would exist if the circum-stance obliging him to pay damages had not occurred."[15] This principle is also referred to as the principle of natural restitution (*Naturalrestitution*), and means that the innocent party must be placed in the same situation as if the breach had not occurred. The innocent party may therefore claim full compensation of all losses irrespective of the degree of fault of the breaching party. Because this provision appears in the General Part of the BGB, it applies to both contracts and torts.

---

[11] Each regulating one moment of life: the general part addresses birth and rights which are inherent to one's existence; obligations addresses the relation to others; property law addresses the acquisition, possession and transfer of property; family addresses the relation among relatives; and inheritance addresses the passing away.

[12] Zweigert and Kotz (n 5) 1BII22. On differences between the German and French variants of the Civil Law family, see further Siems (n 8) 74-76 and Uwe Kischel, *Comparative Law* by (Oxford University Press 2019) Chapters 6 and 7.

[13] Christian Grüneberg, in Palandt *Bürgerliches Gesetzbuch* (79th edn, CH Beck Munich 2020) Introduction para 6, 7. Also Kischel (n 12) 366.

[14] These reforms are described in Zimmermann (n 10) 36.

[15] German Civil Code <http://www.gesetze-im-internet.de/englisch_bgb/index.html> accessed 7 August 2022. Further citations in this chapter of the provisions of this Code are taken from this source.

There has been much discussion on this principle, including during the 66th German Jurists Forum,[16] in which participants resolved that incentives should be introduced into the law for an injured party to act economically and to avoid excessive losses for recovery, following commentators who argue that losses should be allocated so as to minimize the economic costs of the damage by providing incentives for the innocent party to use his or her own resources in order to reduce losses.[17] It has also been argued that the absence of a duty to mitigate loss creates an incentive for the innocent party to take unnecessary and unusually high risks, since the breaching party would have to pay the full amount of losses regardless.[18] However, these suggestions and concerns were not taken up by the legislator and have not been enacted into law so far, although there are certain exemptions to this full recovery principle accepted by the courts,[19] for example in cases of breach of their duty of care by employees, where liability to third parties is in some circumstances distributed proportionately between the employer and the employee.[20] However, these exceptions have nothing to do with mitigation.

Although in German Law, as in many other Civil Law jurisdictions, there is no specific reference to the duty to mitigate loss, courts are given the discretion to evaluate the circumstances and to limit compensation on the basis of existing rules: according to Lopes, "German law grants the judge greater discretion to determine indemnification than the law in Common Law countries" (original version: o direito alemão concede

---

[16] Resolutions of the 66 German Jurists Forum (*Beschlüsse des 66. Deutschen Juristentages*), which took place in 2006, available at <https://www.djt.de/fileadmin/downloads/66/66_DJT_Beschluesse.pdf> accessed 7 August 2022.

[17] Christian Huber, *Fragen der Schadensberechnung* (Springer Vienna 1993); Thüsing, *Die wertende Schadensberechnung* (CH Beck Munich 2001) 39.

[18] Jens Ekkenga and Thilo Kuntz, in Soergel et al (eds) *Bürgerliches Gesetzbuch* Vol 3/2 Schuldrecht 1/2 (14th edn, Kohlhammer Stuttgart 2014) § 254 para 3.

[19] Walter Weidenkaff, Palandt *Bürgerliches Gesetzbuch* (79th edn, CH Beck Munich 2020) § 611 para 157.

[20] BAG NZA 2007, 1230, 1233.

maior liberdade ao juiz para fixar a indenização que os direitos dos países de Common Law).[21] More precisely, although "there is no duty to mitigate per se (...) a similar result is achieved through the regime on contributory negligence",[22] which is regulated in Article 254 of the BGB:

"Article 254:

(1) Where fault on the part of the injured person contributes to the occurrence of the damage, liability in damages as well as the extent of compensation to be paid depend on the circumstances, in particular to what extent the damage is caused mainly by one or the other party.

(2) This also applies if the fault of the injured person is limited to failing to draw the attention of the obligor to the danger of unusually extensive damage, where the obligor neither was nor ought to have been aware of the danger, or to failing to avert or reduce the damage. The provision of article 278 applies with the necessary modifications."[23]

This article is interpreted to enable courts to apply the same treatment to contributory negligence (multiple causes for the losses) and the failure to mitigate (negligence to take steps to reduce or prevent further losses after breach or failure from the other party). In its first part, the rule (1)

[21] Lopes (n 4) 56.
[22] Clare Connellan, Elizabeth Oger-Gross and Angélica André, 'Compensatory Damages Principles in Civil and Common Law Jurisdictions: Requirements, Underlying Principles and Limits' p. 16 available at < https://www.whitecase.com/sites/whitecase/files/files/download/publications/article-compensatory-damages-principle-in-civil-and-common-law-jurisdictions.pdf> accessed 7 August 2022.
[23] German Civil Code (n 15).

deals with the negative aspect of mitigation doctrine (avoidable losses). It states that the court has discretion to determine to what extent losses are indemnifiable, according to the participation of each party in the losses. The second part (2) deals with both (i) unusual losses which the breaching party was not aware of due to failure of the innocent party to warn of such losses;[24] and with (ii) the innocent party's failure to "avert or reduce" the damage. That is: contributory negligence (1), failure to disclose (2.i), and failure to avert or reduce damages (2.ii), all lead to the same result, which is limiting the extent of liability. And whereas the duty to draw attention to the danger of unusually extensive damage and the duty to avert damage apply to the prevention of the damage, the duty to reduce applies to preventing the aggravation of an existing damage.[25] Thus, for all practical purposes the final clause (2.ii) of Article 254(2) is, at least when considered purely on the basis of its wording, functionally equivalent to the Common Law duty to mitigate described above in Chapter 3.[26] Indeed, in German legal terminology, Article 254 (2) is referred to as establishing a *Schadensminderungspflicht,* which translates literally as "duty to mitigate damage".[27]

The fact that mitigation is not treated as an independent principle, as in Common Law systems, but rather as an aspect of contributory fault on the part of the victim, appears to make the German duty less demanding of the victim than its Common Law counterpart. Thus, whereas English law requires a victim of personal injury who has refused an operation contrary to medical advice to show that he acted reasonably in doing so,[28]

---

[24] This is a functional equivalent of the Common Law doctrine of remoteness of loss, especially as reflected in *Hadley v Baxendale* (1854) 9 Ex 341.

[25] Ekkenga and Kuntz (n 18) § 254 para 84.

[26] Guenter H. Treitel and Gyula Eörsi, 'III. Substitutionary relief in Money', in *International Encyclopedia of International Law* Volume VII: Contracts in General Chapter 16 (Brill, 1976) paras 100, 102 and 106.

[27] Basil Markesinis, Hannes Unberath and Angus Johnston, *The German Law Of Contract: A Comparative Treatise* (Oxford, Hart Publishing, 2006).

[28] *Selvanayagam v University of the West Indies* [1983] 1 WLR 585 (PC).

German law does not require such a victim to accept being operated on unless that measure is 'simple and safe, not connected with exceptional pain, and offers the certain prospect of cure or substantial improvement'.[29] The outcome will often be the same in the two systems, but making the duty to mitigate turn on a judgment about whether the claimant' was at fault does seem to set a somewhat higher threshold for action by the victim than the Common Law does.

The duty to mitigate, as stated in article 254 of the BGB is conceptualised not as an actual legally enforceable duty owed to the other party (a *Pflicht*), but rather as a legal obligation imposed in one's own interest (an *Obliegenheit*)[30] – as is acknowledged by courts:

> "The provision of article 254 of the BGB presupposes that the injured party was at fault when the damage occurred (paragraph 1) or that he culpably failed to avert or reduce the damage (paragraph 2 sentence 1 last half sentence), This fault does not mean the blameworthy violation of an existing performance obligation owed to another, but a fault in one's own affairs. It is a matter of fault against oneself, the violation of an obligation existing in one's own interest (cf. BGHZ 179, 55 = NJW 2009, 582 Rn. 31 mwN)' A breach of an obligation of this kind can only be found if, in violation of good faith, the injured party fails to take reasonable measures that a prudent business-minded person would take to prevent or reduce damage

---

[29] BGH 13 May 1953, BGHZ 10, 18. The case is translated in W van Gerven et al, *Ius Commune Casebooks for the Common Law of Europe: Cases, Materials and Text on National, Supranational and International Tort Law* (Oxford, Hart Publishing, 2000) 795.

[30] Hartmut Oetker, in *Münchener Kommentar zum Bürgerlichen Gesetzbuch* Vol 2 Schuldrecht – Allgemeiner Teil (8th edn, Krüger (ed) CH Beck München 2019) § 254 para 3.

to himself (see BGH, NJW 2015, 1685; NJW 2013, 3442; NJW 2013, 684; NJW 2006, 995)."

(original version: „Die Vorschrift des § 254 BGB setzt voraus, dass bei der Entstehung des Schadens ein Verschulden des Geschädigten mitgewirkt hat (Abs. 1), oder er es schuldhaft unterlassen hat, den Schaden abzuwenden oder zu mindern (Abs. 2 S. 1 letzter Halbsatz). Dieses Verschulden bedeutet nicht die vorwerfbare Verletzung einer gegenüber einem aderen bestehenden Leistungspflicht, sondern ein Verschulden in eigener Angelegenheit. Es handelt sich um ein Verschulden gegen sich selbst, um die Verletzung einer im eigenen Interesse bestehenden Obliegenheit (vgl. BGHZ 179, 55 = NJW 2009, 582 Rn. 31 mwN). Von der Verletzung einer Obliegenheit kann nur ausgegangen werden, wenn der Geschädigte unter Verstoß gegen Treu und Glauben diejenigen zumutbaren Maßnahmen unterlässt, die ein vernünftiger, wirtschaftlich denkender Mensch nach Lage der Dinge ergreifen würde, um Schaden von sich abzuwenden oder zu mindern (vgl. BGH, NJW 2015, 1685; NJW 2013, 3442; NJW 2013, 684; NJW 2006, 995)"[31]

From a comparative point of view, this analysis is particularly interesting since, as we saw in Chapter 3, Common Law writers have felt obliged to either deny that the duty to mitigate is a duty at all or to treat it as a duty owed to the other party (for reasons of fairness or paternalistic concern) or to society as a whole (to ensure economic efficiency).[32] German law does however have its own uncertainties about the basis of this duty. In

---

[31] BGH NJW 2018, 20.
[32] As demonstrated in Section 3.3.1 above.

several decisions, the German courts have treated the duty to mitigate loss as a category of the general principle of good faith, set forth in article 242 of the BGB[33], or considered the innocent party's inaction as an improper *venire contra factum proprium* conduct.[34] Although this understanding is shared by some legal commentators,[35] others argue that these are separate principles that would hinder the innocent party from asserting the entire initial claim, while failure to mitigate would only reduce losses that could be claimed.[36]

The rule under article 254 of the BGB applies to both contract and tort law: "§ 254 BGB is applicable to all claims for damages, regardless of their legal ground, to the extent no special rules exist in a certain field. Thus, its application in cases of claims for damages in the event of breach of contract is undoubted."[37] And the standard for determining reasonable steps to mitigate is the general legal principle that a reasonable and prudent person would take measures to mitigate or avert losses at the given case and circumstances.[38] This looks almost identical to the standard applied in Common Law systems,[39] although, as pointed out above, the fact that in Germany this is conceptualised as a fault standard possibly results in a

---

[33] BGH Decision of 14 March 1961 (VI ZR 189/59) NJW 1961, 655; BGH Decision of 18 April 1997 (V ZR 28/96) NJW 1997, 2234.

[34] BGH Decision of 14 March 1961 (VI ZR 189/59) NJW 1961, 655

[35] Grüneberg (n 13) § 254 para 1.

[36] Oetker (n 30) § 254 para 4; Ekkenga and Kuntz (n 18) § 254 para 3.

[37] Tobias Wagner, 'Limitations of Damages for Breach of Contract in German and Scots Law - A Comparative Law Study in View of a Possible European Unification of Law' (2014) 10 *Hanse L. Rev.*, 73. In the same sense, Gustavo Santos Kulesza, *Princípio da mitigação de danos; evolução no direito contratual* (Curitiba, Juruá, 2015) 180: "Just as the other rules in German law which govern indemnification, § 254 of BGB is applicable to contractual and non-contractual civil responsibility" (original version: Assim como as demais disposições do direito alemão que regem a obrigação de indenizar, o § 254 do BGB aplica-se tanto à responsabilidade civil contratual como à extracontratual); Grüneberg (n 13) § 242 para 87.

[38] Grüneberg (n 13) § 254 para 36; Oetker (n 30) § 254 para 3, 4.

[39] According to *British Westinghouse Electric & Manufacturing Co Ltd v Underground Electric Railways Co of London Ltd* (1912) AC 673, it is not necessary to 'take any step

less demanding standard in practice. Three further aspects of the position in Germany are essentially identical to the position in Common Law systems as analysed in Chapter 3. Firstly, the costs of any measures taken by the innocent party in order to mitigate (extra losses) generally fall under the original claim, provided such expenses are deemed appropriate for the case at hand,[40] according to court decisions.[41] Secondly, any savings actually made as a result of mitigating steps will reduce the damages recoverable.[42] And thirdly, under the principle of *Vorteilsausgleichung*, benefits gained from ordinary measures to mitigate will also reduce the damages recoverable where the benefits have a sufficient causal connection with the harm-causing event and taking them into account is compatible with the purpose of compensation.[43]

It is important to note that mitigation plays a subsidiary role to the standard and prevailing remedy of specific performance, which may be claimed by the innocent party in all cases,[44] except for situations in

which a reasonable and prudent man would not ordinarily take in the course of his business.' See further: Section 3.3.6 of Chapter 3.

[40] Grüneberg (n 13) § 254 para 36; Oetker (n 30) § 249 para 178, 179.

[41] BGH Decision of 1 April 1993 (I ZR 70/91) NJW 1993, 2685; BGH Decision of 22 January 1959 (II ZR 321/56) NJW 1959, 933. These cases have a similar outcome to *Banco de Portugal v Waterlow & Sons Ltd* [1932] AC 452 (HL), in which claimant included the face value of genuine notes traded with the forged notes printed by the defendant, which had been put in circulation.

[42] Grüneberg (n 13) § 254 para 36. As in *Cerberus Software Ltd* v *Rowley* [2001] EWCA Civ 78, in which the dismissed employee was not entitled to the full 6-month payment in lieu of notice for the earnings on his new job, in which he began less than a month later, were accrued to the calculation of losses.

[43] Grüneberg (n 13) Preliminary Remarks regarding § 249 para 67. See *British Westinghouse Electric and Manufacturing Co Ltd v Underground Electric Railways Co of London Ltd* (n 39) and *Globalia Business Travel S.A.U. (formerly TravelPlan S.A.U.) of Spain v Fulton Shipping Inc of Panama, the New Flamenco* [2017] UKSC 43, both detailed in section 3.3.6 of Chapter 3 as examples of how the presence and absence, respectively, of causal link between the gain from an action to mitigate and the breach constitute a condition for the accrual of such gains.

[44] Grüneberg (n 13) § 281 para 49; BGH Decision of 20 January 2006 (V ZR 124/05) NJW 2006, 1198; BGH Decision of 9 November 2017 (IX ZR 305/16)

which performance is impossible or not proportional to its consideration. Zimmermann explains that: "This rule has a very long tradition; it ultimately derives from the Roman principle of *impossibilium nulla est obligatio* and corresponds to the basic principle of moral philosophy, that 'ought implies can.'"[45] This is what Article 275 lays down:

"Article 275
Exclusion of the duty of performance

(1) A claim for performance is excluded to the extent that performance is impossible for the obligor or for any other person.

(2) The obligor may refuse performance to the extent that performance requires expense and effort which, taking into account the subject matter of the obligation and the requirements of good faith, is grossly disproportionate to the interest in performance. In determining what efforts may reasonably be required of the obligor, it must also be taken into account whether he is responsible for the obstacle to performance.

(3) In addition, the obligor may refuse performance if he is to render the performance in person and, when the obstacle to the performance of the obligor is weighed against the obligee's interest in performance, performance cannot be reasonably required of the obligor.

NJW 2018, 786
[45] Reinhard Zimmerman, 'Breach of Contract and Remedies under the New German Law of Obligations' Volume 48 of *Saggi, conferenze e seminari, Centro di Studi e Ricerche di Diritto Comparato e Straniero Roma* (May 2002) < https://www.cisg.law.pace.edu/cisg/biblio/zimmerman.html> accessed 7 August 2022.

(4) The rights of the obligee are governed by articles 280, 283 to 285, 311a and 326."[46]

In all cases to which Article 275 does not apply, performance will be the standard remedy, whilst a claim for damages (to which the mitigation principles apply) will be the residual remedy – as stated in Article 281:

"Article 281
Damages in lieu of performance for nonperformance or failure to render performance as owed

(1) To the extent that the obligor does not render performance when it is due or does not render performance as owed, the obligee may, subject to the requirements of section 280 (1), demand damages in lieu of performance, if he has without result set a reasonable period for the obligor for performance or cure. If the obligor has performed only in part, the obligee may demand damages in lieu of complete performance only if he has no interest in the part performance. If the obligor has not rendered performance as owed, the obligee may not demand damages in lieu of performance if the breach of duty is immaterial.

(2) Setting a period for performance may be dispensed with if the obligor seriously and definitively refuses performance or if there are special circumstances which, after the interests of both parties are weighed, justify the immediate assertion of a claim for damages.

---

[46] German Civil Code (n 15).

(3) If the nature of the breach of duty is such that setting a period of time is out of the question, a warning notice is given instead.

(4) The claim for performance is excluded as soon as the obligee has demanded damages in lieu of performance.

(5) If the obligee demands damages in lieu of complete performance, the obligor is entitled to claim the return of his performance under articles 346 to 348." [47]

This primacy of the remedy of specific performance over damages contrasts with the Common Law position, where damages is the primary remedy, and it potentially has implications for the effectiveness of the German mitigation duty. Because Article 254 only applies to liability in damages and not to specific performance, the primacy of specific performance means that the duty to mitigate has a smaller field of application and affects fewer claims in Germany than in Common Law systems. Nevertheless, the possibility in Article 275 (2) of excluding specific performance in some circumstances seems to be broad enough to enable a court to exclude specific performance and award damages instead if awarding specific performance in a particular case would have the effect of enabling the obligee (the victim of the breach) to escape the duty to mitigate.

As we saw in Chapter 3, Common Law systems can require that the victim of the breach takes steps to obtain a substitute performance or sale as a possible way to mitigate loss. [48] German courts have decided that the innocent party is not required to seek alternatives, but only needs to do

---

[47] German Civil Code (n 15).
[48] As demonstrated in Section 3.2.2 above.

what is reasonable and due in the individual case at hand.[49] As pointed out above, this difference in the threshold for action by the victim seems to flow from the conceptualisation of the German duty to mitigate as an aspect of contributory fault on the part of the victim. However, German Law contains specific provisions regarding the auctioning (or in some cases, private sale) of moveable things which are due for delivery where the creditor (obligee) in breach of contract fails to take delivery of the thing. Failure of the victim of the breach (in this case the debtor or obligor) to perform such an auction – in applicable cases – is equivalent to a failure to reduce damages, which will then limit his or her recovery. This can be seen in the following provisions:

> "Article 383
> Auction of things not capable of deposit
>
> (1) If the movable thing owed is not suitable for deposit, the obligor may in case of default by the obligee have it auctioned at the place of performance and deposit the proceeds. The same applies in the cases set out in article 372 sentence 2, if spoilage of the thing is to be feared or safekeeping is associated with disproportionate costs.
>
> (2) If reasonable success is not expected from an auction at the place of performance, the thing is to be auctioned at another suitable place.
>
> (3) The auction must be performed publicly by a bailiff appointed for the place of auction or other official

---

[49] BGH Decision of 26 May 1988 (III ZR 42/87) NJW 1989, 290. That German law demands less of the innocent party in this respect is also noted by Treitel (n 2) par 102.

authorised to conduct auctions or a publicly employed auctioneer (public auction). The time and place of the auction, with a general description of the thing, are to be publicly announced.

(4) The provisions of subsections (1) to (3) do not apply to registered ships and ships under construction.

Article 384
Warning of auction

(1) The auction is permitted only after the obligee has been warned about it; the warning may be omitted if the thing is vulnerable to spoilage and postponement of the auction entails danger.

(2) The obligor must notify the obligee of the auction without undue delay; in the event of his failure to do so, he is liable in damages.

(3) The warning and the notice may be omitted if they are impracticable.

Article 385
Sale by private agreement

If the thing has a stock exchange or market price, the obligor may effect the sale privately at the current price through a commercial broker officially authorised to effect such sales or through a person authorised to sell by public auction."[50]

---

[50] German Civil Code (n 15).

More broadly, Article 326 (2) has implications for mitigation in cases of all reciprocal contracts where the creditor (obligee) has, in breach of contract, failed to accept performance but the debtor (obligor) still wishes to perform and is not for other reasons prohibited from doing so – the scenario dealt with in the English case of *White & Carter (Councils) Ltd. V McGregor.*[51] The relevant portion of Article 362 (2) provides as follows (emphasis added):

> (2) If the obligee is solely or very predominantly responsible for the circumstance due to which the obligor does not, under article 275 (1) to (3), have to effect cure, or if this circumstance for which the obligor is not responsible occurs at a time *when the obligee is in default of acceptance, the obligor retains the entitlement to consideration. However, he must allow to be credited against him what he saves due to release from performance or acquires or wilfully fails to acquire from other use of his labour.*

Thus the victim of the breach is, as in English case of *White & Carter (Councils) Ltd. V McGregor,*[52] discussed in Chapter 3,[53] entitled to insist on remuneration for the services owed. However, in contrast with the position under that case, savings made as a result of not having to perform the services, or which would have been made if the victim of the breach had not "willfully" failed to use his services elsewhere, are deducted from the remuneration payable. This is functionally equivalent to a duty to mitigate,[54] and in practical terms applies the same approach as the courts

---

[51] *White & Carter (Councils) Ltd. v McGregor* [1962] A.C. 413.

[52] *White & Carter (Councils) Ltd. v McGregor* (n 51).

[53] Details of the case in section 3.2 above.

[54] Treitel (n 2) par 102 notes this similarity in respect of Section 324 of the pre-2002 German Civil Code, which contained essentially the same provision as the current section 326.

in the United States, which was also discussed above in Chapter 3.[55] Treitel prefers this to English law's refusal to apply the mitigation principle to such cases.[56]

A special application of the principle laid down in Article 326(2) is found in Article 615, which deals with the wrongful dismissal of employees (and providers of equivalent services):

> "Article 615
> Remuneration in the case of default in acceptance and business risk
>
> If the person entitled to services is in default in accepting the services, then the party owing the services may demand the agreed remuneration for the services not rendered as the result of the default without being obliged to provide cure. However, he must allow to be credited against him what he saves as a result of not performing the services or acquires or willfully fails to acquire through use of his employment elsewhere. Sentences 1 and 2 apply with the necessary modifications in cases in which the employer bears the risk of loss of working hours."[57]

This is, for all practical purposes, the same as in English law, where the duty to mitigate obliges an employee to take reasonable steps to find alternative employment.[58]

Moreover, Articles 326 (2) and 615 give effect to what in Germany is referred to as the principle of *Vorteilsausgleichung*. As can be seen from the wording of these provisions quoted above, savings and gains which actually

---

[55] Details of the case in section 3.2 above.

[56] Treitel (n 2) par 103.

[57] German Civil Code (n 15).

[58] *Cerberus Software Ltd* v *Rowley* (n 42). This similarity is noted by Treitel (n 2) par 102.

were made in consequence of the fact that the victim was freed from his obligation to perform are deducted from the sum recoverable. As pointed out above in the discussion of Article 254, this German principle covers much the same ground as the Common Law principle that savings and gains actually made by the innocent party in the course of mitigating their loss must be deducted from the damages recoverable.[59]

Finally, as to the burden of proof, "the prevailing rule is that the defendant must prove that the amount which needs to be paid to the claimant to indemnify his loss is reduced by losses avoided as well as that losses that could have been avoided" (original version: prevalece a regra de que o devedor inadimplente deve provar que o montante indenizatório do credor deve ser minorado de acordo com as perdas evidads ou com os prejuízos que poderiam ter sido evitados).[60] However, even though the burden of proof generally lies with the defendant (breaching party),[61] the innocent party might be required to demonstrate the measures he or she has taken in order to avert or mitigate the losses.[62]

4.2.2 France

The French Civil Code, based on early drafts of Jean-Jacques Régis de Cambacérès (from 1793, 1794 and 1799), was promulgated in 1804, and renamed the Napoleonic Code (between 1807-1817 and 1852-1871) to honour Napoleon, who had brought the project to completion, but is since 1870 simply referred to as the "Code Civil". Its content was classified into three categories: persons, property (and its acquisition) and civil procedure (later moved into a separate code). Besides standardizing the court system and providing a comprehensive enactment of all valid principles and rules for the French civil law, "It formed the basis of the law systems across most

---

[59] See also Treitel (n 2) par 105.

[60] Kulesza (n 18) 187.

[61] BGH Decision of 28 February 1996 (XII ZR 186/94) NJW-RR 1996, 1079.

[62] Grüneberg (n 13) § 254 para 72; BGH Decision of 24 January 2018 (XII ZR 120/16) NJW-RR 2018, 714.

of continental Europe and has had a lasting impact on Civil Law codes in other regions of the world, including the Middle East where it has been combined with the Islamic law."[63] When compared to the BGB, it style of drafting appears terse and non-technical, leaving more 'gaps' to be supplied by interpretation and judicial development, and its structure and content is closer to Roman law.[64]

According to Treitel, "the whole topic of mitigation is not well developed in French law."[65] It has been observed that, when dealing with losses, "French law focuses exclusively on the interest of the victim, to the detriment of those of the party in breach of duty."[66] Its Code applies the full recovery principle, as established in Article 1240:[67]

> "Any act whatever of man, which causes damage to another, obliges the one by whose fault it occurred to compensate it"
>
> (original version: "Tout fait quelconque de l'homme, qui cause à autrui un dommage, oblige celui par la faute duquel il est arrivé à le réparer.")[68]

---

[63] The Napoleonic Code, available at <https://courses.lumenlearning.com/suny-hccc-worldhistory2/chapter/the-napoleonic-code/> accessed on 7 August 2022. The previous sentences also draw on "Napoleonic Code", Encyclopaedia Britannica, available at https://www.britannica.com/topic/Napoleonic-Code.

[64] See the literature cited in notes 8 and 12 above, and John Bell, 'Introduction: The Spirit of French Law' in John Bell, Sophie Boyron and Simon Whittaker, *Principles of French Law* Second Edition (Oxford, Oxford University Press) 8.

[65] Treitel (n 2) par 71.

[66] Solene Le Pautremat, 'Mitigation of Damage: a French perspective' (2006) 55 International Comparative Law Quarterly. London, 205.

[67] French Civil Code, available at <https://www.legifrance.gouv.fr/affichCode.do?cidTexte=LEGITEXT000006070721&dateTexte=20190304> accessed 7 August 2022. Unless otherwise indicated, the numbering and content of the articles of the Code set out in this thesis are as they have been since the 2016 reforms which are described below in 4.2.2.1.

[68] French Civil Code (n 67).

Contributory negligence, provided for in Article 1241, might be argued to limit full recovery, [69] but strictly in cases in which the role of the innocent party also represents the direct cause of the losses (not of only their aggravation – as in mitigation cases). Moreover, as Treitel points out, contributory negligence and mitigation are distinct concepts: "It can be said that in the contributory negligence situation the plaintiff is partly responsible for bringing about the event which causes the loss, while in the mitigation situation the plaintiff can only be charged with failing to take positive steps to avoid the harmful effects of an event brought about solely by the defendant's default."[70] Legal commentator Larroumet argues causation would play a similar role to mitigation,[71] but – again – this rule is limited to analyzing cause, not to regulating how and when one is expected to act in order to mitigate (that is, its focus is on the result, not on the prevention). Although French legal writers have long questioned the recoverability of avoidable losses,[72] the mitigation doctrine has not been accepted in the French legal framework – neither in contracts, nor torts. On the contrary: the duty to mitigate has been expressly rejected by French courts, preventing its development in France, with no more than "occasional appearances in discrete areas of French Law."[73]

In recent cases, decided in 2003, the Court of Cassation reaffirmed twice the non-existence of a binding rule in the French legal framework that demands from the aggrieved party to take actions to mitigate losses

---

[69] Art. 1241. Everyone is responsible for the damage they have caused not only by their act, but also by their negligence or carelessness (original version: Chacun est responsable du dommage qu'il a causé non seulement par son fait, mais encore par sa négligence ou par son imprudence).

[70] Treitel (n 2) par 71.

[71] Christian Larroumet, 'Obligation de modérer le dommage et arbitrage du point de vue du droit français' (2008) 290 *Gaz. Pal.*, 5.

[72] See Jean Domat, *Le droit civil dans l'ordre naturel* (t. 1, Paris: Rollin el Fils 1745) and Robert Joseph Pothieu, *Traité des obligations, selon les regles, tant du for de la conscience, que du for extérieur* (t. 3, Paris: Debure pere, 1761).

[73] Solène Rowan, *Remedies for Breach of Contract: A Comparative Analysis of the Protection of Performance* (Oxford University Press, 2012) 147.

in the interest of the breaching party. In the first case, [74] the claimant was seeking compensation for a mental disorder developed following an accident for which the defendant had been held liable. The court of appeal granted partial compensation, based on the claimant's failure to follow the advice of two doctors which could have improved her condition. The Court of Cassation, however, reversed the decision and granted full recovery, on the basis of the specific argument that the innocent party was under no duty to mitigate. In the second case, [75] the manager of a bakery sought recovery of loss of income for the period in which she could not work due to injuries suffered in a car accident for which the defendant had been held liable. The court of appeal rejected part of the claim, based on the argument that the claimant could have hired a temporary manager to run her business. However, the Court of Cassation, again, rejected any trace of the mitigation doctrine and granted full recovery. Both decisions were based on current article 1240 of the Napoleonic Code, cited above. As a result, Pautremat comments that: "The interests of the defendant have been relegated to such an extent that the relationship of victim and tortfeasor has become more imbalanced than ever."[76]

In the words of Rowan, "None of the cases laid down a refined mitigation principle comparable to the significantly more developed English equivalent. Nor was there any attempt to set a standard of conduct for the victim. The reasonableness of his actions was not considered."[77] As stated by legal commentator Ballot Lena[78] in reference to such decisions:

---

[74] Cass 2ème civ (19 juin 2003) No 931 FS-PRBI, Dibaoui c; Flamand, Bull Civ II No 203, D 2003 Jur 2396.

[75] Cass 2ème (19 juin 2003) No 930 FS-PRBI, Xhauflaire C/ Decrept, D 2003 Jur 2396.

[76] Pautremat (n 66) 205, 210.

[77] Rowan (n 73) 148.

[78] Aurélie Ballot Léna, 'Consécration d'une obligation, pour la victime, d'éviter l'aggravation de son préjudice en matière contractuelle (art. 1263)' (2016) Blog Réforme du droit des obligations – Dalloz <http://reforme-obligations.dalloz.fr/2016/08/10/consecration-dune-obligation-pour-la-victime-deviter-laggravation-de-son-prejudice-en-matiere-contractuelle-art-1263/> accessed 28 February 2020.

"This position of the jurisprudence isolates French law, as attested by comparative law studies (V. S. Reifegerste, Pour une obligation de minimiser le dommage, PUAM, 2002, n° 26 et seq, which presents, in addition to the notion of Common Law countries of 'duty to mitigate the damage', the solutions of certain countries of written law), but also the solutions of international and European law and those of European doctrine (see art. 77 of the Vienna Convention of 11 April 1980 on the International Sale of Goods, art. 7.4.8 of the Unidroit Principles, art. 9.505 of the Principles of European Contract Law and the Draft Common Frame of Reference (DCFR), both in matters relating to tort [VI, art. 6:202, 'Reduction of liability'] and contract [III, art. 3:705, 'Reduction of loss'])"

(original version: "Cette position de la jurisprudence isole le droit français, comme l'attestent les études de droit comparé (V. S. Reifegerste, Pour une obligation de minimiser le dommage, PUAM, 2002, n° 26 et s., qui présente, outre la notion des pays de Common Law de 'duty to mitigate the damage', les solutions de certains pays de droit écrit), mais également les solutions de droit international et européen et celles de la doctrine européenne (V. art. 77 de la Convention de Vienne du 11 avril 1980 sur la vente internationale de marchandises, art. 7.4.8 des Principes Unidroit, art. 9.505 des Principes du droit européen des contrats et le Draft Common Frame of Reference (DCFR), tant en matière délictuelle [VI, art. 6 :202, 'Reduction of liability'] qu'en matière contractuelle [III, art. 3:705, 'Reduction of loss '])").

The prevailing opinion – and current rule in force – in French law is that the innocent party shall not be called to act upon the other party's breach, nor shall justice succumb to the breaching party's economic interest,[79] for this is "(…) a regime which, through robust remedial devices also including specific performance and replacement, is wedded to upholding the subjective preferences of the promise."[80] Thus, as Lopes states, "there is no rule, in French law, that imposes to the creditor the onus of entering a substitute transaction" (to mitigate his or her own losses), but only the creditor's right to claim the transaction to be executed by a third party – this solution is considered a type of specific performance remedy.[81] Importantly, the Civil Code from the start provided that a creditor is not free to obtain a substitute performance from a third party, but must first obtain permission from a court to do so.[82] This requirement, which reflects the traditional preference of French law for enforcing performance of the contract by the parties, is incompatible with the duty to mitigate as it operates in Common Law systems, and has been said to explain why French law does not have a duty to mitigate.[83] As explained below, this requirement has very recently been abandoned as part of a reform process which makes French law more receptive to mitigation (see 4.2.2.1).

Nevertheless, French courts have handed down decisions in which recoverability is limited on the basis of causation, remoteness and good-faith:[84]

> "(…) the duty to mitigate loss finds its way in through the back-door in French law (…). The better legal justification appears, however, to be the requirement for a casual link

---

[79] Pautremat (n 66) 209.

[80] Rowan (n 73) 121.

[81] Lopes (n 4) 72.

[82] Art 1144 CC (original version prior to the 2016 reforms outlined below).

[83] Rowan (n 73) 98; Simon Whittaker, 'Contributory Fault and Mitigation, Rights and Reasonableness: Comparisons between English and French law' in Libus Tichý (ed) *Causation in Law* (Prague, 2007) 149 at 168.

[84] Lopes (n 4) 68-69.

to establish the damages. If the amount of damages would have been lower had the aggrieved party taken some action or, on the contrary, refrained from taking any, then the aggrieved party should not be entitled to the amount of damages that it requests. This reasoning can be easily applied in connection with the judge's full discretion to assess damages."[85]

Besides these situations, only in specific – and exceptional – situations are duties (to act) imposed on innocent parties. For example, the beneficiaries of insurance contracts are considered liable for fault or negligence when they do not take protective measures against third parties; they are required to act, in order to prevent further losses caused by third parties, and their compensation will be limited in situations in which this duty is not met:

> Art. L-172-23 of the French Code of Insurance – "The insured must help to salvage insured property and take all protective measures of his rights against third parties liable. He shall be liable to the insurer for damage caused by the non performance of said obligation, which is attributable to his fault or negligence" (original version: L'assuré doit contribuer au sauvetage des objets assurés et prendre toutes mesures conservatoires de ses droits contre les tiers responsables. Il est responsable'I envers l'assureur du dommage causé par l'inexécution de cette obligation résultant de sa faute ou de sa négligence).[86]

But this legal position – similar to Brazil, as to the absence of specific

---

[85] Connellan, Oger-Gross and André (n 22) 17-18.
[86] Insurance Code available at <https://www.legifrance.gouv.fr/content/location/1744> accessed 7 August 2022.

provisions regarding mitigation, and even stricter as to the number of situations which limit compensation based on a duty to act of the innocent party – might be subject to change, as successive law reform projects have aimed, among other changes, to include the mitigation doctrine in the Civil Code.

4.2.2.1 Reform of the French Law of Obligations

The provisions in the Civil Code on the law of obligations remained stable and unchanged since the enactment of the Code in the late 19th Century. However, from 2005 to 2017 – a period in which France has had been politically led by right, left and center parties – four different law reform projects have been presented: Catala-Viney (2005),[87] Béteille (2010),[88] Terré (2009-2013)[89] and the most recent, the 2017 Reform Bill on Civil Liability, presented by the Minister of Justice at that time, Jean-Jacques Urvoas (2017).[90] The last of these is the result of a public consultation carried out during the second trimester of 2016 and takes the former projects as its starting point. The scope of the most recent reform, as stated, is a response to the fact that "the current civil liability

---

[87] *Avant-projet de réforme du droit des obligations et de la prescription* (Proposals for Reform of the Law of Obligations and the Law of Prescription). Translation into English available at
<http://www.justice.gouv.fr/art_pix/rapportcatatla0905-anglais.pdf> accessed 7 August 2022. John Cartwright, Stefan Vogenauer and Simon Whittaker (eds), *Reforming the French Law of Obligations: Comparative reflections on the avant-projet de réforme du droit des obligations et de la prescription ('the avant-projet catala')* (Oxford, Hart Publishing, 2009) contains detailed critical assessments of these proposals as well as the translated text.

[88] Available at <http://www.textes.justice.gouv.fr/art_pix/avant_projet_regime_obligations.pdf> accessed 7 August 2022.

[89] Divided in three sources: Terré, François, *Pour une réforme du droit des contrats* (Dalloz 2009); *Pour une réforme du droit de la responsabilité civile* (Dalloz 2011); and *Pour une réforme du régime général des obligations* (Dalloz 2013).

[90] Projet de réforme de la Responsabilité civile (Reform Bill on Civil Liability (March 2017)). English translation available at <http://www.textes.justice.gouv.fr/art_pix/reform_bill_on_civil_liability_march_2017.pdf> accessed 7 August 2022.

law becomes increasingly inaccessible and hard to understand for any person, lawyer or layman, French or foreigner. As it stands, the current reform of the civil liability regime does improve accessibility of sources and predictability of the law."[91] So far, this long process has resulted in amendments to the Code in 2016, which have significantly reformed the general regime of obligations and proof of obligations, as well as the general law of contract.[92] However, importantly for the purposes of this thesis, the law of damages has not yet been reformed, but is addressed in the 2017 Reform Bill on Civil Liability which has not yet become law.[93] Although the proposals relevant to the topic of this thesis have therefore not yet resulted in legislative reforms, they do serve as academic indicators of current legal thinking in France.

Before considering the relevant provision in the 2017 Reform Bill, it is important to note that one of the changes introduced in the 2016 reform of contract law already makes French law more hospitable to a duty to mitigate, although it does not by itself introduce such a duty. This is the new article 1222, which (in most cases) removes the requirement for court authorization in the old article 1144 and so makes it easier for the victim of a breach of contract to enter into a substitute transaction with a third

---

[91] Ozan Akyurek, 'The preliminary draft of the civil liability reform in France' (Financier Worldwide, October 2016) <https://www.financierworldwide.com/the-preliminary-draft-of-the-civil-liability-reform-in-france#.XlPiYmhKiUk> accessed 7 August 2022.

[92] Ordinance n°2016-131 of February 10, 2016, which came into force on October 1, 2016. See Simon Whittaker and John Cartwright 'Introduction' in John Cartwright and Simon Whittaker (eds), *The Code Napoléon Rewritten French Contract Law after the 2016 Reforms* (Oxford, Hart Publishing, 2020) 4; Solene Rowan 'The New French Law of Contract' (2017) 66 I.C.L.Q. 805-831. An English translation, commissioned by the French Ministry of Justice, of the new provisions introduced into the Code by the 2016 reforms is available at <https://www.trans-lex.org/601101/ /french-civil-code-2016/> accessed 7 August 2022. The Ordinance was ratified by Law n° 2018-287 of April 20, 2018, which amended some of the 2016 reforms but not in a way that affects mitigation.

[93] Whittaker and Cartwright (n 92) 4: Rowan (n 92) 831.

party.[94] As pointed out above, the need under the old law to obtain court authorization for a substitute transaction was incompatible with a duty to mitigate. That incompatibility has now disappeared, opening the door to the development of such a duty in this context.

With regards to mitigation, the 2017 Reform Bill introduces a specific provision in the section of damages – as long demanded by legal commentators such as Rowan:

> "Loss mitigation has advantages and disadvantages. From the point of view of the performance interest, the main disadvantage is that it removes the deterrent value of full compensatory liability. Its main advantages are the encouragement of proactivity in the injured promisee, and that the defaulting promisor is not overburdened in circumstances where a satisfactory alternative is available to the promisee. These advantages have convinced French law reformers that mitigation can have a positive role to play."[95]

This follows the proposal in the *avant-projet Catala*[96] for the introduction of a duty to mitigate, which was welcomed because it is "similar to the position in both English law and Article 254(2) of the BGB, and furthermore responds to a concern to raise moral standards as a matter of both law and equity (not to allow a 'victim' to profit from a

---

[94] Art. 1222: "Having given notice to perform, a creditor may also himself, within a reasonable time and at a reasonable cost, have an obligation performed or, with the prior authorisation of the court, may have something which has been done in breach of an obligation destroyed. He may claim reimbursement of sums of money employed for this purpose from the debtor. He may also bring proceedings in order to require the debtor to advance a sum necessary for this performance or destruction." For the original version of Art. 1144 see note 82 above and the accompanying text.

[95] Rowan (n 73) 155.

[96] Note 88 above.

situation) as well as of economic logic".[97] It has also been argued that the introduction of the mitigation doctrine would potentially bring benefits to the whole society, as "imposing a duty to mitigate damages to a victim, especially when it comes to tort, would allow a limitation on the cost of compensation for society as whole" (original version: "imposer à la victime de limiter l'étendue de son préjudice devrait permettre, spécialement en matière délictuelle, un encadrement du coût de l'indemnisation pour l'ensemble de la société").[98]

The proposed provision is part of "Chapter IV – The effects of liability". It applies to contractual and tort cases, but excludes damages for personal injuries. The rule (in the proposed article 1263) allows the reduction of damages to the extent that the victim did not take safe and reasonable measures to avoid its aggravation:

> Except in the case of personal injuries, damages are reduced where the victim did not take safe and reasonable measures, notably having regard to his ability to pay, appropriate to avoid an increase in his own loss.

> (original version: "Sauf en cas de dommage corporel, les dommages et intérêts sont réduits lorsque la victime n'a pas pris les mesures sûres et raisonnables, notamment au regard de ses facultés contributives, propres à éviter l'aggravation de son préjudice.")

The limited applicability of the rule when compared to Common Law formulations explored in Chapter 3 as well as the German law examined above – as a result of the exclusion of claims for personal injury – may

---

[97] Pauline Rémy-Corlay "Damages, Loss and the Quantification of Damages in the *Avant-Projet de Reforme*" in Cartwright, Vogenauer and Whittaker (eds) (n 87) 316.
[98] Alain Anziani and Laurent Béteille 'Rapport d'information' (2008-2009) 558 available at <https://www.senat.fr/rap/r08-558/r08-5581.pdf> accessed 7 August 2022.

be justified by the legal context of French law, which is known to be protective of victims. The exclusion of personal injury claims from the duty to mitigate was nevertheless criticized by Rémy-Corlay when it appeared in the earlier Catala proposals. She considered that the requirement in that proposal that mitigating measures must be reliable, reasonable and proportionate provided a sufficient safeguard to victims of personal injuries.[99] Secondly, the proposed article states that the claimant is expected to avoid an aggravation of its loss which is not quite the same as imposing an obligation on them to minimise their loss. The extent of the claimant's obligation would therefore be narrower "than under Common Law, where the claimant is required to reduce its loss if reasonably possible."[100] Moreover, the wording of this rule restricts the impact of the duty to mitigate to claims for damages and does not cover claims for specific performance. A similar limitation in the Catala proposals was criticized on the ground that:

> "The profound justification of the duty to mitigate the loss consists in the will to manage resources efficiently. However, these economic considerations are not limited to assessing damages. They apply likewise to enforced performance in kind. As the system is at present, a creditor who thinks he has failed in his duty to mitigate the loss will therefore be well advised not to claim damages, but rather to apply for performance in kind. In that way he will escape the consequences of his omission, whatever its pernicious effects."[101]

---

[99] Rémy-Corlay (n 97).

[100] Pierre-Louis Merer, 'The dawn of a duty to mitigate damages in French law' available at < https://www.shipownersclub.com/pierre-loius-merer-the-dawn-of-a-duty-to-mitigate-damages-in-french-law/> accessed 7 August 2022.

[101] Yves-Marie Laithier, "The Enforcement of Contractual Obligations: A French Perspective" in in Cartwright, Vogenauer and Whittaker (eds) (n 87) at 136 (internal references omitted).

Here it is important to consider that, under the reformed French law, specific performance is (in contrast with the position in Common Law systems) the primary remedy for breach and/or available at the option of the victim of the breach. As to this matter, Laithier states that "French law has long recognized the right of the creditor to obtain an order for performance in kind against the debtor on the sole condition that this is possible".[102] And the current version of article 1222 of the French Civil Code clearly treats the specific performance as an immediately available remedy, at the choice of the creditor (except for situations in which it is impossible or disproportionally costs to the debtor).[103] This confirms the French regime to be similar to the German (as well as many other jurisdictions, as Spain, Italy, Swiss and the Netherlands),[104] in which mitigation ends up playing a subsidiary role since the creditor may seek performance in lieu of damages, thereby avoiding triggering his or her duty to mitigate.

Another consequence of the restriction of mitigation to claims for damages is that it appears to create a position that is similar to the position in English law as established in *White & Carter (Councils) Ltd. v McGregor*,[105] although, it differs from American law as well as German law.[106] Another possible similarity with the Common Law can be found in the standard of conduct imposed by this proposal on the innocent party. The requirement to "take safe and reasonable measures" looks essentially similar to the Common Law duty to take reasonable steps to mitigate loss.[107] Interestingly, this seems to place the French proposal

---

[102] Yves-Marie Laithier, "Exécution Forcée en Nature" in Cartwright, Vogenauer and Whittaker (eds) (n 87) 276.

[103] Art. 1222: A creditor of an obligation may, having given notice to perform, seek performance in kind unless performance is impossible or if there is a manifest disproportion between its cost to the debtor and its interest for the creditor.

[104] Laithier (n 102) 276-277.

[105] As debated in Section 3.3.5 of Chapter 3. Note however that even after the 2016 reforms French law does not contain a doctrine of anticipatory breach: Rowan (n 92) 829-830.

[106] See the discussion in Secion 4.2.1 above.

[107] As debated in Section 3.3.5 of Chapter 3.

closer to the Common Law position than to the German approach with its focus on contributory fault and (as we saw in the previous section) a less demanding threshold for action by the innocent party. Although one French commentator praised the earlier Catala proposals for being closer to the German than to the Common Law approach in this regard,[108] the wording adopted by the 2017 Reform Bill is different from the Catala proposal,[109] and it is significant that the Reform Bill proposal does not follow the German example of referring to fault on the part of the innocent party. However, it is too early to express a firm view on this since "safe and reasonable measures" is such a broad concept that its concrete meaning will ultimately depend on how the French courts interpret this phrase. A final feature that is noteworthy from a comparative point of view is that this French proposal does not expressly impose a *duty* to mitigate, but merely states that damages will be reduced if mitigating measures are not taken. In this respect it differs from the prevailing formulations in the Germanic and Common Law systems.

This reform – if and when ever enacted – would allow France to harmonize its law to neighboring common and Civil Law countries and to the United Nations Convention on Contracts for the International Sale of Goods (1980) – to which France is a signatory and that includes specific mitigation provisions (to be analyzed later in this Chapter in section 4.4). And it would certainly represent a turning point from where the mitigation doctrine would develop to fit the country's legal scenario and cultural context when regulating further issues related to the duty to mitigate (such

---

[108] Remy-Corlay (n 97) who considers that the German requirement that it must be shown that the victim is at fault in not seeking to mitigate his loss "corresponds better to the general spirit of French law, which favours the compensation of victims".
[109] The Catala proposal was as follows: "Art. 1373: Where the victim had the possibility of taking reliable, reasonable and proportionate measures to reduce the extent of his loss or to avoid its getting worse, the court shall take account of his failure to do so by reducing his compensation, except where the measures to be taken were of a kind to have compromised his physical integrity." Translation taken from Cartwright, Vogenauer and Whittaker (eds) (n 87) 859.

as clarification of what would constitute reasonable steps and the effects of successful and unsuccessful measures to mitigate).

4.3 Argentina

Brazil is the largest country in South America, and the only one on the continent colonized by the Portuguese (from whom the mother language was inherited). In all other countries, Spanish colonization resulted in a common Spanish mother language. But apart from this historical difference, Brazil has much in common with Argentina, one of its neighbors and the second largest country – in territory and economy (only behind Brazil) – in South America.[110] The two countries also have commercial trade agreements, share membership of the Common Market of the South (MERCOSUR) and compete in all sports. Despite their different colonial origins, they also share some post-independence legal history: the authors of Argentina's first Civil Code drew extensively on Teixeira de Freitas's draft Civil Code for Brazil (1856-1865),[111] which, though never enacted, also provided the basis of Brazil's own first Civil Code of 1916.[112] Associated with this, these first post-independence Civil Codes of the two countries reflected significant influence from both the German and French civilian traditions as a result of extensive engagement by the drafters of these Codes with the leading contemporary scholarship from both countries, resulting in a German-inspired structure, although in both cases it was the French Civil Code rather than its German counterpart that helped shape the text of the provisions adopted.[113] There were, of course, also important differences between these codifications, in content as well

---

[110] Available at < https://www.nationmaster.com/country-info/groups/Latin-America-and-Caribbean> accessed on 7 August 2022.
[111] M. C. Mirow, *Latin American Law: A History of Private Law and Institutions in Spanish America* (University of Texas Press 2004) 139.
[112] Kleinheisterkamp (n 6) 272-273. On the legal system of Brazil, see also Chapter 2 above.
[113] Kleinheisterkamp (n 6) 272-274.

as structure and style,[114] but these commonalities, which persisted through the enactment of new Codes in both countries, developed new dimensions as a result of the influence of English and especially American commercial law and practices across the whole continent.[115] Thus, Lopez-Medina has observed that:

> "despite evident linguistic differences Brazilians and Hispanic American lawyers do share a rather common map of legal influences, institutions, and ideologies. Their conversations, at a certain abstract level, show a common ground in history, in legal theory, in bibliographical references, and in institutional and political values and commitments."[116]

This provides a strong reason for paying particular regard to the treatment of mitigation of loss in Argentinian law, which represents the largest and most developed of the Hispanic American legal systems.

Bordering the south of Brazil, Argentina was culturally influenced by its Spanish colonizers and later English invaders, before achieving its independence in 1874. As a Civil Law country, its first Civil Code was written by Dalmacio Vélez Sársfield, and reflected great influence

---

[114] Not least because "the Brazilian Code was predominantly an indigenous product: more than a third of its provisions are based on the pre-existing law, and another third are new provisions of original Brazilian pedigree", while the Argentinian Code had eclectic sources, including French, Belgian and German authors, the codes of several other Latin American Countries, as well as the Russian Civil Code and the Roman *Corpus Iuris Civilis*. See Kleinheisterkamp (n 6) at 273 and 270. Moreover, the Brazilian Code followed the German example of including a General Part at the beginning of the Code, but the Argentian Code did not do so: ibid.

[115] Kleinheisterkamp (n 6) at 274-280.

[116] Diego López-Medina, 'The Latin American and Caribbean legal traditions: Repositioning Latin America and the Caribbean on the contemporary maps of comparative law' in M Bussani and U Mattei (eds), *The Cambridge Companion to Comparative Law* (Cambridge, Cambridge University Press, 2012) 344 at 351.

of Roman Law (as in the case of property transmitted by tradition) and the Napoleonic Code (145 articles were copied from it).[117] It was in force between 1871 and 2015, until – on August 1st, 2015 – it was replaced by the new *Código Civil y Comercial de la Nación*.[118] To develop the new Code "a broadly participative method was used, which had never been done before. Relevant precedents of comparative law, the scholarship of prestigious national and foreign legal commentators, the opinion of legal congresses and the criteria applied by jurisprudence were employed".[119] The Code is structured in six books: general part, family law, property law, inheritance law and personal and property common sections.

4.3.1 Mitigation of Loss in Argentina

In respect of damages, "Full recovery is one of the pillars upon which our liability system rests, and this supposes reasonable equivalence between the loss and the recovery".[120] This is reflected in its article 1740 of the 2015 Civil and Commercial Code:

---

[117] For detail, see Kleinheisterkamp (n 6) at 268-270 and Mirow (n 111). The Civil Code of Argentina available at <https://www.oas.org/dil/esp/Codigo_Civil_de_la_Republica_Argentina.pdf> accessed 7 August 2022.

[118] Civil and Commercial Code of the Argentinian Nation available at <http://servicios.infoleg.gob.ar/infolegInternet/anexos/235000-239999/235975/norma.htm> accessed 7 August 2022.

[119] Fundamentos del Anteproyecto de Código Civil y Comercial de la Nación available at < http://www.nuevocodigocivil.com/wp-content/uploads/2015/02/5-Fundamentos-del-Proyecto.pdf> accessed 7 August 2022 (original version: "se utilizó un método ampliamente participativo, como nunca antes se había hecho. Se há tenido a la vista los antecedentes más significativos del derecho comparado, la doctrina de los autores nacionales y extranjeros com mayor presitigio académico, la opiniós de los congresos de juristas, y los critérios de la jurisprduencia")

[120] Carlos A. Calvo Costa, *Código Civil y Comercial de la Nación concordado, comentado y comparado com los códigos civill de Veléz Sarsfield y de Comercio* (1ª Ed., 2ª reimpresión, Ciudad de Buenos Aires, LaLey, 2015) 725 (original version: "La reparación plena o integral es uno de los pilares fundamentals sobre los que se erige nuestro sistema de responsabilidad por daños, y supone la necesidad de una razonable equivalencia jurídica entre el daño y su reparación")

Art. 1740. Full recovery.

Recovery must be full. The victim shall be placed in the position he or she was in before the harmful fact, through either payment money or specific performance. The victim may choose specific performance, unless it is not possible or excessively expensive or abusive, in which case monetary compensation will be paid (...)"

(original version: "Reparación plena.

La reparación del daño debe ser plena. Consiste en la restitución de la situación del damnificado al estado anterior al hecho dañoso, sea por el pago en dinero o en especie. La víctima puede optar por el reintegro específico, excepto que sea parcial o totalmente imposible, excesivamente oneroso o abusivo, en cuyo caso se debe fijar en dinero (...)).

Legal commentator Mostajo observes that the interpretation of the current Argentinian Civil Code is that "the legislator has unequivocally expressed the functions of the law of damages, which are, exclusively, the functions to prevent and to repair" (original version: "el legislador se ha pronunciado inequívocamente acerca de las funciones del derecho de daños en general y ha establecido que ellas son, exclusivamente, la función de prevención y la función de reparación"). [121] Thus, the rule in Argentinian law, according to Ormaechea, is that "in case of breach by one of the parties, the other obtains a right to require specific performance of the

---

[121] Daniel Ugarte Mostajo, 'La mitigación de daños en la responsabilidad por incumplimiento contractual: breve análisis comparado en el derecho civil de Argentina y Perú' (2018) avaliable at < http://www.scielo.org.pe/pdf/derecho/n80/a04n80.pdf> accessed 7 August 2022.

contractual obligation and the option of seeking indemnification for losses and damages".[122]

For cases in which the remedy sought is damages, art. 1710 (which appears in the section on Personal Rights, Other Type of Obligations, Civil Liability) includes a mitigation rule, which represents a limitation to the full recovery principle. This is an entirely new provision for Argentinian law, first introduced by the 2015 Code. This article provides that:

> Art. 1710. Duty to prevent loss
>
> Every person has the duty to, in so far as it depends on him:
>
> a) Avoid causing unjustifiable damage;
> b) Adopt, in good faith and in accordance with the circumstances, reasonable measures to prevent damage from occurring, or to decrease its magnitude; if such measures avoid or reduce the magnitude of a damage for which a third party would be liable, he has the right to be reimbursed for the value of the expenses incurred, in accordance with the rules of unjust enrichment;
> c) Not aggravate the damage, if it occurred already.
>
> (original versión: Artículo 1710. Deber de prevención del daño
>
> Toda persona tiene el deber, en cuanto de ella dependa, de:
>
> a) evitar causar un daño no justificado;

---

[122] Andres Ormaechea, 'Obligación de mitigar el daño' (2016) avaliable at <https://www.abogados.com.ar/obligacion-de-mitigar-el-dano/18372> accessed 7 August 2022.

b) adoptar, de buena fe y conforme a las circunstancias, las medidas razonables para evitar que se produzca un daño, o disminuir su magnitud; si tales medidas evitan o disminuyen la magnitud de un daño del cual un tercero sería responsable, tiene derecho a que éste le reembolse el valor de los gastos en que incurrió, conforme a las reglas del enriquecimiento sin causa;

c) no agravar el daño, si ya se produjo.)[123]

Legal commentators have provided a variety of explanations and justifications for the imposition of this duty. According to López Mesa, the "preventative dimension of civil liability is acquiring ever greater importance, given that, if the damage is avoided before it occurs, a significant saving in means, time and costs is achieved".[124] Fiorenza places the duty to mitigate loss as "a derivation of the generic duty of not harming" (original version: "una derivación del también genérico deber de no dañar"),[125] founded on article 19 of the National Constitution, which provides:

Article 19. The private actions of men that do not offend public order and morals, nor cause harm to any third party, are reserved for God's sole judgement, and exempted

---

[123] Civil and Commercial Code of the Argentinian Nation (n 117) (original version: "frente al incumplimiento de una de la partes, la otra tiene el derecho de exigir el cumplimiento específico de la obligación asumida en el contrato como opción a la indemnización de daños y perjuicios")

[124] Marcelo López Mesa, 'La aplicación de um nuevo fator de atribuición: la causación de um daño evitable' (2013), Biblioteca Juridica Online, DC 1C1E (original version: "La faceta preventiva de la responsabilidad civil está adquiriendo cada vez mayor importancia, dado que si se suprime el daño antes de producirse se logra un importante ahorro de medios, tiempos y costos").

[125] Alejandro Alberto Fiorenza, 'El deber de prevenir el daño. Análisis del art. 1710 del Código Civil y Comercial' (2018) *El Derecho* <http://www.elderecho.com.ar/includes/pdf/diarios/2018/05/24052018.pdf> accessed 7 August 2022.

from the authority of judges. No citizen of the Nation will be obliged to do whatever is not imposed by law, nor prevented from doing what the law does not forbid.

(original version: Las acciones privadas de los hombres que de ningún modo ofendan al orden y a la moral pública, ni perjudiquen a un tercero, están sólo reservadas a Dios, y exentas de la autoridad de los magistrados. Ningún habitante de la Nación será obligado a hacer lo que no manda la ley, ni privado de lo que ella no prohíbe).

Ossola makes clear that the broad wording of Article 1710 is wide enough to include a duty to mitigate, in his observation that the "generic duty to act to prevent losses has been extended to 'all people' (including the victims themselves), and not only those upon whom lies a specific legal duty" (original version: "deber genérico de actuar a fin de prevenir daños se ha extendido a 'toda persona' (incluidas las propias víctimas), y no solo a aquellas sobre quienes pese un deber jurídico específico").[126]

In a comment that echoes the conceptualization of the duty in German legal thought as an *Obliegenheit* owed to oneself rather than a *Pflicht* owed to the other party,[127] Fiorenza acknowledges that the duty to mitigate "is in no way an obligation (because it cannot be claimed), but a general and abstract duty".[128] Based on the wording of Art 1710, it appears the duty covers both, limitation of loss (paragraph "b") and non-aggravation of loss (paragraph "c"). From a comparative point of view, it is also interesting to note that this provision looks like a hybrid of the German and the Common Law approaches: paragraph "b" treats contributory fault and the duty to limit loss as aspects of the same principle (as in Germany), while

---

[126] Federico Ossola, *Responsabilidad civil* (AbeledoPerrot, 2017) 175.

[127] See Section 4.2.1 above.

[128] Fiorenza (n 125) (original version: "no es de ningún modo una obligación (porque no es exigible), sino un deber general y abstracto").

the duty not to aggravate loss is treated by paragraph "c" as an independent duty (as in the Common Law). As in both the Common Law and German law, commentators agree that the duty is applicable to both contractual and non-contractual (that is, tort) liability.[129] Again, as in both of these systems, application of the duty results in the reduction of the amount of damages awarded.[130] As to the expenses incurred in the course of mitigation, article 1710 refers to the general rule for unjust enrichment in article 1794: "Every person who without cause is enriched at the expenses of another, is obliged to, to the extent of his or her own benefit, reimburse the expenses of the other."[131] Since the breaching party benefits from such expenditure because it reduces the damages he has to pay to the innocent party, this provision may make such expenditure recoverable, which it is in both German law and the Common Law. Mostajo comments that "Such losses (...) are known to the parties at the moment they enter the agreement (art. 1728(19)) and, as such, are indemnifiable by the breaching party. Always considering whether such measures and the corresponding expenses are reasonable to the nature of the obligation (type of contract) and circumstances of the case (people, time and place)".[132] Importantly, the rule in article 1794 can work so as to benefit either party, and could

---

[129] Edgardo López Herrera, *Código Civil y Comercial de la Nación Comentado* (La Ley, 2015) 996; Roberto Vázquez Ferreyra, 'La función preventiva de la responsabilidad civil' (2015) La LAey, Cita Online AR/DOC/1447/2015, p. 6.

[130] "La reducción de la indemnización es una consecuencia implícita en la norma argentina"; Daniel Mostajo, 'Apuntes en torno a las medidas mitigadoras en el Código Civil y Comercial argentino, con especial atención a la responsabilidad civil por incumplimiento contractual' <http://www.elderecho.com.ar/includes/pdf/diarios/2017/10/26102017.pdf> accessed 7 August 2022.

[131] Original version: "Toda persona que sin una causa lícita se enriquezca a expensas de otro, está obligada, en la medida de su beneficio, a resarcir el detrimento patrimonial del empobrecido".

[132] Mostajo (n 130). (Original versión: "Estas pérdidas (...) pasan a ser previsibles para las partes desde el momento mismo de la celebración del contrato (art. 1728(19)) y, como tales, indemnizables por el deudor. Esto último, teniendo siempre en consideración que las medidas mitigadoras y los gastos de ellas derivadas deben cumplir con el requisito de razonabilidad medido en función de la naturaleza de la

therefore also serve as a gateway for taking into account any gains made by the victim of the breach as a result of the mitigating action, as is achieved by the German principle of *Vorteilsausgleichung* and illustrated for the Common Law by the decision in *British Westinghouse Electric and Manufacturing Co Ltd v Underground Electric Railways Co of London Ltd*.[133]

Since there is no rule recognizing anticipatory repudiation of contracts, Ormaechea affirms that the duty to mitigate – in such case – will arise at the time the obligation becomes due. This means that the parties "must wait until the obligation becomes due, and then upon one party's breach the duty to mitigate will arise for the other party".[134] This looks rather similar to the current position in French law, which, as was noted above, is not compatible with the duty, in both the Common Law and German law, on the victim of a repudiatory breach to enter into a substitute transaction in order to mitigate his loss.

In contrast with Common Law jurisdictions, where damages is the primary remedy available as of right and specific performance is only available at the court's discretion, the victim of a breach of contract in Argentina has a *right* to require specific performance, with indemnification and damages being available at the victim's option.[135] It therefore appears that the victim can avoid the duty to mitigate loss by choosing specific performance, as there is no equivalent in the 2015 Civil and Commercial Code for the restriction on specific performance in section 275 (2) of the BGB discussed in 4.2.1 above. On the other hand, the victim's right to performance seems to support an outcome similar to *White & Carter*

---

obligación (tipo de contrato) y las circunstancias del caso concreto (personas, tiempo y lugar").

[133] See Section 3.2.3 in Chapter 3.

[134] Ormaechea (n 122). Original version: deberán esperar hasta el vencimiento del plazo pactado para el cumplimiento de las prestaciones, y recién en ese momento ante el incumplimiento de cualquiera de las partes nacerá en cabeza del cumplidor la obligación de mitigar.

[135] See above n 123.

(Councils) Ltd. v McGregor,[136] leaving the victim of an early repudiation free to perform his obligations in order to secure his right to full performance by the other party.

Although the 2015 Civil and Commercial Code is fairly new, the decisions of the courts (mostly lower courts) already indicate the interpretation of article 1710 so as to extract from its rationale a requirement for the innocent party to enter substitute transactions in order to prevent additional losses. In a case decided in 2017, the claimant, who had been provided, by the defendant, with unsuitable cattle feed, sought to increase the damages granted by the first-instance judge, which had been reduced for the reason that the claimant had failed to prevent additional losses by buying substitute cattle feed. The Appeal Court dismissed the case stating that "the claimant should have bought feed to substitute the defective one, so as to contribute to the non-aggravation of losses".[137]

Another decision citing article 1710 – though denying its application – from 2016, refers to a case in which the victim died buried by gravel, and defendants were accused of not having avoided this outcome/loss. The court ruled that nothing further was expected from defendants, as it was the victim who had invaded private property.[138] The facts of the case, however, indicate that this did not constitute an application of the mitigation doctrine, as this refers to actions taken to mitigate the aggravation of an existing loss, whereas the case concerned failure to prevent the occurrence of a loss.

Other than that, research on precedents has confirmed Ormaechea's

---

[136] See chapter 3 section 3.3.3.

[137] Expte. Nº 1-62119-2017 - "Fal María Cristina c/ Rindes y Cultivos Das SA S/ daños y perj. incump. contractual (exc. Estado)" – CÁMARA DE APELACIONES EN LO CIVIL Y COMERCIAL DE AZUL (Buenos Aires) – SALA PRIMERA - 19/09/2017 (original version: "la actora debería haber adquirido alimento para sustituir el faltante, para de ese modo contribuir a la no agravación del daño").

[138] Expte. Nº 2-60404-2015 - "Fal Teves Alberto Ariel c/ Ferrosur Roca SA S/daños y perj. autom. c/les. O muerte (exc. Estado)" – CÁMARA DE APELACIONES EN LO CIVIL Y COMERCIAL DEPARTAMENTAL (AZUL) – SALA II – 16/05/2016.

warning that the duty to mitigate loss is "a subject matter practically unknown until now to our legal culture",[139] and its newness certainly means that there is still some uncertainty. An example of this uncertainty can be seen in legal commentator Casermeiro's linking of mitigation to article 43 of the Argentinian Constitution, which provides the basis for the so called "preventive action"[140] (article 43: "Any person may institute an expedited preventive action, when no other more suitable legal means is available, against any act or omission of public authorities or individuals which in an arbitrary or manifestly illegal manner injures, restricts, alters or threatens, rights and guarantees recognized by this Constitution, a treaty or a law or may imminently do so..").[141] The same link is made by Argentinian courts when interpreting the "measures to prevent" (mentioned in article 1710) as judicial claims filed to avert potential losses. In a decision from 2019, regarding a case in which the claimant sought an order from the court for the defendant to delete social media posts potentially capable of causing losses, the court granted the order, making express reference to article 1710 as the basis for a judicial claim aiming to avoid the occurrence of loss

---

[139] Ormaechea (n 122) (original version: un tema prácticamente desconocido hasta ahora en nuestra cultura jurídica).

[140] Luis Adolfo Alavila Casermeiro, 'La acción preventiva em el nuevo Código Civil y Comercial' (2017), Biblioteca Juridica Online, DC 22B7. In the same sense, Jose Antonio Reviriego, 'La tutela preventiva y la acción preventiva en el derecho argentino (2011), Biblioteca Juridica Online, DC 16CE: "There is no doubt that the constitutional ground for the preventive action is article 43 of the National Constitution (original version: "No hay duda del fundamento constitucional de la tutela preventiva em el artículo 43 de nuestra Constituición Nacional").

[141] Argentinian Constitution, available at <http://servicios.infoleg.gob.ar/infolegInternet/anexos/0-4999/804/norma.htm>, accessed on 7 August 2022. Original version: "Toda persona puede interponer acción expedita y rápida de amparo, siempre que no exista otro medio judicial más idóneo, contra todo acto u omisión de autoridades públicas o de particulares, que en forma actual o inminente lesione, restrinja, altere o amenace, con arbitrariedad o ilegalidad manifiesta, derechos y garantías reconocidos por esta Constitución, un tratado o una ley"

(original version: "evitar la producción de un daño").[142] This evidences a certain level of distortion of the mitigation doctrine, which deals with the prevention of additional losses by the victim's own actions rather than with the judicial remedies available to victims.

Regarding the victim's behaviour, discussion of what constitutes reasonable actions to mitigate point to the directions in article 1710 regarding good-faith and state that the burden on the innocent party must not be as heavy as it is on the breaching party. Thus, Fiorenza has written that:

"Good faith, understood as truth and the basis of juridical relations, is the great measuring rod for the conduct of legal subjects. And when discussing the avoidance (prevention), or the decrease (mitigation or no aggravation) of harm, it provides support to the principle of prevention and criteria to the mitigation of losses".[143]

On the same aspect, according to Mostajo:

"When assessing the reasonableness of actual mitigating steps, it must be taken into account that the standard of conduct required from the creditor is not the same as that usually employed to assess the conduct of the debtor

---

[142] Expte. N° 13-04825788-1 (012053-303952) - "Fal María Nilva Dias Ephima Palacio y Otros c/ Monica Beatriz Molina /acción preventiva" – TRIBUNAL DE GESTION ASOCIADA-TERCERO PODER JUDICIAL MENDOZA – 23/10/2019 (original version: "evitar la producción de un daño").

[143] Fiorenza (n 125). (Original version: La buena fe, entendida como verdad y fundamento de las relaciones jurídicas, es la gran vara con la que se mide el comportamento del sujeto de derecho. Y em matéria de evitación (prevencón), o disminución (mitigación o no agravamento), es el fundamento insígnia, donde se han apoyado el pricipio de prevención, y el critério de mitigación del daño).

in complying with its obligations: the standard expected from the creditor will be relatively lower".[144]

A final matter worth considering is whether article 1710 also covers cases like *White & Carter (Councils) Ltd. v McGregor*;[145] in other words, whether it could prevent someone from insisting on the right to perform the contract, and thus to receive the contract price, if doing so would have the result that the sum payable by the party in breach is larger than it would have been if the victim of the breach cancelled the contract and merely claimed damages. As was seen above, Germany found it necessary to include two specific provisions in the BGB to deal with such cases, whilst the current French proposals for a new duty to mitigate fail to cover this scenario.[146] Although one must be cautious at this early stage of the life of this new Argentinian rule, it does seem to be the case that the wording of article 1710 is broad enough to cover not only claims for damages, but also claims for specific performance, including the contract price. If this is in future confirmed by the cases, that would mean that Argentina has opted for the same solution as Germany and the United States.

4.4 Transnational Legal Instruments

Transnational instruments have been conceived in order to harmonize and bind different legal jurisdictions to a common set of rules, especially in respect of international sales.[147] In Latin America itself, some tentative

---

[144] Mostajo (n 130). (Original version: al momento de determinar la razonabilidad o no de una concreta medida mitigadora, debe tenerse presente que el estándar de conducta con el que se mida la actuación del acreedor no puede ser el mismo que usualmente se utiliza para evaluar la conducta del deudor en el cumplimiento de sus obligaciones: el estándar de conducta exigido al acreedor será relativamente más bajo)

[145] *White & Carter (Councils) Ltd. v McGregor* (n 51).

[146] Section 4.2.1 above.

[147] Peter Huber, 'Comparative Sales Law' in Reimann and Zimmermann (n 6) 934-967.

steps towards legal unification and harmonization have taken place.[148] Such initiatives have grown as trade and all kind of business among different countries began to demand rules and solutions that could be mutually accepted and enforced among parties from different jurisdictions. Reflecting the work of international groups of legal experts, these instruments typically represent both state-of-the-art proposals about best practice in law and shared thinking across the divides of national borders and legal traditions. Given this, it is important to observe and analyze if and how the mitigation doctrine has been codified and established in such instruments, for this will reflect the experience and lessons learned from different legal systems.

4.4.1 Hague Uniform Law of International Sales ("ULIS")

The development of these supranational instruments started with the work of the International Institute for the Unification of Private Law (UNIDROIT), established in 1926 with the purpose to "study needs and methods for modernising, harmonising and co-ordinating private and in particular commercial law as between States and groups of States and to formulate uniform law instruments, principles and rules to achieve those objectives".[149] Its work resulted in the Hague Convention relating to a Uniform Law of International Sales (ULIS), which entered into force in 1972, but has been ratified by only a very limited number of (mostly European) states and has not been widely applied in international trade.[150] Much more successful has been an instrument developed out of this experience by the United Nations Commission on International Trade Law (UNCITRAL), which had been established in 1966: the 1980 UN

---

[148] Kleinheisterkamp (n 6) 276-282.

[149] Unidroit information available at <https://www.unidroit.org/about-unidroit/overview> accessed 7 August 2022.

[150] Huber (n 147) 936-937.

Convention on Contracts for the International Sale of Goods—CISG.[151] Before looking in more detail at the latter, it is worth noting that ULIS already contained an express duty to mitigate in its Article 88:

> The party who relies on a breach of the contract shall adopt all reasonable measures to mitigate the loss resulting from the breach. If he fails to adopt such measures, the party in breach may claim a reduction in the damages.

4.4.2 Vienna Convention on Contracts for the International Sale of Goods ("CISG")

The United Nations Convention on Contracts for the International Sale of Goods ("CISG") 1980, aims to establish uniform rules applicable to international trade of goods. According to its preamble, "the adoption of uniform rules which govern contracts for the international sale of goods and take into account the different social, economic and legal systems would contribute to the removal of legal barriers in international trade and promote the development of international trade."[152] The steps of its historic and technical development are described in the explanatory note, with credits to the International Institute for the Unification of Private Law (UNIDROIT), in Rome, and the United Nations Commission on International Trade Law (UNCITRAL).[153] Currently, over 80 countries have become signatories and acknowledged the Convention as binding rule for international trade, including Brazil (since April 1st, 2014).[154] That makes its treatment of mitigation of great importance to this thesis.

With regards to breach of contract by either party, the CISG establishes

---

[151] CISG available at <https://www.uncitral.org/pdf/english/texts/sales/cisg/V1056997-CISG-e-book.pdf> accessed 7 August 2022.

[152] CISG (n 151) preamble.

[153] CISG (n 151) 33-34.

[154] See <https://www.cisg.law.pace.edu/cisg/countries/cntries.html> accessed 7 August 2022.

that it is the innocent party's choice to claim performance or damages (arts. 45 and 61). This approach is similar to that of the Brazilian Civil Code,[155] indicating a possible compatibility between CISG rational and Brazilian existing rules.

> Article 45
>
> (1) If the seller fails to perform any of his obligations under the contract or this Convention, the buyer may:
>
>   (a) exercise the rights provided in articles 46 to 52;
>   (b) claim damages as provided in articles 74 to 77.
>
> (...)
>
> Article 61
>
> (1) If the buyer fails to perform any of his obligations under the contract or this Convention, the seller may:
>
>   (a) exercise the rights provided in articles 62 to 65;
>   (b) claim damages as provided in articles 74 to 77.

This express authorization for the innocent party to seek performance suggests that the issue raised in the *White & Carter (Councils) Ltd. v McGregor* case[156] could be decided in the same way under the CISG, leaving the victim of an early repudiation free to perform his obligations in order to secure his right to full performance by the other party. In other words, the victim of the breach can avoid the duty to mitigate by choosing to claim performance rather than damages. Moreover, the victim has this right not only in cases of anticipatory repudiation, but in respect of any breach of contract. This contrasts with the position in Common Law systems, in which, as seen in Chapter 3, damages is the primary and

---

[155] See reference to article 475, in Section 2.2 of Chapter 2.
[156] *White & Carter (Councils) Ltd. v McGregor* (n 51).

usual remedy. Significantly, the CISG does not include an equivalent to the restrictions on specific performance found in section 275 (2) of the BGB or in article 7.2.2 of the PICC (discussed below), although articles 46 and 62 add the disclaimer that the performance-oriented remedies may be chosen "unless the buyer has resorted to a remedy which is inconsistent with this requirement."

In the event that damages are sought, article 77 presents the duty to mitigate as a limitation on damages to be awarded under the CISG:

> Article 77
> A party who relies on a breach of contract must take such measures as are reasonable in the circumstances to mitigate the loss, including loss of profit, resulting from the breach. If he fails to take such measures, the party in breach may claim a reduction in the damages in the amount by which the loss should have been mitigated.

In contrast to the German BGB, in which the duty to mitigate is embedded in contributory fault, here the mitigation doctrine is regulated as an independent principle, as in Common Law systems. In this case, the rule clearly refers to the prevention of the aggravation of an existing loss. Besides, the brief formulation regarding reasonableness expected from the innocent party indicates a low threshold, equivalent to that established in *British Westinghouse Electric and Manufacturing Co Ltd v Underground Electric Railways Co of London Ltd.*[157] In a case decided by Austrian Supreme Court (10 Ob 518/95), in which the buyer could not meet his obligation of obtaining a letter of credit due to the seller's failure to provide the necessary details, the court defined reasonable measures as

---

[157] *British Westinghouse Electric and Manufacturing Co Ltd v Underground Electric Railways Co of London Ltd.* (n 39)

"those which under the circumstances of the individual case could have been expected in good faith".[158]

Chapter 3 of this thesis has explained that the duty to mitigate in Common Law systems requires of the victim of a breach of contract to enter into a substitute transaction in order to limit the loss caused by the breach.[159] The CISG gives effect to this principle in an indirect way in the provisions regulating the recoverability of losses in cases in which the contract is avoided for breach: the innocent party is entitled to recover the difference between the original price and the current price at the time of avoidance (arts. 75 and 76 – "recover the difference between the price fixed by the contract and the current price"). This rationale has been applied to decisions grounded on the CISG,[160] which have also acknowledged the inclusion of extra costs incurred when taking reasonable steps to mitigate in the claim for losses from the aggrieved party.[161]

In addition to these two Conventions (ULIS and CISG) there are also several relevant "soft law" instruments that have included provisions on mitigation.

---

[158] Available at <http://cisgw3.law.pace.edu/cases/960206a3.html> accessed 7 August 2022.

[159] See section 3.2.2 of Chapter 3.

[160] Available at <http://cisgw3.law.pace.edu/cases/091217s1.html> accessed 7 August 2022: If the buyer did not purchase replacement goods and if it would have been reasonable to do so, the damages [and interest] are reduced to the amount that would be due if he had purchased the replacement goods.

[161] In a case decided by Swiss Commercial Court (HG. 1999.82-HGK), in which plaintiff sought to recover the advance payment made before becoming insolvent and avoiding the contract, and the court acknowledged the defendant's right to set-off his own damages from the restitution owed to claimant, "[t]he court also acknowledged a right to compensation for the loss resulting from additional expenses incurred for transport, containers, storage and disassembly as well as for the loss on exchange caused by the increase in the value of the United States dollar since the time of the advance payment." Available at <http://cisgw3.law.pace.edu/cases/021203s1.html> accessed 7 August 2022.

4.4.3 Principles of International Commercial Contracts ("PICC")

In 1994, the International Institute for the Unification of Private Law (UNIDROIT) published its Principles of International Commercial Contracts ("PICC" – revised 2004, 2010 and 2016).[162] This is not a binding legal instrument. According to the Preamble, the Principles *shall* be applied when the parties have agreed that their contract is to be governed by them and that they *may* be applied (inter alia) if the parties have chosen the lex mercatoria (or general principles of law) to apply to their contract or have not made any choice of rules at all. The Principles are also intended to serve as a model for national legislatures and to be used to interpret or supplement international legal instruments or domestic law. They have in fact been applied in a number of arbitration proceedings as well as in some court decisions.[163] They include an article dealing expressly with "mitigation of harm":

> Article 7.4.8
>
> (Mitigation of harm)
>
> (1) The non-performing party is not liable for harm suffered by the aggrieved party to the extent that the harm could have been reduced by the latter party's taking reasonable steps.

---

[162] For a brief description, see Huber (n 147) 949. For comprehensive treatment, see Stefan Vogenauer (ed), *Commentary on the UNIDROIT Principles of International Commercial Contracts (PICC)* 2nd Edn (Oxford, Oxford University Press, 2015).

[163] These are available at http://www.unilex.info/instrument/principles.

(2) The aggrieved party is entitled to recover any expenses reasonably incurred in attempting to reduce the harm.[164]

The uncomplicated wording of the rule is limited to setting out the two main aspects of mitigation: that the avoidable losses are not recoverable, and that reasonable expenses incurred in trying to mitigate will be recoverable. The official comment of this article tackles the reasonableness aspect and the argument of the economic waste, revealing a low threshold for the aggrieved party by stating that:

> "Evidently, a party who has already suffered the consequences of non-performance of the contract cannot be required in addition to take time-consuming and costly measures. On the other hand, it would be unreasonable from the economic standpoint to permit an increase in harm which could have been reduced by the taking of reasonable steps."[165]

With no details as to burden of proof – after all, this is not meant to be a full and detailed code – this Article provides only the starting point for the application of the doctrine. In addition, like the CISG, the PICC includes provisions dealing specifically with mitigation through substitute transactions. And the official comment on this article expressly includes "damages for additional harm which it may have sustained" in favour of the aggrieved party.

---

[164] Unidroit Principles of International Commercial Contracts available at <https://unidroit.org/english/principles/contracts/principles2016/principles2016-e.pdf> accessed 7 August 2022. The Official Comment summarises the effect: "Any harm which the aggrieved party could have avoided by taking reasonable steps will not be compensated".

[165] Available at <http://www.unilex.info/principles/text> accessed 27 June 2020.

Article 7.4.5
(Proof of harm in case of replacement transaction)

Where the aggrieved party has terminated the contract and has made a replacement transaction within a reasonable time and in a reasonable manner it may recover the difference between the contract price and the price of the replacement transaction as well as damages for any further harm.

Article 7.4.6
(Proof of harm by current price)

(1) Where the aggrieved party has terminated the contract and has not made a replacement transaction but there is a current price for the performance contracted for, it may recover the difference between the contract price and the price current at the time the contract is terminated as well as damages for any further harm.

(2) Current price is the price generally charged for goods delivered or services rendered in comparable circumstances at the place where the contract should have been performed or, if there is no current price at that place, the current price at such other place that appears reasonable to take as a reference.

When these provisions are compared to the treatment of mitigation in the jurisdictions analysed earlier in this Chapter and in Chapter 3, the following is noteworthy: First, there is a clear distinction between mitigation and contributory negligence (unlike the German rationale), with each treated separately in an independent section.[166] This approach reinforces the argument presented in section 2.3.3 of Chapter 2 and section 3.3.2 of Chapter 3, which recognizes that the two rules bring a similar outcome (that is, limiting recovery), but each applies at a different moment (whilst contributory negligence is one of the original causes for the loss, failures to mitigate causes the aggravation of an existing loss). Second, the express reference to substitute transactions as a way to mitigate clarifies the expectation on the aggrieved party as to this issue; and, when compared to Civil Law countries, represents a level of detail that is in between the absence in Argentina and the procedural provisions found in Germany.

Further, the PICC deals with both remedies available to the aggrieved party upon breach: damages (article 7.4.1) and performance (7.2.2), denoting some similarity amongst the transnational instruments analysed in this Section.[167] And again, as to this aspect, it resembles the CISG in its comparison to the *White & Carter (Councils) Ltd. v McGregor*[168] outcome, confirming the possibility of one of the parties upholding performance even in the case of anticipatory repudiation.[169] On the other hand, article

---

[166] Contributory negligence is regulated in Article 7.4.7: "Where the harm is due in part to an act or omission of the aggrieved party or to another event for which that party bears the risk, the amount of damages shall be reduced to the extent that these factors have contributed to the harm, having regard to the conduct of each of the parties."

[167] Comment 2 on article 7.4.1 refers to the possibility of claiming damages in conjunction with other remedies: "This Article also states that the aggrieved party may request damages either as an exclusive remedy (for example, damages for delay in the case of late performance or for defective performance accepted by the aggrieved party; damages in the event of impossibility of performance for which the non-performing party is liable), or in conjunction with other remedies. Thus, in the case of termination of the contract, damages may be requested to compensate the loss arising from such termination, or again, in the case of specific performance, to compensate for the delay with which the aggrieved party receives performance and for any expenses which might have been incurred."

[168] *White & Carter (Councils) Ltd. v McGregor* (n 51).

[169] Official comment 2. to article 7.4.1 points out a difference between PICC and the CISG: "This Article also states that the aggrieved party may request damages either

7.2.2, in contrast with the CISG, imposes restrictions on the availability of specific performance that are similar to the restrictions in Article 275 (2) of the BGB, indeed going somewhat further in 7.2.2(c). The latter in particular means that the victim of a breach cannot easily avoid the duty to mitigate by opting for specific performance instead of damages.[170]

> Article 7.4.1
> (Right to damages)
>
> Any non-performance gives the aggrieved party a right to damages either exclusively or in conjunction with any other remedies except where the non-performance is excused under these Principles.
>
> Article 7.2.2
> (Performance of non-monetary obligation)
>
> Where a party who owes an obligation other than one to pay money does not perform, the other party may require performance, unless
>
> (a) performance is impossible in law or in fact;
> (b) performance or, where relevant, enforcement is unreasonably burdensome or expensive;

---

as an exclusive remedy (for example, damages for delay in the case of late performance or for defective performance accepted by the aggrieved party; damages in the event of impossibility of performance for which the non-performing party is liable), or in conjunction with other remedies. Thus, in the case of termination of the contract, damages may be requested to compensate the loss arising from such termination, or again, in the case of specific performance, to compensate for the delay with which the aggrieved party receives performance and for any expenses which might have been incurred."

[170] Official comment 2. to article 7.2.2 lays out five hypothetical situations as "Exceptions to the right to require performance".

(c) the party entitled to performance may reasonably obtain performance from another source;

(d) performance is of an exclusively personal character; or

(e) the party entitled to performance does not require performance within a reasonable time after it has, or ought to have, become aware of the non-performance.

Finally, as to the burden of proof, a decision from the Tribunal Supremo of Spain, involving two local electricity companies, based on the PICC, which granted A damages from B due to unjustified refusal to connect B to its distribution network, stated that mitigation "cannot lead to an unreasonable reversal of the burden of proof by forcing the aggrieved party to prove that it could have avoided or reduced the harm". The decision reflects the Common Law approach on this matter, as seen in *Lombard North Central v Automobile World (UK) Ltd*,[171] which is to place the burden to prove failure to mitigate on the breaching party.

4.4.4 Principles of European Contract Law ("PECL")

A similar "soft law" instrument – but with its geographical reach restricted to Europe – is the Principles of European Contract Law ("PECL").[172] According to Article 1:101 PECL, these principles are intended to be applied as general rules of contract law in the EU, to provide rules which parties may incorporate into their contract, to be applied as part of "general principles" or "lex mercatoria", and to provide solutions for issues which are not resolved by the applicable (national) law. Like the PICL, the

---

[171] *Lombard North Central v Automobile World (UK) Ltd* (2010) EWCA Civ 20.

[172] Available at <https://www.trans-lex.org/400200/_/pecl/> accessed 7 August 2022. For a brief discussion of its development, see Huber (n 147) 945. For comprehensive treatment, see Ole Lando and Hugh Beale (eds), *Principles of European Contract Law* Parts I and II (Kluwer, 1999); Ole Lando, Eric Clive, André Prüm, and Reinhard Zimmermann (eds), *Principles of European Contract Law* Part III (Kluwer, 2003).

PECL includes a specific provision on mitigation; indeed, it uses identical wording:

> Article 9:505: Reduction of Loss
>
> (1) The non-performing party is not liable for loss suffered by the aggrieved party to the extent that the aggrieved party could have reduced the loss by taking reasonable steps.
>
> (2) The aggrieved party is entitled to recover any expenses reasonably incurred in attempting to reduce the loss.

Again like the PICC, the PECL distinguished between mitigation and contributory fault by including a separate provision on the latter, and it also provides specifically for substitute transactions:

> Article 9:504: Loss Attributable to Aggrieved Party
>
> The non-performing party is not liable for loss suffered by the aggrieved party to the extent that the aggrieved party contributed to the non-performance or its effects.
>
> Article 9:506: Substitute Transaction
>
> Where the aggrieved party has terminated the contract and has made a substitute transaction within a reasonable time and in a reasonable manner, it may recover the difference between the contract price and the price of the substitute transaction as well as damages for any further loss so far as these are recoverable under this Section.
>
> Article 9:507: Current Price

> Where the aggrieved party has terminated the contract and has not made a substitute transaction but there is a current price for the performance contracted for, it may recover the difference between the contract price and the price current at the time the contract is terminated as well as damages for any further loss so far as these are recoverable under this Section.

Because of the high degree of similarity between PECL and PICC, the comparative remarks made above in respect of PICC also apply to PECL. There is no need to repeat them.

4.4.5 Developments towards a Common European Sales Law (CESL)

The most ambitious transnational harmonization process to date has taken place in Europe. The European Union has not only implemented sector-specific regulatory measures, but has also attempted (so far unsuccessfully) to create a common European contract law, at least in respect of contracts of sale.[173] The most important example of sector-specific measures is the Consumer Sales Directive, which was strongly influenced by the CISG, and has had a major impact on national contract laws.[174] The broader and more ambitious harmonization programme led to the publication in 2009 of a Draft Common Frame of Reference (DCFR) as a preparatory step for a common European Code of Private Law. However, this was overtaken in 2011 by a less ambitious proposal, an optional instrument in the field of sales law: the Proposal for a Regulation of the European Parliament and of the Council on a Common European Sales Law (CESL), which was a condensed version of part of the DCFR

---

[173] For a brief overview, see Huber (n 147) 939-945.

[174] Huber (n 147) at 941. A good example of its extensive impact is that it inspired and helped shape the fundamental reform of German contract law in 2002 noted above in 4.2 as well as the current French reform efforts discussed in 4.3.1.

and meant to apply to international sales contracts if it was chosen by the parties. In a further reduction of ambition, the CESL proposal was withdrawn in 2015, and subsequent harmonisation developments have dealt with relatively narrow sector specific topics such as contracts for the online and other distance sale of goods and contracts for the supply of digital content.[175] Despite this political failure of the DCFR and CESL, they are of great importance to this thesis as they are the product of a long period of concentrated effort by the leading academic experts in Europe to find solutions that would be acceptable across borders and different legal families/traditions. In a sense, they represent the best current international opinion.[176]

In terms that are identical to the DCFR, the CESL contains a general provision on mitigation of loss, as well as specific provisions regarding mitigation through substitute transactions:

Article 163
Reduction of loss

1. The debtor is not liable for loss suffered by the creditor to the extent that the creditor could have reduced the loss by taking reasonable steps.

2. The creditor is entitled to recover any expenses reasonably incurred in attempting to reduce the loss.

---

[175] For an overview of all these developments, see Huber (n 147) 941-944.

[176] Official text of CESL available at <https://eur-lex.europa.eu/legal-content/EN/TXT/?uri=CELEX%3A52011PC0635> accessed 7 August 2022. The DCFR is available in: C Von Bar, E Clive, H Schulte-Nölke et al. (eds.), *Principles, Definitions and Model Rules of European Private Law — Draft Common Frame of Reference (DCFR)* (Munich, Selier, 2008). A draft version is available at <https://www.ccbe.eu/fileadmin/speciality_distribution/public/documents/EUROPEAN_PRIVATE_LAW/EN_EPL_20100107_Principles__definitions_and_model_rules_of_European_private_law_-_Draft_Common_Frame_of_Reference__DCFR_.pdf> accessed 27 June 2020.

Article 164

Substitute transaction

A creditor who has terminated a contract in whole or in part and has made a substitute transaction within a reasonable time and in a reasonable manner may, in so far as it is entitled to damages, recover the difference between the value of what would have been payable under the terminated contract and the value of what is payable under the substitute transaction, as well as damages for any further loss.

Article 165

Current price

Where the creditor has terminated the contract and has not made a substitute transaction but there is a current price for the performance, the creditor may, in so far as entitled to damages, recover the difference between the contract price and the price current at the time of termination as well as damages for any further loss.

These provisions coincide with the general availability of specific performance as a primary remedy at the option of the victim of a breach – which does not exclude the application of the section that regulates the reduction of loss – provided for in Articles 106.1 (buyer), 131.1 (seller), 155.1 (customer) and 157.1 (service provider) – according to the person who claims:

Article 106

Overview of buyer's remedies

In the case of non-performance of an obligation by the seller, the buyer may do any of the following:

(a) require performance, which includes specific performance, repair or replacement of the goods or digital content, under Section 3 of this Chapter;
(b) withhold the buyer's own performance under Section 4 of this Chapter;
(c) terminate the contract under Section 5 of this Chapter and claim the return of any price already paid, under Chapter 17;
(d) reduce the price under Section 6 of this Chapter; and
(e) claim damages under Chapter 16.

Article 131
Overview of seller's remedies

In the case of a non-performance of an obligation by the buyer, the seller may do any of the following:

(a) require performance under Section 2 of this Chapter;
(b) withhold the seller's own performance under Section 3 of this Chapter;
(c) terminate the contract under Section 4 of this Chapter; and
(d) claim interest on the price or damages under Chapter 16.

Article 155
Remedies of the customer

In the case of non-performance of an obligation by the service provider, the customer has, with the adaptations set out in this Article, the same remedies as are provided for the buyer in Chapter 11, namely:

(a) to require specific performance;

(b) to withhold the customer's own performance;

(c) to terminate the contract;

(d) to reduce the price; and

(e) to claim damages.

Article 157

Remedies of the service provider

In the case of a non-performance by the customer, the service provider has, with the adaptations set out in paragraph 2, the same remedies as are provided for the seller in Chapter 13, namely:

(a) to require performance;

(b) to withhold the service provider's own performance;

(c) to terminate the contract; and

(d) to claim interest on the price or damages.

This contrasts with the position in the Common Law, where specific performance is a secondary remedy only available at the discretion of the court, and it may be wondered whether this general availability is compatible with the duty to mitigate. As was seen in 4.2.2.1 above, this is one of the objections raised against the French proposal. Commenting on the relationship between the mitigation doctrine and the remedy of specific performance on the DCFR, Rowan states that: "The co-existence of specific performance and loss mitigation is not unusual. An example can be found in the DCFR, which proposes both the primacy of specific performance and the adoption of a principle of mitigation."[177] However, it must be asked: does this option not enable the victim to by-pass the duty to mitigate by claiming specific performance rather than damages? It is noteworthy that, like the CISG, the CESL does not contain restrictions on the availability of specific performance comparable to those found in Article 275 (2) of the BGB and article 7.2.2 PICC. Perhaps the willingness to accept the potential by-passing of the duty to mitigate reflects the traditional Civil Law commitment to performance of the contract.

The CESL distinguishes between mitigation and contributory fault, dealing with the latter in a separate article: "Article 162 CESL makes it clear that the debtor is not liable for loss suffered by the creditor to the extent that the latter has contributed to the non-performance and its effects."[178]

Article 162

Loss attributable to creditor

The debtor is not liable for loss suffered by the creditor to the extent that the creditor contributed to the non-performance or its effects.

Finally, as to one party's right to insist on performance even if termination would limit its losses (the issue dealt with in *White & Carter*),[179] the solution in the CESL is similar to the CISG and PICC (therefore, different from American Common Law approach but similar to that in England), which allows the innocent party to choose performance in the face of breach.

---

[177] Rowan (n 73) 154.

[178] Matthias Lehmann, 'Damages and interest' in Javier Plaza Penadés and Luz M. Martínez Velencoso (eds), *European Perspectives on the Common European Sales Law* (Springer 2015) 255.

[179] *White & Carter (Councils) Ltd. v McGregor* (n 51).

4.4.6 Principles of Latin American Contract Law ("PLACL")

Los Principios Latinoamericanos de Derecho de los Contratos ("PLDC" or, in English, "PLACL") is the product of collaboration between academic experts and universities from the various Latin American countries, including Brazil, and draws inspiration from PICC, PECL, CISG CESL and local national Civil Codes, especially the new Argentinian Code discussed above, as well as the current French reform of the law of obligations, also discussed above.[180] The methodology of its development and the approach adopted is very similar to the creation of the PICC and PECL[181] and so are its objectives.[182] The PLACL is clearly of great importance to a thesis concerned with the law of Brazil, not least because it represents state-of-the-art current legal thought in Latin America.

In common with the PICC and PECL, the PLACL contains an express provision on mitigation, which is distinguished from contributory fault, dealt with separately in the immediately preceding article:Article 108. Contribution of the obligee to its harm

---

[180] Carlos Pizarro Wilson, 'Presentación', in Íñigo De la Maza, Carlos Pizarro Wilson and Álvaro Vidal Olivares (eds), *Los Principios Latinoamericanos de Derecho de los Contratos: Texto, presentación y contenidos fundamentales* (Madrid, Agencia Estatal Boletín Oficial Del Estado, 2017) 15. This book includes an English translation of the text. (Available at <https://www.boe.es/publicaciones/biblioteca_juridica/abrir_pdf.php?id=PUB-PR-2017-44> accessed 19 January 2020). For the background, context and development of this initiative as well as analysis in English of its proposals by international experts, see Rodrigo Momberg, Stefan Vogenauer (eds), *The Future of Contract Law in Latin America: The Principles of Latin American Contract Law* (Oxford, Hart Publishing, 2017).

[181] Jan Peter Schmidt, 'The 'Principles of Latin American Contract Law' Against the Background of Latin American Legal Culture: A European Perspective', in Momberg and Vogenauer (eds) *The Future of Contract Law in Latin America: The Principles of Latin American Contract Law* (Oxford, Hart Publishing, 2017), 57, 87–95.

[182] Thus Articles 1 and 2 are in combination essentially similar to the Preamble of the PICC and Article 1:101 of the PECL.

Compensation is subject to reduction when the obligee has contributed to the non-performance by way of its acts or omissions.

Article 109. Mitigation of loss

(1) Compensation is subject to reduction when the obligee has failed to take reasonable measures to mitigate loss in good faith. Reduction shall correspond to the amount by which the loss could have been mitigated.

(2) The obligee is entitled to compensation for what it has allocated towards mitigating the loss, even if these measures have been ineffective.

Maza, Wilson and Olivares refer to articles 108 and 109 as two additional reasons (besides non-foreseeability) for limiting recovery, both originating from the creditor's conduct, whether an action or an omission, and criticize the absence of any reference to reasonability on the measures taken in section (2) of article 109.[183] Still, the two-part structure of Article 109 is identical to the structure of the equivalent provisions in the PICC and PECL. However, the wording of paragraph (1) is different, as both the PICC and PECL formulate the principle by reference to the liability of the party in breach ("The non-performing party is not liable (…)"), whereas the PLACL formulates it by reference to the determination of the compensation payable ("Compensation is subject to reduction (…)"). In this respect, the PLACL formulation is closest to that adopted by the French law reform proposals[184] and similar to ULIS Article 88 and CISG Article 77.

A further contrast with the PICc and PECL is that it does not

183 Maza, Wilson and Olivares (n 180) 73-74.
184 See Section 4.2.2.1 in Chapter 4.

make separate and express provision for mitigation through substitute transactions. However, this should not make any difference in practice: it is clear from the experience of Common Law systems, discussed in Chapter 3, as well as from the 2017 judicial decisions in Argentina discussed in 4.3.1 above, that this can be derived from the general mitigation principle. Apart from this, the high degree of similarity between the PLACL and the PICC and PECL means that the comparative assessment made in 4.4.3 and 4.4.4 above is equally applicable here.

4.5 Conclusion

The research on Civil Law jurisdictions evidenced that the mitigation doctrine has not developed as much in these countries as it has developed in Common Law countries – in which every new case is a new opportunity to revisit, rethink and develop the doctrine. The most relevant finding in this section was that not only most recent supranational instruments (formulated with contributions from many jurisdictions), but also individual countries, have found in the acknowledgment and inclusion of the mitigation doctrine – preferably as an autonomous principle – a way to improve their codes and existing rules. This tendency (observed in Brazil's neighbour and cultural partner Argentina, and in highly traditional France) points towards an answer to one of the main questions in this thesis, which concerns the importance of filling the legislative gap in Brazil on the duty to mitigate.

Although many Civil Law countries have not gone so far as to adopt an express provision for the duty to mitigate, there is very little practical difference between Common Law systems and Germanic systems, with the latter using an expanded notion of contributory negligence to achieve the same results in practice as the Common Law duty of mitigation. As to the leading member of the French family of Civil Law systems, there is both a clear desire among lawyers for adopting an approach very similar to the Common Law, and a well-developed law reform project in that direction.

This tendency towards convergence, following the Common Law lead, is reinforced by the inclusion, in the new Argentinian Civil and Commercial Code – dated 2015 – of a specific provision regulating mitigation. All of these aspects provide support for the proposal put forward in this thesis for the development of the Brazilian legal system.

The research has revealed that Germany includes the duty to mitigate with its contributory negligence rule, while French law reserves no space in its current legislation or judicial practice for the mitigation doctrine. These formulations differ from Common Law countries (at least in the United Kingdom and the United States), where mitigation plays an effective role and the cases that represent the binding precedents for the doctrine treat it as an autonomous principle. Legal practice, however (considering the German interpretation of the contributory rule and the French law reform project), in both cases, limits recovery. This outcome is similar to the one observed in the Common Law countries analyzed in Chapter 3, and reinforces the argument that Civil Law countries – even those with no express reference to the mitigation doctrine – have experienced a veiled application or are in the process of introducing the duty to mitigate (even if based on different conceptual grounds).

The French law reform project as well as the reforms already implemented in Argentina suggest that there is an increasing tendency for express regulation of the duty to mitigate in Civil Law countries, acknowledging and setting its role as an autonomous principle (like in Common Law countries) to be fully addressed in codes and rules, allowing its development and application by courts, with respect to aspects like reasonableness, burden of proof and treatment of extra losses and gains. Such regulation is – in fact – advisable, as it removes the need for courts to engage in discussions (such as those Chapter 2 identified in Brazil) about whether the mitigation principle should be applied and on what it requires. Once its application is fully accepted – and a matter of law – the doctrine is able to mature and develop in each Civil Law country according to its context and the will of its legislators and courts.

The research on Argentinian law resulted in several findings from a jurisdiction that has, only recently, incorporated the duty to mitigate loss, which found its ground in the constitutional principle of not causing harm. The mitigation doctrine was crafted as an abstract duty, recognizing the economic argument of avoiding waste of resources, and limiting – at some point – the full recovery principle. The rule on mitigation was made effective in relation to both torts and contract claims, and applicable to situations in which the remedy picked by the innocent party is damages (and not specific performance, which is made available at the party's choice). Reasonable action from the innocent party is based on good faith, and considers the burden of acting – including substitute transactions – according to each situation. As to the expenses incurred in mitigation, the rule applies the unjust enrichment rationale to prevent the "unjust impoverishment" of someone reasonably acting to mitigate.

Although there is a limited number of precedents applying the mitigation doctrine (and many of them apply article 1710 in the sense of preventive judicial claims), the successful reception on the Argentinian side so far can also be projected for Brazil, especially considering the cultural and legal contexts of both countries. Argentina's experience suggests that a proper formulation of the mitigation principle could fit into the Brazilian Civil Code, which is not much more than a decade older than the Argentinian Civil and Commercial Code and has significant similarities in provisions as to damages and liability. This would represent a positive development of Brazilian legislation – not to mention its alignment with the other jurisdictions.

As to the transnational legal instruments, their relevance is unquestionable as they resulted from profound studies, made by multinational groups – with different backgrounds, culture and relevant experience – intending to formulate state-of-the-art guidance and provisions. In this context, it is particularly important to observe that all of them deal with the mitigation doctrine as an autonomous principle, with minor differences as to how to regulate substitute transactions and the treatment of extra losses and/or gains. Another relevant finding regarding these instruments is that all of them grant to the creditor/innocent party the choice between the remedies of specific performance and damages, which represents a similar scenario to the Brazilian legal scene. And although mitigation does not apply when the party chooses performance, its field of application is preserved when the remedy chosen is damages.

The similarity in the formulation and wording of the transnational instruments, noted by Keirse,[185] provides useful indications regarding how to best regulate mitigation doctrine. The resemblance referred to suggests a two-statement rule as the best approach to formulate the provision: first setting a limitation on recovery as a consequence of the failure to take reasonable action to avoid the aggravation of losses, and secondly including expenses incurred in mitigating in damages owed to the innocent party. Also noteworthy to bear in mind is that the mitigation doctrine is already present and binding in Brazil, to the extent that the CISG applies – as the country is one of the signatories of this instrument.

Evidently, the level of abstraction and details reflected in the formulation of a rule to regulate the mitigation doctrine must reflect the legal and cultural background of the jurisdiction, as seen in this Chapter. General provisions can be a solution to resolve the main picture (whether there is a duty to act on the innocent party; whether it applies to contracts and torts); detailed ones can try to guide future discussions (what constitutes reasonable actions; whether substitute transactions are

---

[185] Keirse describes CESL's article 163 as being "identical to Article 3:704 of the *Draft Common Frame of Reference* (DCFR), which in turn is identical do Article 9:505(1) by the *Lando Commission's Principles of European Law* (PECL), which, again, resembles Article 77 of the *United Nations Convention on Contracts for the International Sale of Goods* (CISG) (1980)", in Anne Keirse, 'Why the Proposed Optional Common European Sales Law Has Not, But Should Have, Abandoned the Principle of All or Nothing: A Guide to How to Sanction the Duty to Mitigate the Loss' (2011) 19 *European Review of Private Law*, 961

expected; extra losses and gains that result from mitigation; who bears the risk of mitigating). Nevertheless, the clear international tendency to stipulate an express duty to mitigate leads to one conclusion: the first step must be taken. The next chapter explores how that may be done in Brazil.

CHAPTER 5

217

5.1 Introduction

After focusing the research on Common and Civil law jurisdictions in Chapters 3 and 4, either experienced or inexperienced in applying the mitigation doctrine, it is time now to go back to the starting point of the present research: the finding that Brazilian courts repeatedly apply a so-called duty to mitigate loss, not expressly referred to in the existing legislation, nor duly debated by legal commentators, when deciding cases of breach of contract and torts. This chapter therefore answers the research question as to the most appropriate way to regulate the duty to mitigate in Brazil. It was found in Chapter 2 that this application is not uniform as to either the grounds or the effects of the mitigation principle, as both court decisions and writers refer to different existing rules in the Brazilian Civil Code (good faith, causation, contributory negligence, among others) as bases for limiting the full recovery principle. This led to the conclusion that the absence of express regulation of the duty to mitigate constitutes a gap in the national legislation, especially as Brazil is a Civil Law jurisdiction, in which the ideal holds that all rules must pre-exist and be expressed in codes and laws.

Thus, with the comparative research methodology developed during the elaboration of the thesis having focused on the application of the mitigation principle in each of the jurisdictions selected, it is time to present the final conclusions and the proposal to amend the Civil Code of Brazil so as to regulate the mitigation doctrine.

5.2 Summary of findings

The research analysed in Chapter 2 confirmed the hypothesis presented in Chapter 1 that the lack of express regulation of mitigation of loss leaves a gap in the Brazilian Civil Code. It showed that uncertainty as to the application of the mitigation doctrine, divergence as to its ground, a lack of rules defining its main requirements and practical aspects, and differences in how the courts interpret the duty to mitigate, together create the need for an express provision in order to meet the requirements of a Civil Law system for a clear legal basis for judicial decisions as well as to harmonize its understanding by parties and their legal advisers and its application by the courts.

Subsequently, Chapter 3 put the spotlight on the evolution of the duty to mitigate in different Common Law jurisdictions – with special focus on English and American courts. This formed the starting point of the investigation as Common Law systems have the longest and most extensive experience of applying an express duty to mitigate. Practical and procedural aspects were detailed, such as its application in tort and contract law, the circumstances in which substitute transactions would be required or not, the treatment of extra losses or extra benefits arising from reasonable mitigating conduct, and the location of the burden of proof on the defendant as to a potential failure to mitigate. The main tensions raised by legal commentators regarding theoretical aspects and controversial cases were also investigated: good faith, altruism, fairness and efficient use of resources were presented as possible grounds for the mitigation doctrine that could justify placing both a burden to mitigate and the risk in mitigating on the innocent party, and defending it against the accusations that it threatens the binding force of contracts. Two justifications were found to be especially persuasive: looked at from the perspective of the parties, mitigation ensures fairness between them, while from the perspective of society mitigation promotes economic efficiency.

The moment the duty arises was identified, it was explained that the duty is limited to incurring reasonable expenses and making reasonable efforts to mitigate the extent of the loss, and the relation between the duty to mitigate and the remedy of specific performance was analyzed. The chapter also investigated how the standard of reasonable conduct expected from the innocent party is conceptualized in relation to expenses, litigation and reputation, and, finally, the relationship (and distinction) between the duty to mitigate loss and other doctrines which limit recovery of damages. This chapter provided both insight into issues which will have to be considered in the drafting of a Brazilian mitigation provision and provided a basis for comparing functional equivalents in Civil Law systems.

Finally, Chapter 4 focused on how selected Civil Law jurisdictions deal with the duty to mitigate. Three different models and moments in legislation were analyzed. These ranged from European France where there has been much criticism from legal commentators of the absence of an express mitigation rule, leading to recent law-reform proposals to include mitigation as an express limit to the full recovery principle, through Germany where the mitigation doctrine is present in the Civil Code but disguised under the contributory negligence label, to Brazil's neighbour Argentina with its recently enacted Civil Code containing an express mitigation provision. This analysis revealed an increasing trend for Civil Law countries to follow the Common Law example by adopting express provisions regarding mitigation, each in their particular way. It showed that a duty to mitigate is no longer considered to be inconsistent with the principle of full compensation which is traditionally regarded as fundamental in Civil Law countries, including Brazil. As Anne Keirse, a supporter of the mitigation doctrine in Civil Law countries has pointed out, "a flexible apportionment of the damage is called for, as the liability of the defendant does not entail that the aggrieved party is freed from any responsibility to take reasonable care for his own interest."[1] Indeed, the main justifications in Common Law jurisdictions for the duty to mitigate, fairness between the parties and economic efficiency, are now also endorsed in Civil Law jurisdictions, as the example of the French law reform project shows particularly clearly.[2] This would conveniently

---

[1] Anne Keirse, 'Why the Proposed Optional Common European Sales Law Has Not, But Should Have, Abandoned the Principle of All or Nothing: A Guide to How to Sanction the Duty to Mitigate the Loss' (2011) 19 *European Review of Private Law* 976.
[2] See 4.2.2.1 above.

match with the values present in the Brazilian legal context.[3] Additionally, transnational instruments – which aim to harmonize rules for different countries – were compared, confirming the general trend for legislative instruments to expressly deal and regulate the mitigation doctrine. In addition to revealing this trend, the chapter highlighted difficulties arising from the absence of an express duty to mitigate as well as further issues which will have to be considered in the drafting of a Brazilian mitigation provision, including various possibilities for the structure and wording of such a provision.

Taken together, this comparative research allows the duty to mitigate to be confirmed as an autonomous doctrine, with increasing application in most jurisdictions belonging to both the Common Law and Civil Law families as well as in relevant international instruments. Importantly, this includes Argentina, with which Brazil shares a close legal relationship, and the Principles of Latin American Contract Law (PLACL). This confirms the initial hypothesis that the inclusion of an express provision regarding the mitigation doctrine would represent a step forward in the development of the Brazilian legal framework. The reasons why Brazil should regulate the duty to mitigate, according to the findings of this research, are numerous: First, it is the way to provide an express provision to ground and harmonize the application of the principle by the courts. Second, because doing so would allow a uniform application of the doctrine, supported by its own provision, with a precise definition of the content of the rule, which will identify the trigger for its application and specify what would be expected from parties. Third, because to acknowledge the mitigation doctrine as an autonomous principle by regulating it expressly would place Brazil alongside the most up-to-date legal trend and would promote individual

---

[3] The pursuit of fairness finds a perfect complement in article 422, of the Civil Code, which expressly imposes the parties the duty of good faith throughout their entire relation (see section 2.2 above). Similarly, the economic argument of efficiency perfectly relates to the limited availability of resources inherent to an emerging country as Brazil.

justice in the sense of fairness between the parties (that is to say, good faith) as well as the social goal of efficient use of economic resources. And finally, because such a provision would harmonize the local framework with that of the CISG,[4] to which Brazil is a signatory.

5.3 Issues arising from the research

The research conducted in the previous chapters not only supports the express regulation of a duty to mitigate in Brazil, but also reveals a range of practical issues which need to be addressed when drafting a new provision and provides a basis for deciding how to do so. Ten such issues will be outlined in this section, along with conclusions on how to address them, in both cases drawing on the previous chapters. This will provide a firm foundation for developing in the next section a concrete proposal for a new provision for inclusion in Brazil's Civil Code.

5.3.1 Should the mitigation rule form part of a provision on contributory fault or should it be an independent provision?

The Civil Law jurisdiction where mitigation of loss has been expressly required the longest, and where the mitigation principle is consequently most firmly established – Germany – treats this as an aspect of the reduction of damages for contributory negligence.[5] This has been followed in a number of other jurisdictions and has recently been supported by Anne Keirse, a thoughtful proponent of requiring mitigation in Civil Law systems.[6] The approach followed in Argentina's new art. 1710 is very close to this: although it expressly refers to duties to adopt measures to decrease the magnitude of damage and not to aggravate damage, it sets these out

---

[4] CISG available at <https://www.uncitral.org/pdf/english/texts/sales/cisg/V1056997-CISG-e-book.pdf> accessed 7 August 2022.

[5] Section 4.2.1 above.

[6] Keirse (n 1).

alongside and in the same paragraph as the duty to adopt "reasonable measures to prevent damage from occurring".[7] The advantage of this approach is that it associates the mitigation principle with a doctrine which is well-established in Civil Law jurisdictions, including Brazil.[8]

However, the most recent trend is to treat mitigation as an autonomous principle regulated independently of contributory negligence in a separate article. This is the case in the French law reform proposal[9] as well as in all transnational instruments, including the CISG, to which Brazil is a party, and the Principles of Latin American Contract Law (PLACL).[10] Moreover, Treitel has convincingly shown that contributory negligence and mitigation are distinct concepts, as the former is concerned with partial responsibility for bringing about the event causing the loss, while the latter concerns the need to take positive steps to limit the loss caused by the defendant's default.[11]

For these reasons it is proposed that the mitigation principle should be regulated in an independent, separate provision in Brazil's Civil Code rather than as an aspect of contributory negligence. An important point to bear in mind when accommodating the duty to mitigate loss, will be that it is relevant to define the moment when it arises, for this differentiates mitigation from other applicable doctrines.

5.3.2 Should the mitigation rule apply to both contract and tort?

In Common Law jurisdictions the duty to mitigate applies to victims of both breaches of contract and of torts. This is also the position in Germany, where section 254 appears in the General Part of the Civil

---

[7] Section 4.3.1 above.
[8] Section 4.2.2.1 above.
[9] Section 4.2.2.1 above.
[10] Section 4.4 above.
[11] Guenter H. Treitel, *Remedies for Breach of Contract: A Comparative Account* (Oxford University Press 1988).

Code,[12] in the French law reform proposal,[13] and in Argentina, where art. 1710 imposes broad and general duties to limit and to avoid aggravating loss.[14] Because they focus exclusively on contracts, the various transnational instruments do not provide any direct help in this regard, but they do not appear to be incompatible with applying the duty to torts as well.[15] Perhaps most importantly, the most significant rationales for a duty to mitigate – fairness between the parties and economic efficiency – are equally applicable regardless of whether a loss is caused by a breach of contract or a tort.[16] Finally, because some courts and commentators In Brazil have already required mitigation in respect of both contract and tort,[17] there is a need to provide a clear legislative basis in respect of both.

Accordingly, the new mitigation principle in Brazil should apply to both breaches of contract and tort.

5.3.3 Should the mitigation principle be conceptualized as a duty?

Although it is usual in Common Law jurisdictions to refer to "the duty to mitigate", it has been questioned whether the mitigation principle truly imposes a duty on the victim of the breach of contract or tort since it does not give an enforceable claim-right to the other party but merely leads to a reduction in the victim's claim against the latter.[18] In Germany it is accordingly referred to as on "Obliegenheit" rather than a "Pflicht".[19] Interestingly, the proposed French provision does not use the language

---

[12] 4.2.1 above.
[13] 4.2.2.1 above.
[14] 4.3 above.
[15] 4.4 above.
[16] See the discussion of the rationales in Common Law systems in chapter 3.
[17] See chapter 2 and specifically Daniel Pires Novais Dias, 'O duty to mitigate loss no direito civil brasileiro e o encargo de evitar o próprio dano' (2011) 12 *Revista de Direito Privado*, 89, 99.
[18] Chapter 3 above.
[19] 4.2.1 above.

of duties to articulate the mitigation principle but simply sets out the consequences of a failure to mitigate,[20] whereas the new Argentinian provision expressly imposes a duty.[21] The various transnational provisions reflect both approaches: ULIS art. 88 and CISG art. 74 both use the language of duty by respectively stating that the victim "shall adopt" or "must take" reasonable measures to limit loss; but the more recent soft-law instruments, PICC, PECL, CESL and PLACL all follow the same approach as has been proposed in France.[22] In addition, the latter group can be sub-divided further: on the one hand, PICC, PECL and CESL describe the consequences of a failure to mitigate in terms of its effect on the liability of the defendant,[23] whereas PLACL art. 109 simply states that, "Compensation is subject to reduction when the obligee has failed to take reasonable measures to mitigate loss in good faith".[24]

The choice between these different approaches is not easy. Brazil's legal-cultural links to Argentina, as well as its membership of CISG, point towards adopting a duty-formulation in the proposed new provision. However, the most modern position is simply to set out the consequences of a failure to mitigate, and this is the approach that was preferred by the influential group of leading Latin American academics (including from Brazil) who drafted the PLACL. The latter shows that an important advantage of this approach is that it makes it possible to set out in a clear and elegant way the various consequences of a failure to mitigate,[25] which will help to advance the goal of bringing certainty and clarity to Brazilian

---

[20] Section 4.2.2.1 above.
[21] Section 4.3 above.
[22] Section 4.4. above.
[23] Sections 4.4.3,4.4.4 and 4.4.5.
[24] Section 4.4.6.
[25] In full, Article 109 provides:
(1) Compensation is subject to reduction when the obligee has failed to take reasonable measures to mitigate loss in good faith. Reduction shall correspond to the amount by which the loss could have been mitigated.
(2) The obligee is entitled to compensation for what it has allocated towards mitigating the loss, even if these measures have been ineffective.

law. The PLACL approach should therefore also be followed in Brazil (with suitable adjustments).

5.3.4 What standard of conduct should be expected of the innocent party?

In both, the Common Law and Civil Law jurisdictions, the innocent party is expected to act reasonably. But the standard of what constitutes reasonable action, in both legal families and in the many jurisdictions analyzed in this thesis, is far from strict. With reference to the jurisdictions analyzed, the Common Law experience shows that the duty to mitigate should not be a very demanding one, in order not to impose a heavy additional burden to the already aggrieved party.[26] As to Civil Law systems, the German approach of assimilating mitigation to contributory negligence also seems to require a low standard of care, expressly detailing some specific situations in which action will be required.[27] In fact, as was observed in Chapter 4, the German duty appears to be less demanding of the victim than its Common Law counterpart. In Argentina, where reasonable action is expressed in article 1710 of the Civil and Commercial Code with the reference to "the circumstances and according to good faith", legal commentators have unanimously stated the standard of reasonableness to be relatively low.[28] Finally, what exactly is required by the broad French formulation referring to "safe and reasonable measures", will ultimately depend, as argued in Chapter 4,[29] on how the French courts interpret the rule and apply it to concrete cases.

This indicates that no jurisdiction has moved forward in regulating the abstract concept of reasonableness, at least not specifically for the

---

[26] See Section 3.3.2, *Banco de Portugal v Waterlow & Sons Ltd* [1932] AC 452 (HL) and Dori Kimel, *From Promise To Contract: Towards A Liberal Theory Of Contract* (Hart Publishing 2003).
[27] Section 4.2.1 above.
[28] See Section 4.3.1. and notes 419 and 420.
[29] Section 4.2.2.1 above.

purposes of applying it to mitigation.[30] There is a positive side to this, for it allows this standard to connect with other situations which also call for reasonable action, thereby harmonizing its meaning throughout the legal system, according to each jurisdiction's legal and cultural context.

As for the new Brazilian rule, the same applies: whilst the innocent party should be required to act reasonably, it is not within the scope of the proposed mitigation provision to define what reasonable action means. Existing interpretations of reasonableness will be considered and each concrete situation will call for the judgement of the parties and courts: on one side, there will be situations in which the party will be required to act by existing law, and on the other side there will be situations in which excessively risky or expensive action will not be expected. And between those, reasonableness should remain a matter of fact, and not law. It is also worth pointing out that Article 422 of the Brazilian Civil Code makes reference to probity and good faith in the execution and conclusion of contracts, and thus provides a resource that the courts can draw on in considering what are reasonable steps, in a way that harmonizes a new duty to mitigate with other pre-existing rules. Further resources are provided by Articles 421, which refers to the social function of contracts, and Article 187, which provides that an unlawful act is committed if the holder of a right, when exercising it, manifestly exceeds the limits imposed by his economic or social purpose, good faith or good customs.

5.3.5 How far should the mitigation principle reach?

Differences regarding the reach of the mitigation doctrine exist as to its application beyond the prevention of the aggravation of loss: should the duty also cover the reduction of the loss caused? Common Law systems have uniformly developed to consider that the duty to mitigate encompasses both the reduction of the loss and avoidance of the

---

[30] Section 3.3.6 above.

aggravation of the losses.[31] The same is true for most Civil Law countries and transnational instruments, some of which make express reference to the reduction of losses (besides the prevention of their aggravation): Article 254 (2) of the BGB mentions "to avert or reduce the damage";[32] article 1710 of Argentinian Civil and Commercial Code also mentions "to avoid or reduce";[33] the PICC,[34] the PECL[35] and the CESL [36] all refer to "reduction of losses"; and, finally, the ULIS,[37] the CISG[38] and the PLACL[39] mention the mitigation of damages in a broad sense.

The only exception to this found in the research was the French law reform project,[40] whose provision restricts the mitigation concept to "avoid the increase" of one's own loss. The French project also limits the provision on mitigation in a further respect: is not applicable to personal injury claims (the French system is notable for being protective to victims). These restrictions are subject to criticism from legal commentators, as it places France a step behind to the international trend for a broader mitigation rule.

In this regard, there is absolutely no reason for the Brazilian provision to differentiate between the reduction and the non-aggravation of losses in the application of the mitigation rule, nor to restrict it from applying to personal injuries. There is no local reason to justify such a move, and, as we have seen, this would be out of line with the international tendency.

---

[31] Chapter 3.
[32] Section 4.2.1.
[33] Section 4.3.1.
[34] Section 4.4.3.
[35] Section 4.4.4.
[36] Section 4.4.5.
[37] Section 4.4.1.
[38] Section 4.4.2.
[39] Section 4.4.6.
[40] Section 4.2.2.1.

5.3.6 Should mitigation apply only to the remedy of damages or should it also affect specific performance?

In Common Law systems, damages is the primary remedy and specific performance is exceptionally available when damages would be inadequate.[41] In Civil Law systems, specific performance is the primary remedy or at least available at the option of the victim of the breach.[42] This means that, whereas in a Common Law jurisdiction the duty to mitigate would affect most claims for breach of contract, in a Civil Law system, on the other hand, its application could be avoided by a victim who opts for claiming specific performance rather than damages (except for the situations mentioned in article 275 of the German Civil Code,[43] 1740 of the Argentinian Civil and Commercial Code,[44] 1222 of the French Code[45] and 46 and 61 of the CISG).[46]

The tension between specific performance and mitigation is to be resolved in light of the local existing rules. As in other Civil Law systems, Article 475 of the Brazilian Civil Code,[47] as mentioned in Chapter 2 section 2.2, grants the victim of a breach of contract the discretion of choosing between specific performance of the contract or its resolution. However, unlike the Codes mentioned in the previous paragraph, it does not contain limitations to this discretion. If the choice is to be preserved in the hands of the innocent party, a new provision on mitigation should

---

[41] Section 3.3.5 above.

[42] Chapter 4.

[43] Section 4.2.1 above.

[44] Section 4.3.1 above.

[45] Section 4.2.2 above.

[46] Section 4.4 above.

[47] "A party injured by non-performance may apply for dissolution of the contract, if he does not prefer to demand performance of it, and in either case, the injured party has the right to indemnification for losses and damage" (original version: A parte lesada pelo inadimplemento pode pedir a resolução do contrato, se não preferir exigir-lhe o cumprimento, cabendo, em qualquer dos casos, indenização por perdas e danos).

not restrict this choice and should therefore only apply to the innocent party's claim for damages. Whilst this may mean that the duty to mitigate could be "evaded" by the innocent party in circumstances where this would not be possible in a Common Law system, this is an unavoidable outcome of a difference in approach between Brazil and the Common Law tradition when it comes to specific performance. Moreover, once a duty to mitigate has been included in the Civil Code, the courts could consider whether this means that Articles 187, 421 and 422, which require respect for the social function of contracts and good faith, restrict how this choice may be exercised. As explained in 5.3.4, these provisions have important implications for what constitutes reasonable behavior by a contracting party. Here it is also worth mentioning that the binding force of contracts is not absolute, for judicial revision (or even termination) is permitted in "exceptional and limited" situations[48] (for example, where the breaching party establishes that t their failure to perform was due to *force majeure*). And in any case, as in other Civil Law jurisdictions, the mitigation doctrine will play an important role when the remedy sought by the claimant is damages.

Further, in the case of anticipatory repudiation (when a contracting party, before the due date, makes it clear that he will not perform on the due date), the outcome in Common Law jurisdictions might be different according to the country (with England allowing the innocent party to uphold performance, and the United States favouring mitigation).[49] In Civil Law jurisdictions such as Brazil, as much as in Argentina, there is no rule recognizing anticipatory repudiation of contracts, meaning that the innocent party is allowed choose between upholding the contract or seeking damages when performance is due, in which case the duty to mitigate will only arise if and when the other party's obligation becomes

---

[48] Lei n° 10.406, de 10 de janeiro de 2002 (Código Civil). Available at <http://www.planalto.gov.br/ccivil_03/leis/2002/l10406.htm> accessed 7 August 2022, art. 421-A, III.

[49] Section 3.3.5 above.

due. This arrangement should not be affected by the eventual regulation of the mitigation doctrine, and this is therefore not something that would need to be addressed in a new mitigation provision in the Civil Code of Brazil.

5.3.7 Should additional costs caused by mitigating measures be recoverable?

As evidenced in Chapters 3 and 4, whenever the innocent party incurs additional costs in the reasonable attempt to mitigate the losses caused by the other party, such costs will fall under the original claim in case mitigation is not successful. Acknowledged by precedents in Common and Civil Law jurisdictions, this is also reflected in transnational instruments like the PICC (article 7.4.5) and the CISG (articles 75 and 76). Brazilian courts might well come to the same conclusion by themselves, since it seems logical to allow the recovery of such additional loss as these were incurred by the innocent party in the best interest of the other party, as it is the party in breach who would have benefited if the mitigation steps had been successful, and such recovery has been widely permitted with no further questioning. Nevertheless, in order to avoid uncertainty it seems appropriate to address this in the new provision, especially to reinforce the limitation of such additional expenses to what is appropriate under the circumstances of the case.

5.3.8 Should actual savings made and benefits gained as a result of mitigation reduce the compensation recoverable?

Just as much as the additional costs incurred by mitigation should be recoverable, any savings and benefits gained as a result of mitigating should reduce the compensation recoverable. After all, it would make no sense to be compensated twice for the same loss (by the result of the successful action to mitigate and also by the breaching party). Common law courts' precedents are uniform on this matter, and the German Civil Code also includes express provisions regarding this (Articles 326 (2) and 615).

In the Brazilian context, however, it seems unnecessary to address this issue in the new provision, for this situation would be covered by unjust enrichment, regulated in Brazil through article 884 of the Civil Code,[50] which prevents someone from being enriched without just cause at the expense of another person. That would apply in a situation in which the aggrieved party, who successfully reduced or avoided part of the loss, claimed recovery for a part of the loss that was never actually incurred or was later mitigated through a substitutive transaction. The claimant would not be entitled to any compensation regarding this mitigated loss, since it would result in unjust enrichment, prohibited under this provision (which, therefore, limits recoverability in similar situations).

This reasoning has not – at least not yet – been adopted in precedents or books, articles or journals. That is unsurprising, for this specific application of article 884 would be consequential to the concrete application of the mitigation doctrine that is being proposed in this thesis. But the connection between both provisions would undoubtedly arise once a claimant who successfully mitigated part of his loss, as required under the terms of a mitigation provision, were to seek recovery for non-existing losses. Such a claim could then be systematically rejected under the argument that recovery of the avoided losses would represent an unjust enrichment for the claimant.

5.3.9 Is an express provision for substitute transactions needed?

As shown in Section 3.2.2, a substitute transaction can be an effective way to mitigate loss, provided there is an available market. This is

---

[50] Article 884:" Anyone who, without just cause, is enriched at the expense of another person, will be obliged to repay the undue gain, at current monetary value." (original version: Aquele que, sem justa causa, se enriquecer à custa de outrem, será obrigado a restituir o indevidamente auferido, feita a atualização dos valores monetários).

acknowledged in precedents from Common Law countries, [51] is referred to in the BGB (setting out procedural steps in specific situations in which substitute transactions apply),[52] and is mentioned in Argentinian court decisions based on its mitigation doctrine.[53] It is also expressed in some transnational instruments,[54] but is not expressly provided for in PLACL.[55]

The experience in Argentina and in Common Law jurisdictions indicates that the absence of an express legislative requirement to mitigate loss by entering into a substitute transaction does not bring any prejudice. This may well be because it is intuitive that losses can be mitigated by seeking a (fungible) [56] substitute transaction. Indeed, the Civil Code already recognizes in Article 249 a substitute transaction as a permissible and appropriate response to a breach of contract: "In case of repudiation of delay of the debtor, if performance might be executed by a third party, the creditor is free to seek for it and claim from the debtor the costs and losses".[57] Nor is it necessary to regulate the procedural aspects of mitigation, for this concerns the concrete situation rather than the mitigation doctrine itself. Technically speaking, mitigation through a substitute transaction is not part of the mitigation rule itself, but only one of the many ways in which the rule can be applied and given effect. Therefore, the Brazilian rule need not make express provision for mitigation through substitute transaction. This is a matter that can, and should, be left to be dealt with by the courts on the basis of the requirement of reasonableness (explained in 5.3.4 above) in light of Article 249.

---

[51] *Southcott Estates Inc. v Toronto Catholic District School* 2012 SCC 51 and *100 Main Street Ltd. V W.B Sullivan Construction Ltd.* (1978) 88 DLR (3d) (Ont. CA Can).

[52] Section 4.2.1 above.

[53] Section 4.3.1 above.

[54] CISG 75, PICC 7.4.5, PECL 9-506 and CESL 164.

[55] Section 4.4.6 above.

[56] Barry E. Adler, 'Efficient breach theory through the looking glass' (2008) 83 *New York University Law Review* 1679, 1722.

[57] Original version: Se o fato puder ser executado por terceiro, será livre ao credor mandá-lo executar à custa do devedor, havendo recusa ou mora deste, sem prejuízo da indenização cabível.

5.3.10 Which party should bear the burden of proof?

In the context of the mitigation doctrine, the burden of proof concerns the failure to mitigate. This is so because mitigation is raised as a defensive argument by the defendant, which aims to reduce the damages to be awarded on the basis that they could have been mitigated by reasonable action from the claimant. In the Common Law, the question of who bears the burden of proof is answered by numerous precedents, which repeatedly place this burden on the defendant.[58] But commentators and court decisions advert to situations in which the claimant might be called upon to demonstrate that mitigating actions were actually taken.[59] As to transnational instruments, they do not regulate this matter, for their focus is on substantive issues, and not on procedural ones.

In Brazil, this situation is properly addressed by its Civil Procedural Code[60] which, in article 373, stipulates the general rule of distribution of the burden of proof in civil claims:

Art. 373. The burden of proof is on:

I - the claimant, regarding the constitutive fact of his right;

II - the defendant, as to the existence of an impediment, modification or extinction of the author's right.

§ 1st In the cases provided for by law or in view of the peculiarities of the case related to the impossibility or the excessive difficulty of fulfilling the charge under the *caput* or to facilitate obtaining proof of the contrary fact, the judge may assign the burden of proof in a different

---

[58] *Lombard North Central v Automobile World (UK) Ltd* (2010) EWCA Civ 20.
[59] Section 3.2.5 above.
[60] Available at <http://www.planalto.gov.br/ccivil_03/_Ato2015-2018/2015/Lei/L13105.htm> accessed 13 August 2022.

manner, provided that it does so by reasoned decision, in which case it should give the party the opportunity to discharge the burden assigned to it.

(original version: Art. 373. O ônus da prova incumbe:

I - ao autor, quanto ao fato constitutivo de seu direito;
II - ao réu, quanto à existência de fato impeditivo, modificativo ou extintivo do direito do autor.

§ 1º Nos casos previstos em lei ou diante de peculiaridades da causa relacionadas à impossibilidade ou à excessiva dificuldade de cumprir o encargo nos termos do *caput* ou à maior facilidade de obtenção da prova do fato contrário, poderá o juiz atribuir o ônus da prova de modo diverso, desde que o faça por decisão fundamentada, caso em que deverá dar à parte a oportunidade de se desincumbir do ônus que lhe foi atribuído.

Thus, according to this provision, the general rule is that the defendant will bear the burden of proving the facts that limit the claimant's claim, while the claimant might be told to produce evidence when it is easier for him/her to prove the mitigating steps taken at such case. Mitigation claims will fall under this rule, with the result that there is no need to address such matters in the new substantive provision to be proposed.

5.4 How should Brazil regulate the duty to mitigate?

As a Civil Law system, Brazilian law is codified, with all the main principles of private law, including Contract Law and Tort Law, set out systematically in the Civil Code.[61] The appropriate way to incorporate a

---

[61] Section 2.2 above.

duty to mitigate into Brazilian law is therefore through amendment of the current Civil Code,[62] specifically of the sections which deal with recovery of damages (and its limitations) in torts (Article 402) and contracts (Article 945). As already alluded to in the previous section, and as further discussed below, the location of the duty in the Code means that the wording of the proposed provision must take account of existing provisions with which it will interact, such as the duty of good faith in Article 422. To fit systematically into the Code, the amendments will also need to include the duty to mitigate as another limitation on the full recovery principle, using terminology that corresponds to that of the Code. In keeping with the style of the Code, the wording should be concise and, yet, lay down as much as possible of the rationale of the mitigation doctrine, clearly enough for parties to understand and the courts to apply it.

For the reasons outlined in Chapter 4, it is particularly important to take account of the example provided by Argentina.[63] However, although the approach adopted in Argentina has been very useful in answering the questions in the previous section which arose from the comparative research conducted in this thesis, it is less useful when it comes to the wording of a new provision for Brazil. This is because Article 1710 of the Argentinian 2015 Civil and Commercial Code incorporates a duty to mitigate into a broader duty to prevent loss.[64] However, the conclusion reached in the previous section was that the mitigation principle should be regulated in an independent, separate provision in Brazil's Civil Code rather than as an aspect of contributory negligence.[65] As we saw, this is the approach adopted in all transnational instruments, including the CISG, to which Brazil is a party, and the Principles of Latin American Contract

[62] Article 61 of the Federal Constitution indicates those who can propose such amendment: Congressmen, the President, Supreme and Superior Courts, the General Prosecutor and any group of at least 1% of citizens. Available at <http://www.planalto.gov.br/ccivil_03/constituicao/constituicao.htm> accessed 13 August 2022.
[63] Section 4.3 above.
[64] Section 4.3.1 above.
[65] Section 5.3.1 above.

Law (PLACL). As these result from international efforts to come up with systematic guidance as to the mitigation doctrine, they represent the "state of the art". Moreover, it was also concluded that the mitigation principle should not be expressed in terms of a duty, as in Article 1710, but rather, as in PLACL, by setting out the consequences of a failure to mitigate.[66]

In light of this, the following ten conclusions reached on the basis of the comparative research and analysis conducted in this thesis must be reflected in a new provision in the Civil Code of Brazil:

(i) The mitigation principle should be regulated in an independent, separate provision (5.3.1).

(ii) The mitigation principle in should apply to both breaches of contract and to tort liability (5.3.2).

(iii) The mitigation principle should not be formulated as a duty, but rather be expressed by setting out the consequences of a failure to mitigate (5.3.3).

(iv) Whilst the innocent party should be required to act reasonably, it is not within the scope of the proposed mitigation provision to define what reasonable action means (5.3.4).

(v) The mitigation principle should not differentiate between the reduction of loss and the aggravation of loss, or restrict its application to personal injuries. It should apply to all loss (5.3.5).

(vi) The mitigation provision should refer only to claims for damages (5.3.6).

(vii)The provision should provide that an innocent party can recover additional costs incurred in the reasonable attempt to mitigate the losses caused by the other party (5.3.7).

---

[66] Section 5.3.2 above.

(viii) The provision need not deal with any savings and benefits gained by the innocent party as a result of mitigation (5.3.8).

(ix) The Brazilian rule need not make express provision for mitigation through substitute transactions (5.3.9).

(x) There is no need to address the location of the burden of proof in the new proposed new provision as this matter is dealt with by the Civil Procedure Code (5.3.10).

Importantly, the analysis in section 5.3 leading to these conclusions took specific account of existing provisions in the Code with which the proposed new provision will co-exist and interact: Articles 187, 249, 421, 422, 475 and 884; as well as Article 373 of the Civil Procedure Code. These conclusions therefore ensure that the proposal will fit systematically into the Civil Code.

5.5 Proposed wording for a Brazilian mitigation rule

According to the Brazilian Civil Code structure,[67] it is Title IV that deals in general terms with the consequences of contractual breaches and torts. This Title deals with losses and damages specifically in Chapter III – Articles 402 to 405. Within Chapter III, Article 402 sets out what losses or damages are owed to the creditor (that is, are recoverable by the claimant) by expressly including both actual loss and loss of profit. Following the rationale that the function of the mitigation doctrine is to provide part of the specification of what is included in losses and damages, and in light of the conclusions in Section 5.4 above, it is proposed that the Civil Code of Brazil should be amended to finally regulate the mitigation doctrine in the Brazilian legal framework by introducing a new Article 402-A which will complement Article 402's specification of what is included by stating what

---

[67] Described in Section 2.1 above.

is excluded from losses and damages, namely losses that could have been reduced by taking mitigating steps that are reasonable in the circumstances:

GENERAL EXISTING RULE	ADDITIONAL RULE PROPOSED
Art. 402. Unless otherwise expressly provided by law, the losses and damages owed to the creditor include both actual loss and reasonable loss of profit.	**Art. 402-A. Losses that could have been reduced or avoided by the creditor, once aware of the debtor's conduct and factual context, by taking mitigating steps that are reasonable in the circumstances of the case, will be excluded; In case such steps are taken, additional losses incurred in taking them will be included and additional gains will be offset.[512]**

The proposed wording resembles that proposed by Lopes, for it addresses the limitation on avoidable losses and the situation of extra losses.[69] However, it fundamentally differs from his original proposal as Lopes proposed to regulate the mitigation doctrine by adding paragraphs to Article 403, which deals with the remoteness rule – suggesting a common ground between both doctrines, which was rejected in this thesis.[70] He also showed concern to expressly offset eventual gains that the claimant might have received as a result of his mitigating actions; this aspect is not contemplated in the present proposal, based on the understanding,

---

[68] Portuguese version: Perdas e danos que poderiam ter sido evitadas pelo credor, uma vez ciente da conduta do devedor e do contexto fático, mediante tomada de medidas mitigadoras razoáveis para as circunstâncias do caso, serão excluídas da indenização. Caso tais medidas sejam tomadas, perdas adicionais incorridas serão somadas e ganhos adicionais serão deduzidos do valor a ser indenizado.

[69] Section 1.3 above.

[70] Section 3.3.2 above.

explained above, that Article 884 would be sufficient to prevent one from seeking compensation for a loss that has been successfully avoided (totally or partially).[71] Comino's proposal, in turn, was to regulate the mitigation doctrine together with the contributory negligence principle, through amending the wording of Article 945. This proposal is contrary to the argument in this thesis according to which contributory negligence and mitigation should both be contemplated by legislation, but through different rules which not always will have a common application.[72]

Compared with PLACL,[73] the proposed provision is conceptually similar in as much as its starting point is the limitation of the creditor's entitlement to obtain compensation rather than the debtor's liability for the losses caused. This is different from the other transnational instruments examined in Chapter 3 (PICC[74] and PECL), [75] but it appears to be the most appropriate approach since the mitigation doctrine is meant to affect compensation, the remedy, not change the parties' primary liability. Structurally, the proposed provision, like Article 109 of the PLACL, makes no express reference to substitutive transactions, on the ground that this will arise as a reasonable and available mitigating step depending on the practical situation, and therefore will be expected from the creditor without needing to be spelt out. Also, both the proposal above and PLACL find it enough to expressly mention reasonableness in the first sentence, which deals with the creditor's expected conduct, leaving it implicit in the provisions in the second sentence regarding recovery of the costs of mitigation. On the other hand, a clear difference between the proposed provision and PLACL is the reference in the proposal to the moment the duty arises (once the creditor is "aware of debtor's conduct"). The need to spell this out could be countered by an interpretation of Article 402-A

---

[71] Section 5.3.8 above.
[72] Section 3.3.2 above.
[73] Section 4.4.6.
[74] Section 4.4.3.
[75] Section 4.4.4.

according to which it would not be reasonable to expect someone to act in response to conduct that he is not aware of. However, the proposed wording is intended to represent an improvement in the regulation of the mitigation doctrine because it resolves a potential argument between the parties – especially in cases of substitutive transaction in falling markets – by taking a burden from the creditor (the burden to determine and be judged on when it is reasonable to act) and transferring it to the debtor (who will need to bring evidence that the creditor had become aware of his defaulting conduct).

When accommodating mitigation in the overall architecture of the Code, it is necessary to differentiate it from other applicable doctrines, and for this reason it is relevant to define the moment the requirement arises. Therefore the proposed Article 402-A provides that mitigation shall apply when the victim becomes aware of the debtor's default and thus the need for taking action to limit their own losses. In the Brazilian legal system, the new provision will also coexist with articles that prevent unjust enrichment (Article 884, mentioned above) and those that resolve tensions like the discretion to choose specific performance (Article 475), the treatment of unreasonable actions (Article 187) and the burden of proof (Article 373, of the Civil Procedure Code). These provide resources for interpreting the proposed Article 402-A and for resolving the issues identified in earlier chapters.

The tension between specific performance (of contracts) and mitigation,[76] for instance, is to be resolved by applying local existing rules. Article 475 of the Brazilian Civil Code, mentioned in section 2.2,[77] grants discretion to the creditor to choose between specific performance

---

[76] Section 3.2.1.1.

[77] "A party injured by non-performance may apply for dissolution of the contract, if he does not prefer to demand performance of it, and in either case, the injured party has the right to indemnification for losses and damage" (original version: A parte lesada pelo inadimplemento pode pedir a resolução do contrato, se não preferir exigir-lhe o cumprimento, cabendo, em qualquer dos casos, indenização por perdas e danos).

of the contract or its resolution. Therefore, if the choice is to be preserved in the hands of the innocent party, the requirement of mitigation must not suppress the capacity to make this choice. For this reason the proposal will not require mitigation until the innocent party chooses damages. At this point, it is worth mentioning that the binding force of contracts is not absolute, for the judicial revision (or even termination) is admitted in "exceptional and limited" situations[78] (this might be argued by the breaching party, in case such breach derives from *force majeure*, for instance). The principle of mitigation is therefore compatible with the Code's overall treatment of the binding force of contracts.

Also, determining what constitutes reasonable steps to mitigate, including whether substitute transactions are required, by applying a relevant existing provision provides a way to harmonize the duty with other pre-existing rules. For example, Article 422, mentioned in section 2.2, makes reference to probity and good faith in the execution and conclusion of contracts, while Article 249 might also be adopted as reference for such a situation: "In case of repudiation by reason of delay by the debtor, if performance might be executed by a third party, the creditor is free to seek it and claim from the debtor the costs and losses" [original version: Se o fato puder ser executado por terceiro, será livre ao credor mandá-lo executar à custa do devedor, havendo recusa ou mora deste, sem prejuízo da indenização cabível]. Thus the need for substitute transactions can be decided on a case-by-case basis, according to what is deemed to be reasonable in each case, by referring to these existing articles.

Finally, the risks in taking reasonable action to mitigate (Article 187, of the Brazilian Civil Code, classifies as illegal an action that "manifestly exceeds the limits imposed by its economic or social purpose, by good faith or by good conduct"), the burden of proof (Article 373, of the Civil

---

[78] Brazilian Civil Code (available at <http://www.planalto.gov.br/ccivil_03/leis/2002/l10406.htm> accessed 13 August 2022), art. 421-A, III.

Procedure Code,[79] provides for the burden on the defendant over facts that "impede, modify or exclude" the right of the claimant), and the treatment of extra losses or gains (Article 884, of the Brazilian Civil Code, establishes recovery for unjust enrichment) should be dealt with according to the existing provisions.

In these ways, the wording of the proposed new article and its location within the Code's broader complex of norms will provide guidance to the public and their legal advisers as well as to the courts, prevent obscurity, and avoid collisions with other rules.

[79] Available at <http://www.planalto.gov.br/ccivil_03/_Ato2015-2018/2015/Lei/L13105.htm> accessed 13 August 2022.

TABLE OF CASES

Jurisdiction	Year	Case (parties or docket number)	Section
Argentina	2017	Expte. Nº 1-62119-2017 - "Fal María Cristina c/ Rindes y Cultivos Das SA S/ daños y perj. incump. contractual (exc. Estado)" – CÁMARA DE APELACIONES EN LO CIVIL Y COMERCIAL DE AZUL (Buenos Aires) – SALA PRIMERA - 19/09/2017	Argentina
Argentina	2016	Expte. Nº 2-60404-2015 - "Fal Teves Alberto Ariel c/ Ferrosur Roca SA S/daños y perj. autom. c/les. O muerte (exc. Estado)" – CÁMARA DE APELACIONES EN LO CIVIL Y COMERCIAL DEPARTAMENTAL (AZUL) – SALA II – 16/05/2016	Argentina
Argentina	2019	Expte. Nº 13-04825788-1 (012053-303952) - "Fal María Nilva Dias Ephima Palacio y Otros c/ Monica Beatriz Molina / acción preventiva" – TRIBUNAL DE GESTION ASOCIADA-TERCERO PODER JUDICIAL MENDOZA – 23/10/2019	Argentina
Brazil	2004	TJ/PR Appeal 158909-7, 6th Civil Chamber	Chapter 1

Brazil	2006	TJ/SP Appeal 1.029.972-4, 16th Chamber of Private Law	Chapter 1
Brazil	2010	TJ/SP Appeal 992.06.073838, 30th Chamber of Private Law	Chapter 1
Brazil	2009	TJ/SP Incident Appeal 1.288.546-0/2, 31st Chamber of Private Law	Chapter 1
Brazil	2010	STJ Special Appeal 758.518/PR	Chapters 1 and 2
Brazil	2020	Special Appeal 1.819.069/SC	Chapter 1
Brazil	2021	Petition on Special Appeal 1.733.695/SC	Chapter 1
Brazil	2021	Appeal 1019063-59.2020.8.26.0562	Chapter 1
Brazil	2021	Petition 2139107-93.2021.8.26.0000	Chapter 1
Brazil	2021	TJ/SP Appeal 1020621-94.2020.8.26.0100	Chapter 1
Brazil	2021	STF, ARE 1281443STF	Chapter 1
Brazil	2017	STF, ARE 985744	Chapter 1
Brazil	2017	STF, ARE 1070079	Chapter 1
Brazil	2016	STF, ARE 1000876	Chapter 1
Brazil	2009	TJ/RS Appeal 70025267683, 5th Civil Chamber	Chapter 2
Brazil	2009	TJ/MS Appeal 2009.022658-4/0000-00, 3rd Civil Chamber	Chapter 2
Brazil	2009	TJ/RS Appeal 7002.813.8113, 12th Civil Chamber	Chapter 2
Brazil	2007	TJ/RJ 0007994-66.2007.8.19.0087	Chapter 2
Brazil	2008	TJ/RJ Appeal 2008.001.45909	Chapter 2
Brazil	2009	TJ/RS Appeal 70028036465	Chapter 2
Brazil	2009	TJ/RS Appeal 70019328889	Chapter 2

Brazil	2012	TJ/MG Appeal 1.0145.09.532430-0/003	Chapter 2
Brazil	2008	TJ/RS Appeal 70025609579-2008	Chapter 2
Brazil	2017	Special Appeal 1.655.090/MA	Chapter 2
Brazil	2008	TJ/RS Appeal 70024988883-2008	Chapter 2
Canada	2012	*Southcott Estates Inc. v Toronto Catholic District School* 2012 SCC 51	Chapters 3 and 5
Canada	1978	APECO of Canada Ltd. v Windmill Place [1978] 82 DRL (3d) I	Chapter 3
Canada	1978	100 Main Street Ltd. v W.B Sullivan Construction Ltd. (1978) 88 DLR (3d) (Ont. CA Can)	Chapter 5
Canada	1980	*Jack Cewe Ltd. v Jorgenson* [1980] 111 DLR (3d) 577	Chapter 3
Canada	1979	*Asamera Oil Corp v Sea Oil & General Corp* [1979] 1 S.C.R. 633	Chapter 3
Canada	1989	*Forshaw v Aluminex Extrusions Ltd.* 39 B.C.L.R. (2d) 140, 1989 CanLII 234 (BCCA)	Chapter 3
England	1677	*Vertue v Bird* 84 Eng. Rep. 1000, 85 Eng. Rep. 200 (K.B. 1677)	Chapter 3
England	1824	*Gainsford v Carroll* [1824] 2 B & C 624, 107 E.R. 516	Chapter 3
England	1849	*Beckham v Drake* [1849] 2 HLC 579, 9 E.R. 1213	Chapter 3
England	1912	*British Westinghouse Electric & Manufacturing Co Ltd v Underground Electric Railways Co of London Ltd (No.2)* (1912) AC 673	Chapters 3 and 4

England	1961	*White & Carter (Councils) Ltd. v McGregor* [1962] A.C. 413	Chapters 3 and 4
England	1975	*Stutt v Whitnell* [1975] 1 WLR 870 (CA)	Chapter 3
England	1953	*Pilkington v Wood* [1953] Ch. 770	Chapter 3
England	1993	*Bishopsgate Investment Management Ltd v Maxwell* [1993] BCLC 814	Chapter 3
England	1929	*James Finlay & Co., Ltd. v N.V. Kwik Hoo Tong Handel Maatschappij* [1929] 1 K.B. 400 CA	Chapter 3
England	1895	*Brace v Calder* [1895] 2 KB 253 CA	Chapter 3
England	1960	*Shindler v Northern Raincoat Co. Ltd* [1960] 1 WLR 1038	Chapter 3
England	1919	*Payzu v Saunders* [1919] 2 K.B. 581 CA	Chapter 3
England	2007	*Conner v Bradman & Co* [2007] EWHC 2789 (QB)	Chapter 3
England	2004	*Lagden v O'Connor* [2004] 1 A.C. 1067	Chapter 3
England	1957	*Charter v Sullivan* [1957] 2 Q.B. 117	Chapter 3
England	1993	*Kaines (UK) Ltd* v Österreichische Warenhandelsgesellschaft Austrowaren GmbH [1993] 2 Lloyd's Rep 1 (CA)	Chapter 3
England	2017	*Globalia Business Travel S.A.U. (formerly TravelPlan S.A.U.) of Spain v Fulton Shipping Inc of Panama, the New Flamenco* [2017] UKSC 43	Chapters 3 and 4
England	1980	*Nabi v British Leyland (UK) Ltd.* [1980] 1 WLR 529 (CA)	Chapter 3

England	2016	*Thai Airways International Public Co Ltd v KI Holdings Co Ltd.* [2015] EWHC 1250 (Comm); [2016] 1 All ER (Comm) 675	Chapter 3
England	1984	*Metelmann & Co v NBR* [1984] 1 Lloyd's Rep 614 (CA)	Chapter 3
England	1932	*Banco de Portugal v Waterlow & Sons Ltd.* [1932] A.C. 452	Chapters 3, 4 and 5
England	1973	*Grant v Dawkins and Others* [1973] 3 All ER 897	Chapter 3
England	1955	*Ruxley Electronics v Forsyth* [1996] A.C. 344	Chapter 3
England	1962	*O'Grady v Westminster Scaffolding Ltd.* [1962] 2 Lloyd's Rep. 238	Chapter 3
England	2010	*Lombard North Central v Automobile World (UK) Ltd* [2010] EWCA Civ 20	Chapters 3, 4 and 5
England	2017	*Sainsbury's Supermarkets Ltd v Visa Europe Services LLC* [2017] EWHC 3047 (Comm)	Chapter 3
England	1980	*Koch Marine Inc v D'Amica Società di Navigatione, The Elena d'Amico* [1980] 1 Lloyd's Rep. 75 at 88	Chapter 3
England	2004	*Lagden v O'Connor* [2004] 1 A.C. 1067 at [99]–[100]	Chapter 3
England	2008	*Uzinterimpex Jsc v Standard Bank Plc* [2008] EWCA Civ 819 at [56]	Chapter 3
England	1963	*Darbishire v Warran* [1963] 1 WLR. 1067 CA at 1075	Chapter 3

England	2015	*Bunge SA v Nidera BV* [2015] UKSC 43; [2015] 3 All E.R. 1082 at [81]	Chapter 3
England	2007	*Golden Strait Corpn v Nippon Yusen Kubishika Kaisha ("The Golden Victory")* [2007] UKHL 12; [2007] 2 AC 353 at [10]	Chapter 3
England	2002	*Dimond v Lovell* [2002] 1 AC 384 (HL)	Chapter 3
England	1957	*McAuley v London Transport Executive* [1957] 2 Lloyds Rep 500	Chapter 3
England	2015	*Cavendish Square Holdings BV v Talal El Makdessi* [2015] UKSC 67	Chapter 3
England	2015	*ParkingEye Ltd. v Beavis* [2015] UKSC 67	Chapter 3
England	1997	*Insurance Society Ltd v Argyll Stores (Holdings) Ltd* [1997] 2 WLR 898	Chapter 3
England	1996	*Semelhago v Paramadevan* [1996] 2 S.C.R. 415	Chapter 3
England	1984	*Clea Shipping Corp v Bulk Oil International Ltd (The Alaskan Trader) (No 2)* [1984] 1 All ER 129	Chapter 3
England	2012	*London Branch v Geys* [2012] UKSC 63	Chapter 3
England	1929	*James Finlay & Co., Ltd. v N.V. Kwik Hoo Tong Handel Maatschappij* [1929] 1 K.B. 400 CA	Chapter 3
England	1895	*Brace v Calder* [1895] 2 KB 253 CA	Chapter 3
England	1960	*Shindler v Northern Raincoat Co. Ltd* [1960] 1 WLR 1038	Chapter 3
England	2007	*Conner v Bradman & Co* [2007] EWHC 2789 (QB)	Chapter 3

England	2004	*Lagden v O'Connor* [2004] 1 A.C. 1067	Chapter 3
England	2013	*Manton Hire & Sales Ltd v* *Ash Manor Cheese Co Ltd* [2013] EWCA Civ 548	Chapter 3
England	1956	*Heaven & Kesterton Ltd v* *Etablissements Francois Albiac et* *Cie* (1956) 2 Lloyd's Rep. 316	Chapter 3
England	1940	*Liffen v Watson* [1940] 1 K.B. 556 CA	Chapter 3
England	1948	*Dennis v L.P.T.B.* [1948] 1 All E.R. 779	Chapter 3
England	1973	*Cunningham v Harrison* [1973] Q.B. 942 CA	Chapter 3
England	1947	*Redpath v Belfast and County* *Down Railways* [1947] N.I. 167	Chapter 3
England	2004	*Hamilton-Jones v David &* *Snape* [2004] 1 W.L.R. 924	Chapter 3
England	1874	*Bradburn v Great Western* *Railways* (1874) L.R. 10 Ex. 1	Chapter 3
England	1980	*Nabi v British Leyland (UK)* *Ltd.* [1980] 1 WLR 529 (CA)	Chapter 3
England	1980	*Jack Cewe Ltd. v Jorgenson* [1980] 111 DLR (3d) 577	Chapter 3
England	2010	*Choil Trading S.A. v Sahara* *Energy Resources Ltda* [2010] EWHC 374 (Comm)	Chapter 3
England	1973	*Grant v Dawkins and Others* [1973] 3 All ER 897	Chapter 3
England	1962	*O'Grady v Westminster Scaffolding* *Ltd.* [1962] 2 Lloyd's Rep. 238	Chapter 3

England	2013	*Singh v Yaqubi* [2013] EWCA Civ 23 CA	Chapter 3
England	1880	*Brownlie v Campbell* [1880] 5 AC 925	Chapter 3
England	1878	*Davies v London and Provincial Marine Insurance Co* [1878] 8 Ch. D469	Chapter 3
England	1976	*Cehave NV v Bremer Handels GmbH* [1976] QB 44	Chapter 3
England	1962	*Hongkong Fir Shipping Co. Ltd. v Kawasaki Kisen Kaisha Ltd.* [1962] 2 QB 26 (CA)	Chapter 3
England	1995	*Barclays Bank plc v Fairclough Building Ltd (No 1)* [1995] QB 214 (CA)	Chapter 3
England	1983	*Selvanayagam v University of the West Indies* [1983] 1 WLR 585 (PC)	Chapter 4
England	2001	*Cerberus Software Ltd v Rowley* [2001] EWCA Civ 78	Chapter 4
England	1854	*Hadley v Baxendale* (1854) 9 Ex 341	Chapter 4
France	2003	Cass 2ème civ (19 juin 2003) No 931 FS-PRBI, Dibaoui c; Flamand, Bull Civ II No 203, D 2003 Jur 2396	Chapter 4
France	2003	Cass 2ème (19 juin 2003) No 930 FS-PRBI, Xhauflaire C/ Decrept, D 2003 Jur 2396	Chapter 4
Germany	2007	BAG NZA 2007, 1230, 1233	Chapter 4
Germany	1953	BGH 13 May 1953, BGHZ 10, 18	Chapter 4
Germany	2018	BGH NJW 2018, 20	Chapter 4

Germany	1961	BGH NJW 1961, 655	Chapter 4
Germany	1997	BGH NJW 1997, 2234	Chapter 4
Germany	1993	BGH NJW 1993, 2685	Chapter 4
Germany	1959	BGH NJW 1959, 933	Chapter 4
Germany	2006	BGH NJW 2006, 1198	Chapter 4
Germany	2018	BGH NJW 2018, 786	Chapter 4
Germany	1989	BGH NJW 1989, 290	Chapter 4
Germany	1996	BGH NJW-RR 1996, 1079	Chapter 4
United States	1845	*Clark v Marsiglia* (1845) Denio 1 (N.Y.) 317, 43 Am. Dec. 670	Chapter 3
United States	1929	*Rockingham County v Luten Bridge Co.* 35 F. 2d 301 (4th Cir. 1929)	Chapter 3
United States	1982	*Evra Corp. v Swiss Bank Corp.* 673 F.2d 951 (7th Cir. 1982)	Chapter 3

TABLE OF LEGISLATION

Jurisdiction	Instrument	Section
Argentina	Civil and Commercial Code of the Argentinian Nation	Chapter 4
Argentina	Argentinian Constitution	Chapter 4
Australia	Sale of Goods Act	Chapter 3
Brazil	Civil Code (Law no. 10.406/2002)	Chapters 1, 2 and 5
Brazil	Consumer Code (Law no. 8.078/1990)	Chapter 2
Brazil	Brazilian Constitution	Chapters 2 and 5
Brazil	Civil Procedural Code (Law no. 13.105/2015)	Chapter 5
Canada	Sale of Goods Act	Chapter 3
France	French Civil Code	Chapter 4
France	French Insurance Code	Chapter 4
Germany	German Civil Code (*Bürgerliches Gesetzbuch* – BGB)	Chapter 4
Transnational	Convention on Contracts for the International Sale of Goods ("CISG")	Chapters 2 and 4
Transnational	Hague Uniform Law of International Sales ("ULIS")	Chapter 4
Transnational	Principles of International Commercial Contracts ("PICC")	Chapter 4
Transnational	Principles of European Contract Law ("PECL")	Chapter 4
Transnational	Common European Sales Law ("CESL")	Chapter 4
Transnational	Principles of Latin American Contract Law ("PLACL")	Chapter 4

United Kingdom	Law Reform (Contributory Negligence) Act	Chapter 3
United Kingdom	Sale of Goods Act	Chapter 3
United States	Restatement (Second) of Contract	Chapter 3
United States	Restatement (Second) of Torts	Chapter 3

BIBLIOGRAPHY

Adler, Barry E., 'Efficient breach theory through the looking glass' (2008) vol 83 New York University Law Review

Aguiar Júnior, Ruy Rosado de, *Extinção dos Contratos por Incumprimento do Devedor* (2nd Ed., 2003, Rio de Janeiro, Aide Editora)

Akyurek, Ozan, 'The preliminary draft of the civil liability reform in France' (Financier Worldwide, October 2016) available at <https://www.financierworldwide.com/the-preliminary-draft-of-the-civil-liability-reform-in-france#.XlPiYmhKiUk> accessed 7 August 2022.

Alces, Peter A., *A Theory of Contract Law: Empirical Insights and Moral Psychology* (Oxford University Press, 2011)

Alessandri, Arturo, *Responsabilidad extracontractual* (Editorial Universitaria 1943)

Almeida, Juliana Evangelista de, 'A boa-fé no direito obrigacional' (2008) available at <http://www.ambito-juridico.com.br/site/index.php?n link=revista artigos leitura&artigo id=8041> accessed 31 July 2022

Andrews, Neil, *Contract law* (Cambridge University Press 2015)

Antunes, Felipe Martins, 'O duty to mitigate the loss no direito contratual brasileiro' (2013) available at <http://semanaacademica.org.br/system/files/artigos/duty to mitigate the lossev.pdf> accessed 12 June 2021

Anziani, Alain and Béteille, Laurent, 'Rapport d'information' (2008-2009) 558 available at <https://www.senat.fr/rap/r08-558/r08-5581.pdf> accessed 7 August 2022

Atiyah, Patrick S., *The rise and fall of freedom of contract* (first published 1979, Clarendon Press 1985)

Avallone, Patricia Maria Basseto, 'The Award of Punitive and Emotional Distress Damages in Breach of Contract Cases: A Comparison Between the American and the Brazilian Legal Systems' (2002) 8 New Eng. Int'l & Comp. L. Ann.

Avant-projet de réforme du droit des obligations et de la prescription (Proposals for Reform of the Law of Obligations and the Law of Prescription). Translation into English available at <http://www.justice.gouv.fr/art_pix/rapportcatatla0905-anglais.pdf> accessed 7 August 2022

Barnett, Katy, 'Substitutive damages and mitigation in contract law – Tensions between two competing norms' [2016] 28 SAcLJ 808

Barroso, Lucas Abreu, *Contemporary Legal Theory in Brazilian Civil Law* (Juruá, Curitiba, 2014)

Bell, John, 'Comparative Law and Legal Theory' in W Krawietz, N MacCormick & H Von Wright (eds) *Prescriptive Formality and Normative Rationality in Modern Legal Systems* (Duncker & Humblot 1995)

Bell, John, 'Introduction: The Spirit of French Law' in John Bell, Sophie Boyron and Simon Whittaker, *Principles of French Law* Second Edition (Oxford, Oxford University Press)

Berryman, Jeff, 'Mitigation, Specific Performance and the Property Developer: Southcott Estates Inc. v Toronto Catholic District School Board' (2013) 51 Alberta Law Review

Betti, Emilio, *Teoria geral das obrigações* (Campinas, Bookseller, 2005)

Bridge, Michael G., 'Does Anglo-Canadian Contract Law Need a Doctrine of Good Faith?' (1984) Canadian Business Law Journal, 426

Bridge, Michael G., 'Market and damages in sale of goods cases' (2016) Law Quarterly Review 404

Bridge, Michael G., 'Market damages in sale of goods cases - anticipatory repudiation and mitigation' (1994) *Journal of Business Law*, 204

Bridge, Michael G., 'Mitigation of damages in contract and the meaning of avoidable loss' (1989) 105 Law Quarterly Review

Campbell, David, 'Reply to Mark P. Gergen, 'The Right to Perform after Repudiation and Recover the Contract Price in Anglo-American Law', in Larry Dimatteo and Martin Hogg (eds), *Comparative Contract Law* (Oxford University Press 2016)

Carter, J. W., "*White and Carter v McGregor* – How Unreasonable?" (2012) 128 Law Quarterly Review 490

Cartwright, John, Vogenauer, Stefan and Whittaker, Simon (eds), *Reforming the French Law of Obligations: Comparative reflections on the avant-projet de reforme du droit des obligations et de la prescription ('the avant-projet catala')* (Oxford, Hart Publishing, 2009)

Casermeiro, Luis Adolfo Alavila, 'La acción preventiva em el nuevo Código Civil y Comercial' (2017), Biblioteca Juridica Online, DC 22B7

Casermeiro, Luis Adolfo Alavila, 'La acción preventiva em el nuevo Código Civil y Comercial' (2017), Biblioteca Juridica Online, DC 22B7

Chitty, Joseph and Beale, H. G., *Chitty on Contracts* (33rd Ed. Incorporating Second Supplement, London, Sweet & Maxwell, 2020)

Chong, Paulo Araújo, 'O duty to mitigate the loss no direito brasileiro: é justo o credor ser indenizado por prejuízos que deixou de mitigar?' (2017) 1 Cadernos Jurídicos da Faculdade de Direito de Sorocaba

Comino, Tomas Barros Martins, 'As desaventuras do duty to mitigate the loss no Brasil' (2015) Dissertation for the degree of Mestrado Profissional em Direito dos Negócios Aplicado e Direito Tributário Aplicado, Fundação Getúlio Vargas, São Paulo, available at <https://bibliotecadigital.fgv.br/dspace/handle/10438/13610?show=full> accessed 12 June 2021

Connellan, Clare, Oger-Gross, Elizabeth and André, Angélica, 'Compensatory Damages Principles in Civil and Common Law Jurisdictions: Requirements, Underlying Principles and Limits' p. 16 available at <https://www.whitecase.com/sites/whitecase/files/files/download/publications/article-compensatory-damages-

principle-in-civil-and-common-law-jurisdictions.pdf> accessed 7 August 2022

Cordeiro, Antonio Menezes, *Da boa-fé no Direito Civil* (Bd. II, Coimbra, Almedina, 1984)

Costa, Carlos A. Calvo, *Código Civil y Comercial de la Nación concordado, comentado y comparado com los códigos civill de Veléz Sarsfield y de Comercio* (1ª Ed., 2ª reimpresión, Ciudad de Buenos Aires, LaLey, 2015)

Curran, Vivian Grosswald, 'Comparative Law and Language' in Reinhard Zimmermann and Mattias Reimann (eds), *The Oxford Handbook of Comparative Law* (OUP 2006)

Dias, Daniel Pires Novais, 'O duty to mitigate loss no direito civil brasileiro e o encargo de evitar o próprio dano' (2011) 12 Revista de Direito Privado

Dias, José de Aguiar, *Da responsabilidade civil* (Rio de Janeiro, Forense, v. II, 1995)

Didier Jr., Fredie, 'Multa Coercitiva, boa-fé processual e supressio: aplicação do duty to mitigate the loss no processo civil' (2009) Revista de processo, São Paulo, n. 171

Domat, Jean, *Le droit civil dans l'ordre naturel* (t. 1, Paris: Rollin el Fils 1745)

Dourado, Emerson da Silva, 'O dever de mitigar o dano (the duty to mitigate loss)' (2012) available at <http://www.webartigos. com/artigos/o-dever-de-mitigar-o-dano-duty-to-mitigate-the-loss/101882/> accessed 12 June 2021

Drummond, Iain, 'Is 'duty to mitigate loss' a misnomer?' (2016) available at <http://www.shepwedd.co.uk/knowledge/duty-mitigate-loss-misnomer> accessed 12 June 2021

Dyson, Andrew and Kramer, Adam, 'There is no 'Breach Date Rule': mitigation, difference in value and date of assessment' (2014) 130 Law Quarterly Review, 259

Dyson, Andrew, 'British Westinghouse Revisited' (2012) Lloyd's Maritime and Commercial Law Quarterly 412

Dyson, Andrew, 'Choice, benefits and the basis of the market rule' (2016) Lloyd's Maritime and Commercial Law Quarterly, 202

Eberle, Edward J., 'The Method and Role of Comparative Law' (2009) 8 Washington University Global Studies Law Review 451

Eisenberg, Melvin A., 'The duty to rescue in Contract Law' (2002) Fordham L. Rev. 647, 654 <https://scholarship.law.berkeley.edu. facpubs/1412> accessed 8 August 2022

Ekkenga, Jens and Kuntz, Thilo, in Soergel et al (eds) *Bürgerliches Gesetzbuch* Vol 3/2 Schuldrecht 1/2 (14th edn, Kohlhammer Stuttgart 2014)

Farnsworth, E. Allan, *Contracts* (4th edn, Aspen Publishers, 2004)

Fazio, Silvia, 'Corporate governance standards in Brazil: is the country winning the confidence of international investors?' (2013) available at <http://www.lexology.com/library/detail.aspx?g=6400406c-62db-45fe-b444-3e01ccc1236e> accessed 13 August 2022

Fedtke, Jörg, 'Legal Transplants', in Jan M Smits (ed), *Elgar Encyclopedia of Comparative Law* (2nd edn, Edward Elgar Publishing 2014)

Fenn, Paul, 'Mitigation and the Correct Measure of Damage' (1981) 1st Int. J. of Law and Economy

Ferreyra, Roberto Vázquez, 'La función preventiva de la responsabilidade civil' (2015) La LAey, Cita Online AR/DOC/1447/2015

Fiorenza, Alejandro Alberto, 'El deber de prevenir el daño. Análisis del art. 1710 del Código Civil y Comercial' (2018) El Derecho available at <http://www.elderecho.com.ar/includes/pdf/ diarios/2018/05/24052018.pdf> accessed 7 August 2022

Flumignan, Silvano J. G., 'A correlação entre o dano moral, o dano social e o caput do artigo 944 do Código Civil na responsabilidade civil do Estado' (2011) XXXVII Congresso Nacional de Procuradores de Estado, Belo Horizonte

Flumignan, Silvano J. G., 'O dever de mitigar o prejuízo (duty to mitigate the loss) e a responsabilidade civil do Estado' available at <https://jus.com.br/artigos/35654/o-dever-de-mitigar-o-prejuizo-duty-to-mitigate-the-loss-e-a-responsabilidade-civil-do-estado> accessed 13 August 2022

Fradera, Vera Maria Jacob de, 'A contribuição da CISG (Convenção de Viena sobre os contratos de compra e venda internacional) para a atualização e flexibilização da noção de contrato no direito brasileiro' (2012) Revista de Arbitragem e Mediação, v. 34

Fradera, Vera Maria Jacob de, 'Pode o credor ser instado a diminuir o próprio prejuízo?' (2004) 19 Revista trimestral de direito civil

Fradera, Vera Maria Jacob de, *O direito privado brasileiro na visão de Clóvis do Couto e Silva* (Porto Alegre, Livraria do Advogado, 1997)

Fried, Charles, 'The convergence of contract and promise', (2009) Harvard Law Review 7

Fried, Charles, *Contract as Promise: A Theory of Contractual Obligation* (Harvard University Press 1981)

Friedmann, Daniel, 'Economic Aspects of Damages and Specific Performance Compared', in Djakhongir Saidov and Ralph Cunnington, *Contract Damages: Domestic and International Perspectives* (Hart Publishing 2008)

Fundamentos del Anteproyecto de Código Civil y Comercial de la Nación available at < http://www.nuevocodigocivil.com/wp-content/uploads/2015/02/5-Fundamentos-del-Proyecto.pdf> accessed 7 August 2022

Gagaliano, Pablo Stolze and Pamplona Filho, Rodolfo, *Novo Curso de Direito Civil – Contratos* (São Paulo, Editora Forense 2010)

Gagliano, Pablo Stolze, 'Editorial 12 – Duty to mitigate' (2010) available at <www.pablostolze.com.br> accessed 31 July 2022

Gergen, Mark P., 'The Right to Perform after Repudiation and Recover the Contract Price in Anglo-American Law', in Larry Dimatteo and

Martin Hogg (eds), *Comparative Contract Law* (Oxford University Press 2016)

Glenn, H. Patrick, *Legal Traditions of the World: Sustainable diversity in law* (5th edn, OUP 2014)

Góes, Maria Claudia Chaves de Faria, 'Breves considerações acerca da doutrina do abuso do direito' (2014) available at <http://www.tjrj.jus.br/c/document_library/get_file?uuid=a0ff68c7-4cb0-4d86-b33e-c273865fa54d&groupId=10136> accessed 31 July 2022

Goetz, Charles J. and Scott, Robert E., 'The Mitigation Principle: Toward a General Theory of Contractual Obligation' (1983) Virginia Law Review, Vol. 69, No. 6

Gomes, Elena de Carvalho, "Sobre a Cláusula Geral de Boa Fé e sua Abordagem por Pontes de Miranda no 'Tratado de Direito Privado'" (Roma e America, Diritto Romano Comune v. 35, 2014)

Gomes, Elena de Carvalho, *Entre o actus e o factum: os comportamentos contraditórios no direito privado* (Belo Horizonte, Del Rey, 2009)

Grüneberg, Christian, in Palandt *Bürgerliches Gesetzbuch* (79th edn, CH Beck Munich 2020)

Hage, Jaap, 'Legal Reasoning', in Jan M Smits (ed), *Elgar encyclopedia of comparative law* (2nd edn, Edward Elgar Publishing 2014) ch. 42

Hall, George, 'Contract Law, Coherent Legal Theory, and Sound Commercial Practice: the Need for a Balance' (2013) 2 Commercial Litigation and Arbitration Review 1

Hart, H. L. A., *The Concept of Law* (2nd edn, Clarendon Press 1994)

Herrera, Edgardo López, *Código Civil y Comercial de la Nación Comentado* (La Ley, 2015)

Hillman, Robert A., 'Keeping the Deal Together after Material Breach – Common Law Mitigation Rules, the UCC, and the Restatement (Second) of Contracts' (1976) 47 U. of Col. L. R., 558

Hoffman, Eduardo and Helene, Paulo Henrique, 'Duty to mitigate the loss: o dever de mitigar sua própria perda' (2012) available at

<_www.publicadireito.com.br/artigos/?cod=de3f712d1a02c5fb> accessed 31 July 2022

Honnold, John O., 'Uniform Law for International Sales under the 1980 United Nations Convention' (1999) 3rd ed., The Hague: Kluwer Law International available at <http://www.cisg.law.pace.edu/cisg/biblio/honnold.html> accessed 13 August 2022

Huber, Christian, *Fragen der Schadensberechnung* (Springer Vienna 1993)

Huber, Peter, 'Comparative Sales Law' in Reimann, M. and Zimmermann, R. (eds), *The Oxford handbook of Comparative Law* (Oxford University Press 2006)

Jones, Michael A., Dugdale, Anthony M. and Simpson, Mark, *Clerk & Lindsell on Torts* (22nd Ed, Sweet & Maxwell Ltd 2017)

Keirse, Anne, 'Why the Proposed Optional Common European Sales Law Has Not, But Should Have, Abandoned the Principle of All or Nothing: A Guide to How to Sanction the Duty to Mitigate the Loss' (2011) 19 European Review of Private Law, Issue 6, 976

Kelly, Michael Bruce, 'Defendant's responsibility to minimize plaintiff's loss: a curious exception to the avoidable consequences doctrine' (1996) South Carolina Law Review. Columbia, v. 47

Kimel, Dori, *From promise to contract: towards a liberal theory of contract* (Hart Publishing 2003)

Kischel, Uwe, *Comparative Law* by (Oxford University Press 2019)

Kleinheisterkamp, Jan, 'Development of Comparative Law in Latin America' in Mathias Reimann and Reinhard Zimmermann (eds), *The Oxford Handbook of Comparative Law* (2nd Edn, OUP 2019)

Komarov, Alexander, 'The Limitation of Contract Damages in Domestic Legal Systems and International Instruments' in Djakhongir Saidov and Ralph Cunnington, *Contract Damages: Domestic and International Perspectives* (Hart Publishing 2008)

Kramer, Adam, *The Law of Contract Damages* (2nd ed. Hart Publishing 2017)

Kulesza, Gustavo Santos, *Princípio da mitigação de danos; evolução no direito contratual* (Curitiba, Juruá, 2015)

Laithier, Yves-Marie, "Exécution Forcée en Nature" in Cartwright, Vogenauer and Whittaker (eds), *Reforming the French Law of Obligations: Comparative reflections on the avant-projet de reforme du droit des obligations et de la prescription ('the avant-projet catala')* (Oxford, Hart Publishing, 2009)

Laithier, Yves-Marie, "The Enforcement of Contractual Obligations: A French Perspective" in in Cartwright, Vogenauer and Whittaker (eds), *Reforming the French Law of Obligations: Comparative reflections on the avant-projet de reforme du droit des obligations et de la prescription ('the avant-projet catala')* (Oxford, Hart Publishing, 2009)

Lando, Ole and Beale, Hugh (eds), *Principles of European Contract Law* (Parts I and II,1999)

Lando, Ole, Clive, Eric, Prüm, André, and Zimmermann, Reinhard (eds), *Principles of European Contract Law* (Part III, 2003)

Larroumet, Christian, 'Obligation de modérer le dommage et arbitrage du point de vue du droit français' (2008) 290 Gaz. Pal.

Le Pautremat, Solene, 'Mitigation of Damage: a French perspective' (2006) International Comparative Law Quarterly. London, v 55, 205

Legrand, Pierre, 'The impossibility of legal transplants' (1997) 4 *Maastricht J. Eur. & Comp. Law* 111

Lehmann, Matthias, 'Damages and interest' in Javier Plaza Penadés and Luz M. Martínez Velencoso (eds), *European Perspectives on the Common European Sales Law* (Springer 2015)

Leite, Gisele, 'Roteiro sobre o princípio da boa-fé objetiva' (2006) available at <http://www.ambito-juridico.com.br/site/index.php?n link=revista artigos leitura&artigo id=1712> accessed 31 July 2022

Léna, Aurélie Ballot, 'Consécration d'une obligation, pour la victime, d'éviter l'aggravation de son préjudice en matière contractuelle (art. 1263)' (2016) Blog Réforme du droit des obligations – Dalloz available at <http://reforme-obligations.dalloz.fr/2016/08/10/consecration-dune-obligation-pour-la-victime-deviter-laggravation-de-son-prejudice-en-matiere-contractuelle-art-1263/> accessed 13 August 2022

Lenaerts, Annekatrien, 'The General Principle of the Prohibition of Abuse of Rights: A Critical Position on Its Role in a Codified European Contract Law' (2010) 6 European Review of Private Law 1121-1154

Leonard, Thomas M., *Encyclopedia of the Developing World* (Routledge 2013)

Letsas, George and Saprai, Prince, 'Mitigation, Fairness and Contract Law', in Klass, G., Letsas, G., and Saprai, P. (eds), *Philosophical foundations of contract law* (Oxford University Press 2015)

Liu, Qiao, "The *White & Carter* Principle: A Restatement" (2011) 74 MLR 171

Lopes, Christian Sahb Batista, *Mitigação dos prejuízos no direito contratual* (São Paulo, Editora Saraiva, 2013)

López-Medina, Diego, 'The Latin American and Caribbean legal traditions: Repositioning Latin America and the Caribbean on the contemporary maps of comparative law' in M Bussani and U Mattei (eds), *The Cambridge Companion to Comparative Law* (Cambridge, Cambridge University Press, 2012)

MacIntosh, J. G. and Frydenlund, D. C., 'An Investment Approach to a Theory of Contract Mitigation' (1987) 37 U. of Toronto L.J. 113

Mantovani, Alexandre Casanova, 'A mitigação do próprio prejuízo nos contratos administrativos' (2013) available at <https://www.lume.ufrgs.br/bitstream/handle/10183/90488/000914028.pdf?sequence=1> accessed 12 June 2021

Markesinis, Basil, Unberath, Hannes and Johnston, Angus, *The German law of contract: a comparative treatise* (Oxford, Hart Publishing, 2006)

Martin, Lilian Cecilia Neira San, *Del 'deber' del acreedor de evitar o mitigar el daño* (Tor Vergata, Roma, 2010).

Martins, Jose Eduardo Figueiredo de Andrade, *Duty To Mitigate The Loss No Direito Civil Brasileiro* (São Paulo, Verbatim, 2018)

Martins-Costa, Judith, *A boa-fé no direito privado* (São Paulo, Revista dos Tribunais, 1999)

McCormick, Charles Tilford, *A handbook on the law of damages* (West Publishing Company, 1935)

McGregor, Harvey, 'The Role of Mitigation in the Assessment of Damages', in Djakhongir Saidov and Ralph Cunnington, *Contract Damages: Domestic and International Perspectives* (Hart Publishing 2008)

McGregor, Harvey, Edelman, James, Varuhas, Jason and Colton, Simon (general eds), *McGregor on Damages* (21st Ed., London, Sweet & Maxwell, 2020)

McInnes, Mitchell, 'Specific performance in the Supreme Court of Canada' (2013) Law Quarterly Review

McKendrick, Ewan, *Contract Law* (11th edn, Palgrave Macmillan 2015)

McKendrick, Ewan, *Contract law: Text, cases, and materials* (6th edn, Oxford University Press 2014)

Merer, Pierre-Louis, 'The dawn of a duty to mitigate damages in French law' available at < https://www.shipownersclub.com/pierre-loius-merer-the-dawn-of-a-duty-to-mitigate-damages-in-french-law/> accessed on 7 August 2022

Mesa, Marcelo López, 'La aplicación de um nuevo fator de atribuición: la causación de um daño evitable' (2013), Biblioteca Juridica Online, DC 1C1E

Miranda, Francisco Cavalcanti Pontes de, *Tratado de direito privado: tomo XXII – parte especial* (Campinas, Bookseller, 2003)

Mirow, M. C., *Latin American Law: A History of Private Law and Institutions in Spanish America* (University of Texas Press 2004)

Momberg, Rodrigo and Vogenauer, Stefan (eds), *The Future of Contract Law in Latin America:* The *Principles of Latin American Contract Law* (Oxford, Hart Publishing, 2017)

Morgan, Jonathan, 'Smuggling Mitigation in White & Carter v McGregor: Time to Come Clean?' (2015) Lloyds Maritime and Commercial Law Quarterly

Mostajo, Daniel Ugarte, 'Apuntes en torno a las medidas mitigadoras en el Código Civil y Comercial argentino, con especial atención a la responsabilidad civil por incumplimiento contractual' available at <http://www.elderecho.com.ar/includes/pdf/diarios/2017/10/26102017.pdf> accessed 7 August 2022

Mostajo, Daniel Ugarte, 'La mitigación de daños en la responsabilidad por incumplimiento contractual: breve análisis comparado en el derecho civil de Argentina y Perú' (2018) avaliable at < http://www.scielo.org.pe/pdf/derecho/n80/a04n80.pdf> accessed 7 August 2022

Nalin, Paulo and Sirena, Hugo, 'A Convenção de Viena de 1980 e a sistemática contratual brasileira: a recepção principiológica do duty to mitigate the loss' (2002) Revista Trimestral de Direito Civil, v. 49

Nicodemos, Erika, 'Codificação e descodificação: o direito civil e o Código Civil de 2002' (2013) Boletim Conteúdo Jurídico, Coluna Jurídica <http://jus.com.br/artigos25559> accessed 31 July 2022

Noronha, Fernando, *Direito das obrigações: fundamentos do direito das obrigações: introdução à responsabilidade civil* (volume 1. 2. ed. São Paulo, Saraiva, 2007)

Oetker, Hartmut, in *Münchener Kommentar zum Bürgerlichen Gesetzbuch* Vol 2 Schuldrecht – Allgemeiner Teil (8th edn, Krüger (ed) CH Beck München 2019)

Oliveira, Adriane Stoll de, 'A codificação do Direito' (2002) <http://www.egov.ufsc.br/portal/sites/default/files/anexos/11087-11087-1-PB.pdf> accessed 31 July 2022

Olson, Richard J., 'Who Mourns for Specific Performance?' (2013) 71 *Advocate Vancouver* 860

Ormaechea, Andres, 'Obligación de mitigar el daño' (2016) avaliable at <https://www.abogados.com.ar/obligacion-de-mitigar-el-dano/18372> accessed 7 August 2022

Ossola, Federico, *Responsabilidad civil* (AbeledoPerrot, 2017)

O'Sullivan, Janet, 'Mitigation and Specific Performance in the Canadian Supreme Court' (The Cambridge Law Journal, 72, 2013)

O'Sullivan, Janet, 'Repudiation: Keeping the Contract Alive', in Graham Virgo and Sarah Worhington (eds), *Commercial Remedies Resolving Controversies* (Cambridge University Press, 2017) 51-74

Peixoto, Alessandra Cristina Tufvesson, 'Responsabilidade extracontratual – Algumas considerações sobre a participação da vítima na quantificação da indenização' (2008) Revista da Emerj, v.11, n. 44

Pereira, Caio Mario da Silva, *Instituições de Direito Civil* (V. 2, 12. Ed. Rio de Janeiro, Forense 1994)

Pinheiro, Denise, 'Duty to mitigate loss à brasileira: uma questão além do nexo de causalidade' (2012) available at <http://www.publicadireito.com.br/artigos/?cod=3e524bf740dc8cfd> accessed 16 January 2016, published during the XXI Congresso Nacional do CONPEDI/UFF

Pothieu, Robert Joseph, *Traité des obligations, selon les regles, tant du for de la conscience, que du for extérieur* (t. 3, Paris: Debure pere, 1761)

Proença, José Carlos Brandão, *A conduta do lesado como pressuposto e critério de imputação do dano extracontratual* (Coimbra, Almedina, 1997)

Projet de réforme de la Responsabilité civile (Reform Bill on Civil Liability (March 2017)). English translation available at <http://www.textes.

justice.gouv.fr/art pix/reform bill on civil liability march 2017.pdf> accessed 7 August 2022

Rémy-Corlay, Pauline, "Damages, Loss and the Quantification of Damages in the *Avant-Projet de Reforme*" in Cartwright, Vogenauer and Whittaker (eds), *Reforming the French Law of Obligations: Comparative reflections on the avant-projet de reforme du droit des obligations et de la prescription ('the avant-projet catala')* (Oxford, Hart Publishing, 2009)

Reviriego, Jose Antonio, 'La tutela preventiva y la acción preventiva en el derecho argentino (2011), Biblioteca Juridica Online, DC 16CE

Rizzardo, Arnaldo, 'Responsabilidade civil' (5 ed. rev. e atual., Rio de Janeiro, Forense, 2011)

Rodrigues, Silvio, *Direito civil* (v. 4: responsabilidade civil, 20th ed. São Paulo, Saraiva 2003)

Rose, Leslie, *O Código Civil Brasileiro em inglês / the Brazilian Civil Code in English* (Renovar 2008)

Rosenvald, Nelson and Farias, Cristiano Chaves de, *Direito das obrigações* (3rd ed. Rio de Janeiro, Lumen Juris, 2008)

Rowan, Solene, *Remedies for Breach of Contract: A Comparative Analysis of the Protection of Performance* (Oxford University Press, 2012)

Rowan, Solene, 'The New French Law of Contract' (2017) 66 *International Comparative Law Quarterly* 805-831

Saidov, Djakhongir and Cunnington, Ralph, 'Current Themes in the Law of Contract Damages: Introductory Remarks', in Djakhongir Saidov and Ralph Cunnington, *Contract Damages: Domestic and International Perspectives* (Hart Publishing 2008)

Sampaio, Laerte Marrone de Castro, *A boa-fé objetiva na relação contratual* (Barueri, Manole 2004)

Santos, João Manoel de Carvalho, *Código Civil Brasileiro Interpretado* (vol. III, 4th ed., vol. III, Rio de Janeiro, Livraria Freitas Bastos 1950)

Scalescky, Fernanda Sirotsky, 'A Interpretação do Duty to Mitigate the Loss na Convenção das Nações Unidas sobre Contratos de Compra e Venda Internacional de Mercadorias e a sua Recepção pelo Direito Civil Brasileiro' (2013), Cadernos do Programa de Pós-Graduação em Direito UFRGS v. 8 n. 2

Schmidt, Jan. Peter, "The 'Principles of Latin American Contract Law' Against the Background of Latin American Legal Culture: A European Perspective", in Rodrigo Momberg, Stefan Vogenauer (eds), *The Future of Contract Law in Latin America:* The *Principles of Latin American Contract Law* (Oxford, Hart Publishing, 2017)

Schmitthoff, Clive M., 'The Duty to Mitigate' (1961) Journal of Business Law 361

Shiffrin, Seana V., 'The divergence of contract and promise', (2007) 120 Harvard Law Review 724-725

Siems, Mathias, *Comparative Law* (2nd edn, Cambridge University Press 2018)

Siqueira, Carlos André Cassani and Campeão, Paula Soares, 'A cessação dos efeitos do Inadimplemento obrigacional por não mitigação da perda pelo Credor' (2011) Congresso Nacional do CONPEDI, XX, Vitória

Smits, Jan M. (ed), Elgar encyclopedia of comparative law (2nd edn, Edward Elgar Publishing 2014)

Smits, Jan M., *Elgar Encyclopedia of Comparative Law* (2nd edn, Edward Elgar Publishing 2014)

Sotelo, Nicole, 'German Civil Code (Bürgerliches Gesetzbuch, BGB) (1900)' available at <http://hist259.web.unc.edu/german-civil-code-burgerliches-gesetzbuch-bgb-1900/> accessed on 7 August 2022

Swann, Angela and Adamski, Jacub, 'Specific Performance, Mitigation, and Corporate Groups: A Comment on Southcott Estates Inc v Toronto Catholic District School Board' (2014) Canadian Business Law Journal, Vol. 56, Issue 1

Tartuce, Flavio, 'A boa-fé objetiva e a mitigação do prejuízo pelo credor' (2005) available at <http://www.flaviotartuce.adv.br/artigos/Tartuce_duty.doc> accessed 12 June 2021

Tartuce, Flavio, *Função social dos contratos: do código de defesa do consumidor ao código civil de 2002* (2nd ed. São Paulo, Método, 2007).

Tartuce, Flavio, *Teoria Geral dos Contratos* (São Paulo, Editora Método 2008)

Tettenborn, Andrew, 'Damages, Causation Mitigation and the Conduct of the Claimant' in Neil Andrews, Malcolm Clarke, Andrew Tettenborn and Graham Virgo, *Contractual Duties: Performance, Breach, Termination and Remedies* 2nd ed (Sweet & Maxwell Ltd 2012)

Tettenborn, Andrew, 'The conduct of the claimant, avoidable loss and the duty to mitigate' in Neil Andrews, Malcolm Clarke, Andrew Tettenborn and Graham Virgo (eds), *Contractual duties: performance, breach, termination and remedies* (Sweet & Maxwell Ltd 2012)

The Napoleonic Code, available at <https://courses.lumenlearning.com/suny-hccc-worldhistory2/chapter/the-napoleonic-code/> accessed on 7 August 2022

Theodoro Júnior, Humberto, *O Contrato e sua função social* (2nd Ed. Rio de Janeiro, Forense 2005)

Thüsing, *Die wertende Schadensberechnung* (CH Beck Munich 2001)

Timm, Luciano Benetti, 'The social function of contract law in Brazilian Civil Code: distributive justice versus efficiency – lessons from the United States' (2008) <http://escholarship.org/uc/item/29x696kf> accessed 31 July 2022

Treitel, Guenter H. and Eörsi, Gyula, 'III. Substitutionary relief in Money', in *International Encyclopedia of International Law* Volume VII: Contracts in General Chapter 16 (Brill, 1976)

Treitel, Guenter H. and Peel, Edwin, *Treitel on the law of contract* (13th edn, Sweet & Maxwell 2011)

Treitel, Guenter H., *Remedies for Breach of Contract: A Comparative Account* (Oxford University Press 1988)

Valdesoiro, Gabriella Michetti Mora, 'O instituto do duty to mitigate the loss e seu conteúdo eficacional no direito brasileiro em case da causalidade cumulativa do artigo 945 do Código Civil' available at <https://repositorio.ufsc.br/bitstream/handle/123456789/114922/TCC%20-%20FINAL%20-%20REPOSIT%C3%93RIO%20-%20TERMO%20DE%20APROVA%C3%87%C3%83O%20-%20PDF%20A.pdf?sequence=1&isAllowed=y> accessed 13 August 2022

Van Gerven, W. et al, *Ius Commune Casebooks for the Common Law of Europe: Cases, Materials and Text on National, Supranational and International Tort Law* (Oxford, Hart Publishing, 2000)

Veloso, Regina Coeli Soares Oliveira and Vieira, Nathalie Gurgel, 'Duty to mitigate loss: a Brazilian perspective' (2018) Revue libre de Droit

Villas-bôas, Renata Malta, 'Duty to mitigate the loss no Direito Civil pátrio' (2013) Âmbito Jurídico, Rio Grande, XVI, n. 111 available at <http://ambito-juridico.com.br/site/?n_link=revista_artigos_leitura&artigo_id=12702> accessed 12 June 2021

Villas-bôas, Renata Malta, R. M., 'Duty to mitigate the loss no Direito Civil pátrio' (2013) Âmbito Jurídico, Rio Grande, XVI, n. 111 available at <http://ambito-juridico.com.br/site/?n_link=revista_artigos_leitura&artigo_id=12702> accessed 13 August 2022

Villela, João Batista, 'Por uma nova teoria dos contratos' (1975) Revista de Direito e Estudos Sociais, Coimbra, a. 20, n 2-4

Vogenauer, Stefan (ed), *Commentary on the UNIDROIT Principles of International Commercial Contracts (PICC)* 2ⁿᵈ Edn (Oxford, Oxford University Press, 2015)

Von Bar, C., Clive, E., Schulte-Nölke, H. et al. (eds.), *Principles, Definitions and Model Rules of European Private Law — Draft Common Frame of Reference (DCFR)* (Munich, Selier, 2008)

Waddams, Stephen M., *The Law of Contracts* (7ᵗʰ edn, Thomson Reuters 2017)

Waddams, Stephen M., *The law on damages* (Canada Law Book 2004)

Wagner, Tobias, 'Limitations of Damages for Breach of Contract in German and Scots Law - A Comparative Law Study in View of a Possible European Unification of Law' (2014) Hanse L. Rev.,10

Weidenkaff, Walter, Palandt *Bürgerliches Gesetzbuch* (79ᵗʰ edn, CH Beck Munich 2020)

Whittaker, Simon and Cartwright, John, 'Introduction' in Cartwright, John and Whittaker, Simon (eds), *The Code Napoléon Rewritten French Contract Law after the 2016 Reforms* (Oxford, Hart Publishing, 2020)

Whittaker, Simon, 'Contributory Fault and Mitigation, Rights and Reasonableness: Comparisons between English and French law' in Libus Tichý (ed*) Causation in Law* (Prague, 2007)

Wilson, Carlos Pizarro, 'Presentación', in Íñigo De la Maza, Carlos Pizarro Wilson and Álvaro Vidal Olivares (eds), *Los Principios Latinoamericanos de Derecho de los Contratos: Texto, presentación y contenidos fundamentales* (Madrid, Agencia Estatal Boletín Oficial Del Estado, 2017)

Zanetti, Cristiano de Souza, 'A mitigação do dano e alocação da responsabilidade' (2012) Revista Brasileira de Arbitragem, nº 35

Zimmerman, Reinhard, 'Breach of Contract and Remedies under the New German Law of Obligations' (2002) available at < https://

www.cisg.law.pace.edu/cisg/biblio/zimmerman.html> accessed 13
    August 2022
Zimmerman, Reinhard, *The New German Law of Obligations: Historical
    and Comparative Perspectives* (Oxford University Press 2005)
Zweigert, Konrad and Kötz, Hein, *An Introduction to Comparative Law*,
    (Tony Weir tr, 3rd edn, OUP 1998)

"When it gets hard, get harder. That's the deal"

Marcelo Lapolla

Printed in the United States
by Baker & Taylor Publisher Services

Printed in the United States
by Baker & Taylor Publisher Services